"Pittsburgh Police Chief Bob McNeilly has long been considered a le enforcement. During his tenure at the helm of one of the largest pc ments in the nation, he led the department in making progressive cha those changes in accountability and transparency are considered the g in policing. Chief McNeilly has continued to be a valued voice in p and the experiences cited in his book will continue to guide law enf ecutives for years to come."

CHIEF R. GIL I

Seal

"Getting to know Bob by reading of his life experience, that formed his character, explains why he was successful when faced with the difficult task of reaching compliance with a far-ranging federal consent decree. Pittsburgh was the first city to enter into a federal consent decree, and the first to reach compliance. What makes Bob's story stand out is how he addressed the challenges, and the successes he had in improving policing in Pittsburgh. Chiefs who find themselves facing a consent decree, or an oversight board's mandate for change, can learn from Chief McNeilly's approach in Pittsburgh. Members of a city's political leadership will see how important their commitment to meaningful change and support of the chief is to success."

CHIEF DENNIS NOWICKI
Charlotte, NC Police

"Bob McNeilly is one of the most tenacious and driven police reformers I have known. His determination to bring the Pittsburgh Police Department to greater accountability is an important story of what one man can achieve."

CHUCK WEXLER, Executive Director
Police Executive Research Forum

"As is always the case with change, controversy and resistance follows. Chief Bob McNeilly brought the Pittsburgh Police Department from the 1960s into the 21st century. His leadership, commitment to integrity and the tactics he developed for modern policing is a roadmap for police and citizens alike who care about good policing."

TOM MURPHY
Mayor of Pittsburgh, 1994-2006

"Bob was a decent and honest supervisor who I always put complete trust in. He made a real difference as Pittsburgh's Police Chief."

ASSISTANT CHIEF THERESE ROCCO
(First female Assistant Police Chief in the nation.)

THE BLUE CONTINUUM

THE BLUE CONTINUUM

A Police Chief's Perspective on What's Wrong with Policing Today And How to Fix It

ROBERT W. McNEILLY, Jr.

Word Association Publishers
205 Fifth Avenue
Tarentum, Pennsylvania 15084
www.wordassociation.com

1.800.827.7903

The Blue Continuum

Printed in the United States of America.

ISBN: 978-1-63385-424-6
Library of Congress Control Number: 2021915641

Publisher's Cataloging-in-Publication Data

Names: McNeilly, Robert W., Jr., 1951-
Title: The blue continuum : a police chief's perspective on what's wrong with policing today and how to fix it / Robert W. McNeilly, Jr.
Description: Tarentum, PA : Word Association Publishers, 2021. | Illus. ; 12 charts, 1 photo. |
Identifiers: LCCN 2021915641 | ISBN 9781633854246 (pbk.) | ISBN 9781633854390 (ebook)
Subjects: LCSH: Law enforcement -- United States. | Police administration -- United States. | Police chiefs -- United States -- Biography. | Pittsburgh (Pa.) -- Bureau of Police -- Officials and employees -- Biography. | BISAC: BIOGRAPHY & AUTOBIOGRAPHY / Law Enforcement. | POLITICAL SCIENCE / Law Enforcement. | POLITICAL SCIENCE / Public Affairs & Administration.
Classification: LCC HV7935.M36 B58 2021| DDC 363.2068 M36--dc23

To

the hard-working, ethical, and dedicated men and women serving
in law enforcement whose service is too often overshadowed and
impacted by the appalling acts of a small percentage of rogue officers;

those killed in the line of duty and their families, especially those I
served with, including Joe Grill, Tom Herron, and Jim Blair;

my wife, Catherine Vallone McNeilly, whose rising career was
eclipsed only when I was promoted to chief

Contents

	Acknowledgements	xi
	Author's Note	xiii
	Introduction	xv
1	Workers, Lumps, and Bounty Hunters	1
2	Professional Courtesy	11
3	Plainclothes	21
4	Welcome to Supervision	37
5	The Good, the Bad, and the Ugly	53
6	Watch Commander	69
7	District Commander	83
8	Taking the Helm	107
9	The Country's First "Pattern or Practice" Consent Decree	157
10	From Awards to No Confidence	203
11	Urban Legend	237
12	Furloughs	253
13	Moving On	271
14	Best Practices	307

Acknowledgments

I t would be impossible to name all the people I would like to thank, but a few stand out as major influences on my career and on the writing of this book. I will be forever grateful to:

My wife, Catherine, for her unwavering support throughout our careers and our marriage. Our police agency could never have accomplished what we did without her dedication and knowledge, especially regarding management, organization, research, training, and computers.

My daughter, Annie, and my son, Rob, for accepting the hard decisions I had to make without always understanding the reasons behind them and for standing by me in the face of criticism.

My colleagues Therese Rocco and Luanne and Bob Faulkender, for encouraging me to write; Sharon Liotus, for urging me to continue writing after reading my first two chapters; Nan Newell, for editing this book; and Charlotte Lansinger for her guidance.

My mentors, including Public Safety Director Glenn Cannon; Chief Ralph Pampena; Chief Mayer DeRoy; Commanders Tom

Cunningham, Joe Wind, George McComb, and William Medica; Charlotte/Mecklenburg Police Chief Dennis Nowicki; Buffalo Police Commissioner Gil Kerlikowske; Minneapolis Police Chief Bob Olson; and Police Executive Research Forum Executive Director Chuck Wexler.

My outstanding police partners, especially Ray Lenig, Don Haselrig, Bill Joyce, Mike Sippey, Tim Craig, and Steve Calfo.

My friends among the Pittsburgh Police command staff, including Charles Moffatt, William Mullen, William Valenta, Linda Barone, John Warren, Michele Papakie, Tammy Ewin, and my secretaries, Rose Marie Addlespurger, Theresa Cummings, and Nora Bolla.

The best boss I ever served under, Mayor Tom Murphy, an ethical and astute man who never wavered in his support for me during the challenging periods. Also, I am grateful to Township Commissioners Joanne Beckowitz, Donald Similo, Robert Thomas, Robert Keefer, Helen Kochan, and Ed Gronlund, and Township Managers Malisa Migliori and Aaron Sukenik, for their faith in me and continued support.

God's guidance, because without it, I know I would never have accomplished anything on my own.

Author's
Note

This book is a work of nonfiction. The incidents that are re-counted here are based on my personal experience in law enforcement and reflect my recollection of these incidents as they occurred. Most of the names of individuals and locations have been changed in order to protect the privacy of those depicted. Those individuals who are identified by their real names include: my wife; individuals acknowledged in the dedication and acknowledgments; and certain journalists, attorneys, judges, and other public and professional figures, some of whom are quoted in the book. Any similarity between the fictional names in this book and those of real people, living or dead, is strictly coincidental.

Introduction

*"Because if we the storytellers don't do this, then the
bad people will win."*

—CHRISTIANE AMANPOUR

I offer the following assessment of policing from my thirty-seven
years in law enforcement and from many years of consulting
with many other police departments, large and small. I served
with the Pittsburgh Police for twenty-nine years, rising through the
ranks to hold the chief of police position for nearly a decade. Following
that, I was the chief in a small suburban department for another
eight years. For fourteen years my wife, Pittsburgh Police Commander Catherine McNeilly, and I have consulted with many police agencies of all sizes to provide training, management advice, and expert
services.

My hope in writing this book is that the real-life experiences I
recount here will expose serious problems in policing today and I offer
practical ways to fix them. From my experiences working in law enforcement and consulting with law enforcement agencies, I recognize

that many of the problems a department has are present in most law enforcement agencies. I see most problems stemming from two deficiencies.

The first is the department's shortcoming. When most officers get into trouble, it is generally because the department has failed to provide proper policy, training, supervision, and discipline. If the department conformed to those mandates within the department, substandard officer candidates would not be hired, or they would be weeded out of the department if already hired.

The second shortcoming involves the type of people a department employs. From my more than four decades of experience, I contend that officers fall into one of six groups. The police agency providing the proper policy, training, supervision, and discipline will improve the performance of five of the groups and weed out those in the sixth group. The departments who fail will be rife with citizens' dissatisfaction and complaints, lawsuits, improper use of force, excessive vehicle collisions, corruption, and other issues that may result in outside agencies taking some control of the department, disbanding the agency, and terminating personnel, including the chief.

I contend there are five main groups of officers with a sixth group being a subset at the bottom of the fifth group. In the first group are those devoted officers who will continue to provide for the safety of citizens regardless of the obstacles or dangers they confront. At the other end of the spectrum are officers who should never have been hired by any department. They will continually violate police policy, ignore or criticize training, avoid or confront supervisors, and take any action possible, even criminal, to place the responsibility of their unethical and/or criminal behavior on the good officers and supervisors who attempt to hold them accountable.

The 20/80 rule is applicable here, which many police executives explain as *"20 percent of officers do 80 percent of the work while 20 percent of officers create 80 percent of the problems."*

THE BLUE CONTINUUM: LEVELS OF POLICE OFFICERS

1. SKY BLUE–EXCELLENT, STEADY, AND RELIABLE SELF-STARTERS

These officers are committed to their work because they want to make a difference in their community. They will do a good job even if there is poor leadership. They are generally never disciplined. The departments providing awards for officers will recognize these officers frequently. Once this group of officers is given an assignment, minimal oversight is needed. This group is made up of the 20 percent of officers who are responsible for 80 percent of the good police work being done.

2. LIGHT BLUE–GOOD ABILITY FOR LAW ENFORCEMENT

This group is capable of doing good work and will work well under dedicated leadership. They will seldom be disciplined unless they make an unintentional mistake, are still learning the job, or lack good supervision for guidance. With good supervision, the performance of these officers will be raised to mirror the sky-blue officers. Without strong or honest leadership, their work performance will fall off since they do not see anyone caring. Under inadequate supervision, these officers will encounter many more problems and become mediocre officers.

3. BLUE–STANDARD, TYPICAL, OR AVERAGE OFFICERS

Officers in this group appreciate having a job but can take the work or leave it. This group can be greatly impacted by supervisors, whether effective or ineffective. Those with good supervision will avoid any serious discipline, but those with weak supervision will ultimately face disciplinary action that may involve suspension. If the disciplinary measures are effective, this group of officers will be in this position only once in their career. They will do only what is necessary or expected of them unless influenced by supervisors who are strong leaders. If they perform well, it is due to the supervisor insisting upon quality work. If the supervisor doesn't demand quality work or convey that message to officers in this group, the work will tend to be substandard.

4. MEDIUM BLUE–SUBSTANDARD/TEND TO BE INSUFFICIENT PERFORMERS

This group consists of those who accept a job in law enforcement because the pay and benefits are better than anything they had before or may find anywhere else. They are inclined to do little work and may complain about having to do any work at all but will work to avoid trouble in the workplace. This group is affected even more by strong or weak supervisors. Those with weak supervisors and inadequate training will be disciplined repeatedly. Even though the level of discipline may begin with reprimands, the number of times these officers are disciplined will most likely result in progressive discipline leading to suspensions or even termination. Those with strong supervisors and proper levels of training may still face disciplinary action, but the infractions or misconduct will most likely be at the level of oral and written reprimands. This group benefits greatly from an early intervention system.

Depending upon the strength or weakness of their supervisors, the 60 percent of officers in these middle groups (2, 3, and 4) tend to associate either with the better police officers or with the disruptive, disgruntled officers.

5. DARK BLUE–SELF-SERVING OFFICERS

Those officers who really do not want to do police work or possibly any work at all fall into this category. Many do only what they have to do to avoid being fired. Most police officials know it is difficult to terminate an officer in a civil-service, politically connected environment. This group will be responsible for 80 percent of the problems in an agency and can require approximately 50 percent of police managers' time in dealing with the problems they create.

This group is the reason policies must be specific since these officers look for loopholes. They work harder at trying to avoid work than at applying the effort necessary to do the work. These officers may respond to a democratic style of leadership at times, but inevitably need an autocratic style of supervision and discipline; otherwise, they become disruptive to the organization.

This group of officers may reduce the frequency and serious nature of misconduct by having strong supervisors who provide the proper assistance, motivation, and early intervention. They also require continuous training in subjects including ethics, communication skills, regulations, and accountability. This group critically needs early intervention. With some studies showing that up to 25 percent of officers have substance abuse problems, many of those officers will be in this group.

6. MIDNIGHT BLUE–OFFICERS WHO SHOULD NEVER HAVE BEEN HIRED

This subset of the dark-blue group involves a sinister 1-2 percent of officers. They should never have been hired as police officers since they took the job in an effort to be either above the law or to use their positions to further criminal enterprise. They will create turmoil wherever they work. They are self-serving and all their actions will be to hold some power over other officers.

Officers who start in the dark-blue group sometimes end up in this group when they are confronted with the temptations police officers encounter or are pulled into this group by other midnight-blue officers.

Many officers in groups 1-3 generally avoid the criminal officers. Under weak supervision, the officers in the midnight-blue group demoralize most of the officers in the department and damage the reputation of the department before they are finally terminated and/ or arrested.

Midnight-blue officers tend to bully timid supervisors. They will find some weakness or mistake and hold it over the fainthearted supervisor. If they cannot find a supervisor's weakness, they will start a rumor to create one. They want total control of their environment so that they can do whatever *they* want to do rather than what the supervisor wants them to do. The officers in this group have no redeeming value and should be weeded out of a department as quickly as possible before they pollute an entire shift, duty location, or department. These officers eventually get caught in criminal and unethical acts that embarrass the department and the profession of law enforcement. They will create substantial liability for the municipality employing them.

****

Under weak supervision, the officers in groups 2-4 can be influenced by negative attitudes and will ultimately face disciplinary action due to carelessness, attempting to avoid work, or becoming involved in criminal conduct. A weak supervisor having officers in this group will find that officers will ignore their lack of leadership and instead may be impacted by officers in the midnight-blue group. Many in this group will lose their jobs without early identification of problems and early intervention by a responsible supervisor.

A department is best served if officers in the sky-blue group are promoted to supervisory positions. Officers in the light-blue group and the blue group can become good supervisors with the proper training, mentoring, and supervision. Officers in the medium-blue group do not make the best supervisors. They will generally require constant supervision forcing their accountability.

If officers in the dark-blue group become supervisors, serious efforts will be required to overcome the negative impact they will have on their shift or duty location. Actions that should be taken include providing subordinates with a method to anonymously report their supervisor's misconduct, having their own supervisors monitor the deficient supervisor more than his/her other subordinates, Integrity tests, counseling, training, and discipline as warranted. If possible, that supervisor in the dark-blue group should be transferred at intervals to prevent corruption of an entire shift of officers.

****

The police officers I worked with during my long career came in all shades of blue along the continuum. In the following chapters I will relate my experiences with all of them. Fortunately, most of them fell into the first four categories. They were hard-working, ethical individuals and they made me proud. However, I have focused a good bit of my attention on the dark-blue and midnight-blue officers because they can tarnish the reputation of an entire department if they are not identified and properly disciplined. A police department is only as good as those in charge. Under strong leadership, police officers can learn what they need to do to serve and protect with integrity and equanimity.

Many chiefs contend with dramatic events during their time of service. They may have to deal with collective bargaining agreements, no-confidence votes, consent decrees, furloughs, lawsuits or be subject to vicious rumors to damage their reputations. My experience is unique in that I got to experience all these events—and more—during my ten years as police chief in Pittsburgh. Although this book contains material that will be of special interest to other police chiefs, it is also intended to be read as a cautionary tale—to awaken those in the police force to what needs to be done to raise the bar for police work and to educate members of the general public who have the right to demand the very best from their police.

CHAPTER ONE

Lumps, Workers, and Bounty Hunters

"Something is always happening. But when it happens, people don't always see it or understand it or accept it."

—DETECTIVE JOHN HOBBS
(Denzell Washington) in the movie Fallen

Within two weeks of graduation from the police academy I learned not all police officers were the "good guys" I had envisioned. I quickly learned police officers fell into various categories, some good and some bad, including the lumps, the workers, and the bounty hunters.

There was a benefit to being newly assigned to a police district that had not seen a fresh police recruit in seven years. New officers were used to fill in for absent officers who had been permanently assigned to beats and patrol vehicles. The veteran officers worked with regular partners they came to know professionally, and many times personally, since they socialized during their off-duty time. Instead of being assigned to work with only one officer, the recruit would have the opportunity to work with many officers in the first few months to observe how each approached the job of policing. Each day the recruit was assigned to work with a different partner. If new recruits were observant, they could see the good practices of dedicated officers and the bad habits of others.

It was important to learn from officers since many departments didn't employ field training during the 1970s. Field training provided a veteran officer, who was specifically trained to be a post-academy training officer, for recruits so they could obtain practical on-the-job training while answering calls for service in real-life situations. The lack of field training was a departmental deficiency that undoubtedly led to officer failures, complaints from citizens, lawsuits, disciplinary action, and ruined careers.

It was possible to learn from every officer even though our department did not have a field training program. The only difference was that some officers provided a good training experience and others provided examples of what an officer should not do.

THE LUMPS

After my first roll call, I climbed into an older police car driven by a grumpy, balding officer who did not look as though he had ever participated in any type of physical exercise. It was a crisp morning in May but warm enough for short-sleeved shirts. The older officer did not have much to say and did not appear to be amenable to any conversation. It was painfully obvious that having a new rookie officer assigned to him did not fit into his plans for the day. He was assigned as a single officer working the daylight shift. He had to have had many years to obtain an assignment like that and didn't relish the thought of working with an eager, mid-twenties type who was looking for more action than he cared to contend with.

He did provide me, however, with my first lesson. It was rather simple. Officer Marks began with, "Let me tell you something." Expecting my first words of wisdom from an experienced veteran officer,

I listened intently as Officer Marks said, "Don't call the sergeant to a scene. I'll be the one to call one if we need one. I have more than twenty-eight years on this job and I haven't needed to call a sergeant to the scene of anything yet." I had to wonder if Officer Marks was warning me not to seek assistance by going over his head or if he was relaying the directions of the shift sergeant. Possibly it was both.

It did not take long for the radio to crackle with the first call. It was a short drive, only about ten blocks from the station. We were there within ten minutes. And then I got my second lesson: the officer assigned to the police vehicle is the one who operates it. This led to the third lesson: the officer who drives the vehicle never writes the reports. The fourth lesson was obvious: I was going to write every report for every call we answered that day.

Fortunately, the first call was minor—a criminal mischief. During the night someone had damaged a parked car. It did not appear to be a hit-and-run even though the car was parked on a narrow one-way street with cars parked only on one side. There appeared to be scratch marks that someone had intentionally made with a sharp object along the entire side of the car.

Unfortunately, I had never written a police report and had to tell my cantankerous partner that I needed assistance in writing the report. He provided short but direct instructions. "Do you see that first box at the top of the blank report?" After an affirmative reply, the sole direction was, "Well, start there and fill in whatever the box calls for. Once you do that, go down the entire sheet the same way until you are done." I must have done an excellent job because my work did not even require a review. I apparently became an expert in writing reports by the end of my first shift. I was glad when that shift was over and hoped I never had to work with that officer again.

The next day I was assigned to work with an officer who usually walked a beat. He was angry when informed by the shift lieutenant that he would be assigned to work with me, and he let me know it by complaining.

That shift was extremely trying since the officer refused to speak even two words to me. Talk about a long eight hours. From him I learned that the rules of one person driving and one person writing the reports did not apply to cranky veterans or to impressionable rookies who were trying to avert a conflict while on probation. I learned I could drive the car to calls and write any required report.

In a couple of days, I had recognized the first category of police officer I had never imagined existed. They were the lumps. They did the least amount of work possible by failing to volunteer to accept any call, taking eons of time to respond to the calls they could not shirk, and complaining about every bit of work they were compelled to do along with any other responsibility they were inconvenienced to assume such as training a rookie officer.

Although I encountered many lumps along the way, I didn't realize until I was a supervisor that there were actions a supervisor could take to have an impact on officer performance.

THE WORKERS

By the time I had worked my first two weeks, I had worked with ten different officers. I learned many important lessons during those weeks and was left with additional questions for other officers. One of the better officers I had the opportunity to work with was a seven-year veteran, Officer Ryan Green. He was in his late thirties with thinning hair. He was solid and strong, much stronger than one would think at first glance.

Officer Green offered considerable advice regarding policing and life in general. Although he had seven years of service, he was one of the younger officers since the city had not hired for seven years as it downsized the department through attrition. The department had downsized so much that it fell below expected staffing levels and was now attempting to increase the number of officers by hiring new officers in classes that sometimes overlapped.

Green's first guidance I was never to forget. He cautioned me that police work was ever changing due to state legislation and both state and federal court decisions. And the public's expectations of policing were ever changing as society changed. He warned me to remain flexible enough to change or I would go the way of the dodo bird which had failed to adapt to a changing environment.

I noticed he was quick to respond to calls for service. He took the time to explain what an officer should be observing and doing on the way to a call and how to handle various situations. The second sound guidance he provided was to be wary of the advice from certain other police officers. Although some officers were interested in helping a rookie's career, he warned that some had personal, self-serving motives in coaxing a new officer to adopt their policing habits.

Before the shift was over that day, I had hoped I would have the opportunity to work with Officer Green again. I could sense his honesty and genuine desire to mold a rookie officer into a dedicated and respectful public servant. I had witnessed a second category of officer to which I had been naïve to think all officers belonged—the worker. The workers were the officers that immediately accepted each call for service, volunteered for other calls, and interacted with the public with respect and empathy. My wish did eventually come true when he and I were assigned as partners a couple of months later. I would work with him and learn from him for the next two years until I had the opportunity to move to another assignment.

I was grateful to be exposed to a sky-blue officer shortly after graduation from the police academy. I was later to learn that sky-blue officers would always perform well regardless of who supervised them. I would also learn how strong leadership could use positive verbal reinforcement, positive performance evaluations, and awards to encourage more officers to perform better.

THE BOUNTY HUNTERS

I kept Officer Green's advice in mind over the next couple of months while interacting with other officers assigned to the station. I was to learn what he meant by personal motives from two officers, Officers Tim Collins and Bill Kramer.

Officer Collins was tall and of medium build. He was outspoken and had the facial scars to prove he was always amenable to a fistfight. His partner, Officer Kramer, was also of medium build and seemed to have a pleasant nature except that he was quite the follower of his obnoxious partner. He appeared to be enthralled working with him. I was not sure if it was because they seemed to fit the good cop/bad cop pairing or possibly because they had done a considerable amount of police work and had made many arrests.

One night I questioned them as to how they could make so many drug arrests so quickly into their shift. They unabashedly explained they stopped every carful of teenagers as soon as they left roll call and searched the car and its occupants until they discovered any quantity of drugs. Most of the stops led to their seizing a nickel bag of marijuana, a roach (the end of a smoked marijuana cigarette), or a roach clip (the metal clip that holds a roach).

I could not understand why two officers would focus so much of their time on such unimportant activities when there were more serious public safety concerns. It did not dawn on me until later that each of those arrests required the officer to appear for a preliminary hearing at the district justice. The working agreement between the city and the police union mandated that the officer receive three hours of overtime, at a rate of time and one half, for each court appearance. Although the clear majority of their arrests were dismissed or settled with a small fine, the officers were compensated by more than a half-day's pay. If they each had an arrest each night, they could each make more than twenty hours of extra pay each week.

But those officers were not the only ones who had developed a special expertise when it came to making a few extra dollars. Another officer, Ralph Heard, had a DUI (driving under the influence) arrest more nights than he did not. It was not unusual to see Officer Heard parked on one of the main streets as Officer Green and I would drive by. Again, I could not understand how one officer could have so many arrests for just one offense such as DUI. It made much more sense when I learned that Officer Heard parked in the vicinity of one of the local bars and observed patrons as they walked to a parked car. Once the car pulled onto the street, Officer Heard had his arrest for the night. Most DUI arrests in the 1970s were dismissed or the driver received a nominal fine for disorderly conduct and the DUI charge was dismissed. Each arrest meant that a potentially dangerous driver had been removed from the street and Officer Heard would receive three hours of overtime pay from an appearance in Traffic Court.

Not all Traffic Court hearings served the purpose of making the streets safer for motorists and pedestrians. One officer, John Jefferson, admitted that he did not write citations for motorists going through a red light. He said he only wrote citations for motorists who were going through an intersection while the amber light was lit. His rationale was that motorists receiving a citation for running a red light would generally not request a hearing since they knew they were in the wrong. To the contrary, a motorist cited for going through a yellow light would be incensed to receive a citation for running a red light and request a hearing to pursue justice. One will never know how many received justice, but Officer Jefferson received three hours of overtime for showing up at Traffic Court for each one of those appearances.

One will never know how many traffic citations were written due to an actual offense committed and how many were issued for other reasons. Fortunately for motorists, the city changed procedures in 1996. Instead of every officer who issued a citation appearing for Traffic Court, one officer was assigned to Traffic Court to testify in response to the citations issued by all 1,200 department officers. The number of citations issued dropped from 48,000 in 1995 to 13,000 in 1996.

Could 35,000 motorists have been cited unnecessarily each year? One officer, John Berry, who wrote approximately fifty citations per month prior to the change in procedures, failed to write any citations following the change. Other officers who had written large numbers of citations now failed to write any or they wrote only a few once the change was implemented. A large portion of those citations were issued by a few dozen officers.

I came to learn a lot about another category of officers—the bounty hunters. Their level of police activity was directly related to how much overtime was involved. Each citation written and each arrest meant extra overtime pay. There was a bounty on the head of each person they encountered.

Decades later, I would resist the police union's efforts to amend the collective bargaining agreement to include all overtime pay in an officer's pension. I had deep suspicions that the amount of an officer's pension would influence whether a motorist received a traffic citation or faced arrest.

LESSONS LEARNED

1) Not all police officers are the same and not all of them are good guys. Fortunately, the clear majority of police officers I have encountered throughout my career proved to be dedicated and honorable. Those who weren't praiseworthy created a need for detailed department policy, appropriate and effective training, responsible supervision, and swift and sure discipline for violators.

2) A department failing to provide a thorough, documented field training program undermines the new officers' careers, destabilizes the effectiveness of the department, and delivers a disservice to the community who deserves more than what they will be able to receive.

3) The careers of many police officers were greatly hindered or destroyed when they were exposed to improper field training by officers of questionable character. Departments that fail to provide adequate training to new rookies, including field training, are failing to act in the best interests of the community, the department, and the officers who served. The same department would discipline officers for mistakes they were bound to make.

4) When people make blanket statements that they support the police, they cannot know they are also supporting the officers who are lumps being paid for little work and the bounty hunters who see them only as a dollar figure.

5) Elected officials and the public should be wary of increased pensions caused by officers' court appearances following arrests and citations issued.

CHAPTER TWO

Professional Courtesy

"To me, the thing that is worse than death is betrayal. You see, I could conceive death, but I could not conceive betrayal."

—Malcolm X

After making an arrest in a low-income public housing unit, my partner, Officer Green, and I would become involved in one of the longest, most heart-pounding vehicle pursuits of my career. Since we were not equipped with a prisoner cage in our police vehicles, we would need to summon a police van to transport our arrest.

We had just completed the first call of our shift at midnight on the 23rd of December. It was the first Christmas Eve I was to work as a police officer when the police wagon crew informed us that they had witnessed an apparently stolen silver Cadillac operating on a nearby street just outside of the public housing complex. It was amazing how veteran officers could detect a stolen car just from the actions of the car's occupants.

My partner was driving as we pulled up behind the Cadillac only a few minutes later. On the way I had been broadcasting our direction and speed. We did not activate the emergency lights or sirens since we planned to follow while backup moved into the area to assist with the pursuit and apprehensions.

My experienced partner had already taught me considerably about detecting stolen cars and following them, knowing that most pursuits lasted only a few minutes before the occupants bailed out of the car and fled on foot. They were difficult to catch due to their head start and given all the gear an officer had to run with. When they escaped on foot, they generally headed to a place that they knew would harbor them from the pursuing police.

After a few minutes, the three occupants of the Cadillac realized that the marked police car behind them was not coincidentally making all the same turns onto side streets that they were. They gradually picked up speed, well aware that the police car was still behind them. Since it was after midnight and a cold December wind was blowing, there were few cars on the narrow city streets and no pedestrians.

Sparks began flying from the underside of the Cadillac as it bottomed out on the hilly streets. By the time the Cadillac sideswiped a parked car and continued to flee, our emergency lights were on. The pursuit lasted about ten minutes—considered to be a long time in the middle of a large city. It lasted so long that other units got between us and the Cadillac. Eventually, the Cadillac struck a parked car and all three occupants fled on foot. Several assisting officers in the area pursued on foot.

My partner grabbed my arm as I was about to jump from the car and signaled me to get back in. He operated in reverse on the narrow one-way street and drove along side streets until he cut in front of one of the running suspects. Once the suspect realized he had nowhere else to run and was in a neighborhood that would not harbor him, he attempted to hide under a parked car. He was easily caught when the car was surrounded and a police canine forced him out from under the car.

I was fortunate to have a partner who taught me well in so many aspects of policing. Although we had recovered stolen cars regularly, this pursuit and subsequent apprehension gave me the biggest adrenaline dump I had ever experienced. This was an incident that made me realize working smart (remaining in the car to head off the suspect) made much more sense than working hard (pursuing on foot). There were enough officers closer to the suspects than we were who would take up the foot chase and flush the suspects out into a side street where we could head them off at the pass. I was fortunate to be with an experienced officer who cared enough about me, the citizens we served, and our department to take the time and patience to teach the next generation. I learned a lot.

Several months later, I was at the wheel of the police cruiser driving 25 mph as we rounded a bend in the road. Suddenly, a sport utility vehicle driving in the opposite direction crossed into our lane. Had I not swerved the car onto the sidewalk the car would have hit us head on. Fortunately, the sharp bend in the road was in front of a cemetery and with the cemetery closed for the night there were no parked vehicles in the area. The driver was obviously driving beyond the 25-mph speed limit. After my partner and I both breathed a sigh of relief, I reached over and hit the switch to activate our overhead emergency lights. The chase was on.

The black SUV accelerated immediately. It was easy to get the police car turned around since we were already as far right on the roadway as we could have been. I activated the siren using the foot control on the car floor. Even though the sun had set many hours ago, it was not difficult to follow the SUV since its exhaust system could be heard at least a quarter mile away. The SUV had a head start, but we knew it could not maintain its distance from us since the roadway we were on offered only one lane of travel in each direction with cars parked on both sides of the road.

As the SUV rounded a bend in the road, its tires locked up, screeching loudly as the driver jammed on the brakes to make a quick right turn. It appeared he intended to use the side streets in a series of turns to elude us. Even though the driver of the SUV extinguished the vehicle's lights in an evasive maneuver, he was not able to obscure the sound from the exhaust and from squealing tires.

The SUV pulled over to the side of the street on a steep hill. Even before it came to a full stop, two doors on the passenger side opened. This is a common tactic when occupants of stolen vehicles are coming close to capture. Suspects bail out of the moving car to flee on foot while the car is left without a driver. In this case, two fifteen-year-old girls screaming hysterically made a quick exit.

My partner quickly apprehended the two girls as I ran to the driver's door. I grabbed the door handle, yanked hard, and flung the door open as wide as it would go while stopped on the hill. I demanded the driver shut the vehicle off and step out of the car. Instead, the driver sneered at me and shouted, "Just give me my citation and let me the fuck go!" As could be expected, a struggle ensued as I dragged the driver out of his car, got him onto the ground, handcuffed him, and eventually got him into the rear seat of the police car. I learned later the driver's name was Ray Sanchez.

In those days, there were no cages in the back seat of our police cars and the back doors were not equipped to prevent their being opened from the inside. Even though Ray was handcuffed behind his back, he was able to scoot across the rear seat, open the car door on the other side of the police car, and still handcuffed, run down the street. Ray was again captured and confined to the police car.

The story began to unfold as my partner and I investigated what we originally thought was a stolen car. The car was in fact owned by this intoxicated driver. Even though he was well into his twenties, he offered a ride to the two fifteen-year-old girls who knew him from the neighborhood. While they were riding, he offered them some beer and some marijuana. All seemed to be having a good time drinking and smoking until they crossed into the wrong lane of traffic and nearly struck a police car head on.

It was then that Ray decided to make a run for it. The two girls knew they would be in trouble if caught with beer and marijuana, but they also realized they would be in much more danger speeding through city streets with an intoxicated driver while eluding police. They began screaming hysterically, demanding Ray stop the car to let them out. Ray knew that if he stopped, he would certainly not be able to elude the officers since he did not have much of a head start. Eventually, the shrieking of the girls and the possibility they might bail out of a moving car convinced Ray to pull over. Once he pulled over, he knew he would have officers hovering over him.

The entire pursuit lasted only a few minutes. The time spent arresting Ray took twice as long as the pursuit. Obtaining information from the girls and turning them over to their parents would take longer. There also was the matter of obtaining a tow truck and doing the paperwork involved with the inventory. During this time, we waited for additional units to handle some of those duties so we could transport our prisoner to Traffic Division where he would be given a Breathalyzer examination.

As we all waited in the police car, the prisoner continued to berate me and my partner—the arresting officers. My partner and I told Ray to stop before he made any additional comments that could result in more charges and more problems for himself. Ray screamed at my partner and me, "I'm not the one who has problems here. You're the ones who will have problems." Ray continued, "I know many police officers who are friends of mine. You'll be the ones with problems when they hear about this."

My partner this night was David Wood. He and I had attended the police academy together. We both had about six months working the streets at the time. Although we two young officers lacked considerable police experience, we were both highly motivated and had learned a lot from already being involved in many different types of situations.

But neither of us had experienced anything similar to what we were experiencing with Ray. We were still on probation and would be for the next couple of months. I felt confident that any police officer involved in an incident as we had just experienced would have handled the situation the same way that we had. However, it was true that Ray did have police officer friends since he knew their names and their assignments. Apparently, Ray had used his connections in the past, which only served to embolden him to flee the police while driving intoxicated and then to threaten his arresting officers. Although it is virtually impossible to include every detail of an arrest in every police report, I was determined to document as many important details of this arrest as I could without the police report reading like a novel. I included Ray's threatening comments, including that his officer friends would retaliate against my partner and me.

The next week, Ray's preliminary hearing was scheduled in Municipal Traffic Court. I arrived early as I did for every hearing in which I was required to testify. I was obligated to provide testimony during the hearing to substantiate every charge that I had filed against Ray. Failure to provide enough information to justify the charges filed could lead to some or all charges being dismissed.

I waited in the police waiting room for Ray's case to be called. As was usual, a couple dozen officers would wait in the room or in the hallways when the room became full. As I waited, Officer Bill Wolfe approached and asked to speak with me. We exited into the hallway where he told me that Ray was a friend of his. He explained that Ray's business was in home remodeling and that Ray had done work for many police officers including him. Officer Wolfe indicated he would appreciate any "professional courtesy" I could provide to him by my providing inadequate testimony so that the charges would be dropped against Ray.

I told Officer Wolfe that I could not do that and offered a copy of the police report so he knew exactly what occurred the night of the arrest. The veteran officer blurted out a comment about my failure to provide a "professional courtesy," became enraged and demanded to know what I intended to say during the hearing. After I told him I would testify to exactly what happened, including Ray's threat to use his friendship with other officers to retaliate, Officer Wolfe stormed away.

I went back into the waiting room and took a seat. Within a few minutes, Officer Wolfe appeared in the doorway with another officer. He sneered in my direction, pointed toward me, and whispered into the ear of the other officer. A few minutes later Officer Wolfe reappeared with another officer and repeated his actions. Now I understood why Ray displayed such brash and offensive behavior the night he was arrested. Not only did Ray have police friends but they were the type of police friends who would do whatever it took to repay him for some home repairs.

As a rookie officer I was left to wonder what the repercussions were to be. Would it affect any backup I could ever expect to get? Would it affect my career? Would it affect my safety? There was a lot to think about in making just one arrest. I wondered how many times this was going to happen with future arrests. It was obvious I had taken a path that would alienate many other police officers. I felt sure it would not be the last time that would happen.

Months later, our lieutenant at roll call on the night shift announced there were a number of citizens' complaints regarding congregants in front of several bars on the main street of their neighborhood. Instructions were relayed to all officers in attendance to ensure that no one was violating the law or city ordinances by drinking on the street, being loud and disorderly, or by obstructing the sidewalks.

Upon the first pass on the main street, five men were observed drinking in front of one of the bars. As instructed at roll call, my partner and I stopped to inform the men they had to go inside the bar, dispose of their beverages, or leave the area. Four of the men appeared to be in their twenties while one appeared to be about twenty to thirty years older. The men had obviously had their fill of liquid courage long before we encountered them.

It turned out that the older man was the father of three of the younger men. He and one of his sons were the most vocal and defiant. They refused to comply with any request. The older man demanded that my partner and I show him written proof that a complaint had been registered. He argued that the officers should return to their patrol car and leave the area. He informed us that he was a firefighter at the fire station just a few blocks down the street. He told my partner and me that we would be banned from stopping at the firehouse for any reason including use of the restroom or city phone. He informed us that he had police-officer friends who would ensure we paid a price for interrupting his evening with his sons.

All the men refused to comply and one of the younger men threatened to use physical force if I were not the one who left. Of course, this led to a call for backup. The same young man shoved me which resulted in my placing him under attest. The father was also arrested, and father and son were transported to the district station.

It wasn't much longer after that when a gray-haired, slightly balding man in his fifties with a slender but out-of-shape frame strolled into the station. He walked to the front desk to speak with a sergeant and then walked over to my partner and me as we sat writing police reports. He informed us he was an off-duty sergeant, Sergeant Richard Crabbe, from #8 Station, which abutted our district. He verified that the older firefighter had some police friends including at least one sergeant—himself.

Sergeant Crabbe explained that the firefighter was a good friend of his and confirmed that three of the younger men were his sons. He wanted us to turn over the prisoners to him instead of completing the arrest reports. When we explained we could not do so, he informed us that he had a group of officers under his command who would not look favorably on our refusal to do him a favor. We had heard of the group of officers at #8 Station. My partner and I stood our ground and refused, probably due to my shock that another police officer, especially a supervisor, would consider his friendship to be more important than our doing our jobs or ensuring our safety.

It was bad enough that I would alienate some officers because I wouldn't drop DUI charges against someone, but now we would be intimidated by a police sergeant who demanded we drop charges against his friends who had threatened us physically on the street.

Fortunately, we had a lieutenant, Gerald Gray, who was conscientious and supportive of his officers. He had worked internal affairs in the past. Once I explained this matter, he recommended I write a memo to the chief of police. Even though I knew I would stir a hornet's nest within the department, I felt I had no choice but to follow the lieutenant's advice.

I submitted an internal memo to the chief of police through our chain of command as required. I eventually heard that the sergeant was called into the chief's office and warned that no action should be taken against us. We never did hear from the sergeant again, but I cannot attest that some of the officers he drank with at the local watering hole did not harbor some animosity and provide various levels of grief during my career.

LESSONS LEARNED

1) It is extremely important to document an incident in as much detail as possible, especially when you know there will be accusations and internal police interference or outside political interference with an arrest you have made.

2) A great deal of improper pressure is placed on some officers who attempt to enforce the law. Inconceivably, the pressure comes from other officers and supervisors within the department. Those officers attempting to enforce the law are actually betrayed by their own colleagues.

3) Many police officers will not report misconduct they have experienced firsthand since they still have to work with the same officers and for the same supervisors. They depend upon the officers for backup in dangerous situations and they can be sabotaged by the supervisors who are supposed to be looking out for them.

4) Officers who rise through the ranks to supervisory positions retain the same shade of blue they had as officers.

5) There should be an internal section of a police department (Integrity Unit) or an external agency to allow officers to report undue pressure from corrupt fellow officers.

6) Having a strong, reliable shift lieutenant looking out for subordinate officers has tremendous impact on ethical policing.

CHAPTER THREE

Plainclothes

"We must create an atmosphere where the crooked cop fears the honest cop, and not the other way around."

—Frank Serpico
testifying at the Knapp Commission

After two and a half years of working a uniformed radio car I had the opportunity to work a plainclothes assignment in the same district. Since no field training was provided when I started working the streets as a police officer, I didn't give a second thought about working what sometimes was an even more demanding and dangerous job—plainclothes—without any additional training.

A LUMP MAKES DEMANDS OF A WORKER

After only weeks working a plainclothes assignment, I received a phone call from a Pittsburgh police detective, Jerry Peters. I had not heard of him before, but he was quick to tell me who he was. He said he worked in the centralized Detective Division. He explained that his home had been recently burglarized. He was requesting that my partner and I drive through his neighborhood, grab as many young people we could see on the street, throw them up against a car or building, and threaten them with continued harassment until they provided the name of the person responsible for burglarizing his home.

Suffice it to say that I was amazed a city detective would ask my partner and me to do something that was not only illegal but also was an ineffective way to investigate a burglary. Of course, none of what he requested was ever going to happen. When asked why he did not do the roundup himself, he said he did not think it would be proper to investigate his own burglary. But he did not have any qualms about asking us to do something that was illegal and could cost us our jobs.

It did not take long to understand his request given his background. He had a reputation of being one of the lumps on the police department who did not do any work. He was able to get away without doing any work because he bragged about the political connections he had that protected him.

★★★★

During my first summer in plainclothes, we would make stops at some of the regular nuisance areas such as large drinking parties, or the district commander would direct us to make those stops after he received neighborhood complaints. The first one was at a public park. Working plainclothes gave us the opportunity to get in close since the drinkers generally left the area when uniformed officers approached, only to return once the marked police car had gone. Uniformed officers found it frustrating to continue to get calls only to have the violators flee when they saw the officers coming and to return once they left.

While my partner, Steve Bush, and I were interacting with a couple of young men we were able to surprise, a large, intoxicated man in his twenties began shouting and daring us to confront him. He was angry and yelled to me, "Why don't you come down here and get me, Rocky?"

Of course, I had to begin walking toward him as he put on a show for all the other drinkers and the neighbors. He was full of liquid courage and I knew I was going to have my hands full with him since he obviously was larger than my frame of five foot ten and 225 pounds and I expected he'd feel no pain due to intoxication and the anger that was seething from his eyes and his clenched fists. He put his hands up in a boxing stance and shouted, "You're not going to kick my ass, Rocky!" I calmly slid my blackjack out of my front pants pocket and swirled the strap around my hand quickly as I had so often practiced. The leather strap was taut as I grabbed the black-leather defensive tool snugly into my hand with only the few inches of leather-wrapped lead exposed. I shouted back to him, "I will if I have to."

I am convinced it was the way I phrased it – "if I have to..."—that changed the situation. He lowered his fists, turned around, and began running away from me. I gave chase and gained on him slowly. After realizing he could not outrun me, he turned around and put his hands into the air to surrender. I was relieved I was not going to have to do combat with this Goliath. After this incident my partner and I would be referred to as Rocky and Bush. I am convinced that because there was no violence during this incident, and due to our reputation for fairness in other interactions, we were able to develop a working relationship with neighborhoods that provided us with informants leading to successes in other more serious investigations.

Sometimes it was not possible to resolve the matter without violence. For example, the commander once told us to investigate groups of loud young men drinking on the street in an area where a bridge had just been demolished. What had been a two-way street with a walkway over the bridge was now sealed with chain-link fence. The vacant area at the intersection where the bridge met the neighborhood provided a small spot for a group of men to gather without having to drink in the wooded areas surrounding the one-way, dog-legged street.

The night we were sent to investigate this matter there were three cars parked at the end of the bridge with the car windows open, music playing loudly, and a half-dozen young men drinking beer while sitting on the cars or lying on the hood of the car. Working plainclothes benefitted us since we were able to ride right up to them in the darkness before announcing our identity. On the other hand, being in plainclothes did not always provide the level of respect some people would provide to a uniformed officer. On this night, we would not know if the defiance was due to our working plainclothes or merely due to bottled courage.

One young, physically fit man with short hair became the spokesman for the group. Since he was a U. S. marine on leave, he believed he was exempt from obeying city police officers since he claimed he was part of the "federal military." He was not the last military person I would meet who mistakenly believed employment by the federal government somehow trumped state or municipal law enforcement.

Unfortunately for this young marine, he was arrested. He briefly offered resistance while my partner and I struggled to handcuff him. Two of the other men jumped in beside the marine. Two officers were now struggling with three men. Fortunately, all the other men drinking in the group stood by to watch and did not further outnumber my partner and me. I was relieved when backup arrived, and three prisoners were transported in a police wagon to the station.

It turned out the two men who jumped in to assist the drunken marine were sons of police officers. Both of their fathers attempted to intercede on their sons' behalf.

One police officer, Officer Arnold Krantz, turned out to be one of the fathers in the bridge incident. He was irate, bellowing that he remembered a day when a police officer would apprehend a juvenile burglar and turn him over to his parents once he learned the burglar was an officer's son. I told Officer Krantz that I had no intentions of ever doing that and I was beginning to understand why his son had been so quick to fight with police officers. I knew his son was destined for some bad things in the future if he did not learn to take responsibility for what he did that night. I came to realize that the children of police officers were either the most courteous or the most ill-mannered. There did not seem to be much in between.

The other officer was Officer Gregory Milton. When he told his son to apologize to the us, the son replied, "No, why should I? They were fighting with my friend. What was I supposed to do, stand there and watch?"

LEARNING FROM THE TOP 20 PERCENT

Even though I learned a lot from bad experiences, I learned much more from the sky-blue officers I had the opportunity to work with. I had made many mistakes throughout the years due to inexperience. I appreciated those officers I worked with who helped pull me up into the light-blue and sky-blue groups. It would take motivation, a desire to learn, experience, and working with the right people to reach the top levels in performance. I owed my partners a great deal. Those experiences would mean more to me than what I learned from any of the dark-blue officer critics I would meet in my career.

Although Officer Bush and I were assigned to address the quality-of-life issues that annoyed neighborhoods, our ability to work plainclothes permitted us to investigate any type of crime except homicides and rapes and proved to be an enormous learning experience. The crimes of homicide and rape required considerable expertise that only the Homicide Section and the Sex Assault Section could provide.

We were permitted to work robberies, burglaries, thefts, assaults, drug offenses, and other serious crimes. Some arrests came just by being out on the street and being observant. We were in a position to get much closer to offenses in plainclothes than we were as uniformed officers.

Officer Ed Diaz was in the passenger seat and I was driving the unmarked car one Saturday night when we stopped at a red light. I mentioned to my partner that a pickup truck had stopped at the light a few cars in front of us and was now sitting through the light even though it changed green. The car behind the pickup truck beeped its horn several times to no avail. After the driver tired of sounding the horn, he began to drive around the pickup truck. As soon as he did, the driver of the pickup truck pulled in front of the car, forcing the car to stop abruptly to prevent hitting the truck. The car again attempted to pass the truck and the truck again pulled in front of the car, forcing it to stop abruptly again. Other vehicles in line remained stopped in the traffic jam during the entire length of the green light.

I thought we might be seeing the beginning stage of a road-rage incident. I was able to drive into the right lane and pull up next to the passenger side of the pickup truck. I shouted to get the attention of the truck's occupants and told them if they were not going to drive the truck they should pull over and let the other vehicles pass.

The driver stretched himself across the steering wheel to look me directly in the eyes as he said, "We'll pull over if you pull over." Of course, I had to say, "Okay." The driver of the truck made a right turn in front of us and drove a short way to the first area where he could pull the truck into a parking spot big enough for two vehicles. We broadcast our situation and location via police radio as we followed the truck but barely had time to get the information out before both occupants of the truck jumped out.

I was to deal with the occupant on the driver side who was armed with a baseball bat while my partner was left to contend with the passenger who exited with a lug wrench. As they stared down the barrel of a revolver in one hand and a police badge in the other hand, they both realized they were at a distinct disadvantage and surrendered.

Being drunk while threatening and intimidating other motorists was not their most serious offense. Once they were handcuffed, an odor of gasoline permeated the area. The source turned out to be an old "pumper," a disposable beer keg made of plastic. These two had found a use for their pumper by filling it with gasoline. Since the plastic container had no lid, the odor of gas was strong when one neared the bed of the truck. Also, in the truck were about a hundred loaves of bread, rolls, and sandwich buns. It did not take the work of a brain surgeon to figure this one out.

There were two bakeries in the neighborhood. The bakeries would bake and package bread and rolls after which the products would be loaded into delivery trucks during the evenings or early morning hours for delivery to stores and restaurants as soon as the daylight shift started work. Every few months someone would break into the trucks to steal the freshly baked goods. While they stole the bread, they also had a habit of siphoning the tanks of the delivery trucks. In those days, the bakeries were not inclined to pay to upgrade facilities, there were no video recordings available, and little evidence was left behind. Solving these crimes was difficult.

These two intoxicated thieves, spoiling for a fight, provided the best evidence we had to date. All we had to do was get the two bakeries to check their trucks to determine which one was the victim. Sure enough, we found the victim and were able to charge the suspects with theft in addition to their other charges. There is an expression in police work that "it's better to be lucky than good." I felt lucky this night.

Sometimes it was a matter of being lucky and being good. Officer Steve Bush and I were regularly reading police reports of burglaries in our district. One night we read a report that had a huge gift attached to it. A suspect had used a welfare card to attempt to jimmy the rear door of a residence. The slight noise from the door handle woke the homeowner who turned on the light to the back porch. The suspect fled, dropping the welfare card with the picture and name of Eddie Williams.

It took a considerable amount of leg work to locate him. We questioned many people working in the area, such as postal carriers, delivery people, and telephone employees. No one had seen him. We were rewarded for putting in the legwork to find him and lucky when a newspaper delivery person remembered seeing him exit a house one morning.

We waited at the house and managed to apprehend him. After he was read his rights, we found he was very cooperative. We drove him through two neighborhoods for hours as he pointed out the houses he had burglarized. He told us that some of the residents of the houses he entered in the middle of the night never knew he was in there. We knew he was telling us the truth since we researched all the burglary reports upon our return to the station.

We located ten reports about burglaries Williams had committed but could not dwell on the unreported offenses since at that time officers had only six hours to have the subject arraigned after a confession was made. Several of those hours were spent driving through the neighborhoods as Williams pointed out the houses he broke into, described how he did it, discussed what he did while there, and described what he took from the house. He did not take much since he was homeless. He generally ate from the homeowner's refrigerator and on one occasion defecated on the living room floor.

If that was not enough, all his life's belongings were with him. These included a duffel bag that contained a notebook of poems he wrote. He also had a guitar pick and a guitar with the name "Kiyee" carved into the wood.

When we got to the Warrant Office, we were met by the sergeant in charge. We had to have our paperwork approved by the sergeant in order to have the prisoner processed for arraignment. There was only about an hour left of the six hours before we would lose Williams's entire confession. The Warrant Office sergeant was an older curmudgeon who had been a sergeant for decades and worked the desk later in his career. He chastised us for taking so much of our six-hour time limit before getting the suspect's paperwork to his office. Even with the great police work that went into clearing ten burglaries, we were left to defend our work. Fortunately, we did have Williams arraigned within the time limit and were able to use his statement for prosecution.

Williams's defense attorney was successful in obtaining many delays, which seemed to be their best tactic to discourage the victims from testifying against the burglar. After some of the victims lost days of work due to the delays, each postponement meant we would have fewer victims when the case eventually made it to the judge. By trial date, four victims had hung in there and we did get a conviction for those burglaries. It probably would not have mattered if there were four or ten, though, since Williams was sentenced to 11½ to 23½ months' confinement.

Nearly a year later my partner and I arrived for work one night at 7:00 PM. Two officers I highly respected were completing a rape report. I had worked with one of them, Officer David Bouchard, years before while in uniform.

David called me to review the report he was taking for a rape call they just had. He acknowledged that my partner and I could not investigate rapes, but he thought we should read the police report he had just taken. It was similar to the rape report he had taken the previous day. We were not sent a copy of that report since only the Sex Assault Unit followed up on rapes.

Both reports read very much the same. A suspect broke into the house and raped the woman resident on both nights. It is not common that a rapist would return to rape the same victim two nights in a row. What is also not common is the fact that the rapist would read poetry to the victim and play a guitar between multiple sexual assaults.

I told David this sounded like Eddie Williams, but that I did not believe he could be out of jail yet. I immediately went to the plainclothes office and retrieved the arrest reports for Williams. Since Williams's jail time prior to his conviction counted as part of his entire sentence, he was out and preying on the same community. I went back upstairs to David and told him that I suspected the owner of the welfare card still in our files was their suspect.

David notified Sex Assault and immediate action was taken. Eddie Williams was obviously deranged, breaking into peoples' houses in the middle of the night to eat from their refrigerator and defecate on their floors. The Sex Assault investigation resulted in obtaining a positive identification from the victim and a warrant for the suspect's arrest. A stakeout was formed for the victim's house. Sure enough, Williams returned a third time. He was apprehended following a foot pursuit. I was left to hope Williams would receive a lengthy prison sentence for the terror he had put his victim through.

★★★★

Another type of crime extended to incidents in two different parts of the city. In both cases, a young man in his twenties approached a woman from the rear as she walked. He would grab her with one hand across her mouth and the other arm around her body as he dragged her to a nearby car. In both instances he lost control of the struggling woman as he attempted to force her into the car.

Ed Diaz and I knew that having two similar incidents in two different communities within days of each other meant there would probably be a third before long. We could not afford to have another incident; he might be successful in getting her into the car the third time.

A person familiar with one of the attempted abductions provided a partial plate of a car he thought matched the description. We then began searching plates of similar cars in the area, starting with the same three digits. We eventually reduced the list to the most promising leads. One of them was a vehicle registered to a woman living within a couple miles of the first attempted abduction. The question we were left with was how we were to proceed. We opted to stake out the house.

We sat on the house throughout the night. Around 3:00 AM a car matching the description with the first three matching digits on the plate pulled up directly in front of the house. We could see there was a man in his twenties operating the car. We pulled up next to him. He did not realize we were the police until we exited the car and flashed our badges. We had achieved the element of surprise. When we asked for identification, we could see that the car had a crowbar, screwdrivers, and other tools that were typically used for burglaries. In addition, it was apparent there were proceeds from some burglary, including a massive number of quarters, dimes, and nickels and a couple hundred packs of various brands of cigarettes.

We had the potential burglar accompany us to the station where we had summoned one of our victims to meet us. She had no idea why she was meeting us at the station, but as she walked into the station full of officers and some people in civilian clothing, she saw our suspect and shouted, "That's him." It all came together quickly for us that night.

I only had about four years on the job while my partner, Officer Diaz, had one year less than I did. There were two sets of plainclothes officers assigned to each district. The other set of plainclothes officers in our district were Officers Sean McInerney and Johnny Hopgood. They were veterans of at least ten to fifteen years with much more investigating experience than we had. There was a spirit of competitiveness that I believed made us all better police officers. All of us wanted to have the arrests for the serious crimes and the most "good arrests," which generally meant felony arrests.

All four of us had been investigating reports that someone was shooting at moving vehicles at a major intersection of the city. Shots were fired sporadically on different nights. Stakeouts had proven to be nonproductive. One suspect thought capable of such dangerous acts was Billy Thomas. Billy was twenty-two years old with no job and always in some sort of trouble. The shots all seemed to come from the direction of his second-floor apartment. Officers McInerney and Hopgood searched the apartment after they obtained a search warrant, but they were not able to locate the rifle used in the shootings. They had no evidence to make an arrest.

There were many close calls. In one, a cab full of passengers was struck in the windshield. The bullet passed through the car and became embedded in the rear window molding. The occupants of the cab realized how close they came to serious injury or death. Another incident involved a public bus. The bullet entered a side window and passed through the driver's jacket that was hanging right behind the driver's seat. It was obvious the bullet was aimed at the driver's head, but the bus was moving slightly faster than the shooter anticipated. Two other cars were also hit within days of each other. All four of us plainclothes officers were not able to link the shootings until an informant's tip on another felony would circle us back to the South Side.

We received information that a former high school student was selling stolen bus passes. We obtained one of these bus passes and our investigation revealed it was taken during a burglary of a local business. The Blue Diamond reported thousands of dollars' worth of jewelry and other items missing, including bus passes. We investigated further and learned where the suspect lived and the car he drove. We obtained a warrant for the eighteen-year-old, whose name was Charlie Chambers.

Officer Diaz and I staked out the car and waited for it to pull out. We waited for the car to commit a traffic violation before pulling the car over. We established a rapport with him very quickly. He was surprised and overwhelmed at the information we knew. We convinced him his best alternative was to work with us to recover as many of the stolen items as we could. He led us to the trunk of his car where we recovered about one third of the stolen jewelry. More importantly, he identified the other two accomplices. One of them was Billy Thomas.

After processing the arrest paperwork for Charlie, we obtained a search warrant for Billy Thomas's apartment to look for the proceeds from the burglary and for the rifle used in the shootings. We also obtained a warrant for Billy's arrest. We went to the desk sergeant at our station to enlist the aid of uniformed officers to serve the arrest warrant and the search warrant. The desk sergeant, who was a friend of the other team of plainclothes officers, mocked our chances of finding anything in the apartment. He bellowed that if the older, more experienced plainclothes officers had not found the rifle, we were not going to find it either.

Billy's apartment was less than a mile from the station. We arrived there quickly since we feared someone might soon learn of Charlie's arrest and deduce where we were headed next. We wasted no time in making sure we got there before Billy knew what was coming. We got him along with the third accomplice who was staying at Billy's apartment. We recovered nearly all the rest of the jewelry and other items stolen from the store. In addition, we recovered the rifle used in the shooting incidents. It was hidden above a ceiling tile in the suspended ceiling.

We were less excited about recovering most of the stolen jewelry than about our other achievements. We not only cleared the burglary with three arrests, but we were able to clear the four vehicle shootings. What gave me the most pleasure was returning to the station, holding the rifle up to the desk sergeant to make sure he could see it, and announcing, "We got the rifle." We may have been younger and less experienced, but we were smart enough to pay attention to detail, dogged in our determination, and smooth enough in our interrogations to obtain sufficient evidence to solve serious crimes and obtain convictions.

PLAINCLOTHES AT THE STRIP DISTRICT STATION

When Commander Tom Cunningham was transferred from #7 Station to #3 Station, he gave my partner and me the opportunity to go with him. We took him up on his offer. I was first on the list to be promoted to sergeant and wanted to continue to work a plainclothes assignment until then. At #3 Station, I had the opportunity to work with several other plainclothes officers who were some of the best police officers I ever had the opportunity to work alongside.

Patrick O'Malley was my first partner at that station. We worked many drug cases and I learned a great deal from him. We were able to turn a person we arrested into an informant for us. The informant was the first person I had wired to make a controlled buy. We served a search warrant, retrieved the marked money, and used the recording to eventually arrest the dealer's supplier. We arrested Steve Woodward for supplying drugs to a neighborhood just outside the city proper, and the search warrant at his apartment turned up approximately 2,000 pills.

Patrick was good at checking the logs at drug stores to see which pharmacists were prescribing the most narcotics. Patrick was later attached to the Drug Enforcement Agency (DEA) for ten years until he was promoted to lieutenant. Patrick eventually was promoted to commander until he retired and took a position doing investigations for another agency.

My last partner at #3 Station was Tom Clark. Prior to my promotion to sergeant, he and I received direction from our commander to investigate a New Year's Eve shooting at an African American church. The church was in a mixed neighborhood. During church services, multiple shots came through the stained-glass windows, ricocheted off the walls, and one struck a woman.

When we arrived at the church, we could see bullet holes through the plexiglass covering the stained-glass windows. Once inside, we could view the holes through the stained-glass windows. Tom had the idea of placing drinking straws through the holes to determine the trajectory of each bullet. Six sets of holes through two windows all led back to the same location where the shooter had to have stood. It was just outside of the back door of a nearby home.

We went to the home to speak with the residents. A woman came to the door and explained that her husband wasn't there but was working at a nearby hospital. After a short discussion with her, we knew we had to immediately speak with her husband if we were to obtain a confession. Tom and I decided we better get to the hospital fast to speak with him before his wife had the chance to let him know we were coming.

Fortunately, the hospital was only blocks away. We asked security to take us to him immediately. As we were being escorted to where he was working, we could hear him being paged. We knew it had to be his wife trying to warn him we would be coming. But we got to him first and had the opportunity to interview him before he could be tipped off.

He admitted shooting into the church on New Year's Eve. He insisted it was not racial, but he said he had been drinking that night and believed he was shooting into the air. My partner's simple solution to use drinking straws to determine the trajectory of the shots allowed us to gain evidence, take quick action, and put into practice good interview skills.

After working with officers of this caliber, I remembered what my first partner, Ryan Green, told me about only being concerned with what the good officers thought about you and not about what the bad officers had to say. I would always remember to determine to which group a critic belonged. I would take seriously any sky-blue officer who offered criticism. I would not take seriously any criticism from a dark-blue officer.

As I went through the ranks, I was determined to provide the good officers with what they needed to get the job done and to ignore the chatter that would circulate from the bad officers.

LESSONS LEARNED

1) The children of police officers whom I encountered were either the best the next generation had to offer or the worst. There did not seem to be much in between.

2) Some senior officers and supervisors will not give younger officers credit for their work. Some of them think having seniority equates to better policing. Senior officers may have more experience, but that does not necessarily make them more motivated or knowledgeable.

3) I am forever indebted to the good officers I worked with. They made the job fun while we learned.

CHAPTER FOUR

Welcome to Supervision

"It takes a great deal of bravery to stand up to our enemies, but just as much to stand up to our friends."

—J. K. ROWLING,
Harry Potter and the Sorcerer's Stone

A t the age of thirty-two, for the first time in my life I was to have the responsibilities of a supervisor. The police officer's ability to take away the liberty of a person by making an arrest, the power to use force, and the ability to legally take another's life are overwhelming concepts. Being a police supervisor with that daunting power over many men and women is even more overwhelming. Being the first to be promoted in years, all I could think of was a line from the movie *Treasure of Sierra Madre*: "Badges? We don't need no stinkin' badges." Except in my case, what I would be up against was more like: "Training? We don't need no stinkin' training."

Sure, I had not received any field training prior to assignments to walking beats in various parts of #7 Station. Sure, I had not received any training when I was assigned to a plainclothes position with only two years of experience as an officer. But I thought I would surely receive supervisory training before I was assigned to supervise men and women who had the authority to use force, even deadly force, to stop, hold, and arrest those they encountered during their shifts.

For the first time in my life I was not only responsible for what I did on the job, but I was responsible for others whom I had to supervise. And some of those officers were not in the sky-blue or light-blue categories. Some were officers who desperately needed oversight and direction. Some of those officers should not have ever been permitted to be officers. Supervision training was not to happen. I would serve nearly four years as a sergeant with no training in supervision, leadership, or management.

FAILURE TO TRAIN, FAILURE TO SUPERVISE, FAILURE TO SERVE

Although I didn't know enough to be able to express how this failure to train was detrimental to me, the department, and the public, I would eventually realize that the vast majority of failures in a department were the fault of the department, the leadership of the department, and the municipality. It was a departmental failure in more than one way.

The first departmental failure was the disservice to those promoted in failing to give them the tools they needed to complete their duties successfully. Newly promoted supervisors were set up for failure. Depending upon the mistake a supervisor made, it could lead to the supervisor being sued, disciplined, demoted, or terminated. Those actions could destroy a supervisor's ability to pursue further promotional opportunities, be career ending, and lead to public embarrassment for the supervisor and the supervisor's family.

The second department failure was the disservice to the department. Without proper training, the department was not able to be as productive and efficient as it should have been. A poorly led police force only gets productivity from the 20 percent of officers who are self-motivated. Without proper supervisory training and supervision of first-line supervisors, a department is, at best, giving little back at the expense of the taxpayers or, at worst, poor or corrupted service with taxpayer dollars.

The third failure was to the public. The public many times fails to get the police service they are entitled to receive or fails to be treated with the respect and dignity they should expect from a professional police agency.

★★★★

After the minimum time of four years to be eligible for a promotional test, I took the test with hundreds of other officers and eventually learned I had placed first on the sergeant's list. I waited another two years and was promoted to sergeant with slightly less than seven years of experience. Most of those years I worked in a plainclothes capacity alongside other highly motivated, intelligent, and resourceful officers. I had minimal working relationships with uniformed officers for four and a half years and was now expected to supervise a shift of those officers. Some of those officers needed strong leadership and direction. Many of those officers were medium-blue officers or dark-blue officers.

I was sworn in as a sergeant on a Friday in January 1984 and was working the following Monday as a patrol supervisor in #6 Station. Within a couple of weeks, when no lieutenant was working one Sunday morning, I was in charge of all officers working in the district since I was the only supervisor working and was designated as the acting lieutenant. I thought surely the department had time to prepare supervisory training since they had not promoted any sergeants for two years and they were making dozens of new sergeants on the same day in January.

Many municipalities, I was to learn later, hire police officers to demonstrate they are making a commitment to public safety, but they fail to provide them with adequate equipment or proper training to make them effective at providing public safety.

While serving as the acting lieutenant one Sunday morning shift, I first had to relieve the night shift officers. I reviewed the list of officers due to be relieved and noticed that although there were two officers assigned to a wagon crew, only one of them reported into the station for relief. (A police wagon crew consists of two officers assigned to work a vehicle, which was essentially a truck body with a steel box behind the cab that could hold multiple prisoners.)

I asked the officer where his partner was, and he told me he was still outside waiting to be relieved. I instructed him to have his partner come in. He went outside, and I assumed he intended to have his partner come in for relief. The officer came back in and informed me his partner had already left. I could see what was happening. Since the new, young, inexperienced sergeant was struggling with his new duties, some officers would leave work early and have their partners cover for them. I had to send the message that no officers would leave before I checked them at the end of their tour of duty. I could see I had a lot to learn and I had to learn it fast and learn it the hard way.

I am sure some of the officers had some choice names for me when they saw I would not accept cutting corners. I could see it was not going to be an easy task learning how to supervise on my own. I had to learn quickly, or I would be set up for failure. Although I did not know enough at the time, I later learned I was vulnerable since the city and department were guilty of failure to train and I was guilty of a failure to supervise since I didn't know how to supervise.

My patrol supervision was short-lived since I was transferred after only two months. I was transferred in March 1984 to the Service Branch, which included support services including the Warrant Office and the Communications Section.

THE WARRANT OFFICE

The Warrant Office had been created by the department a few years earlier when police officials realized there were too many errors related to charges filed for those arrested. The creation of the Warrant Office was to avoid negligent appointment, negligent training, and negligent supervision.

Since the desk sergeants at the stations were oftentimes police officers working as acting sergeants, they did not always properly review the charges placed against someone arrested or they found insufficient narrative to support the charges the officers were asserting. The Warrant Office was created to be a central location in the city, near the lockup and the city magistrate, where officers would bring their paperwork after dropping off their prisoner at the lockup. The Warrant Office was supposed to always be staffed with knowledgeable sergeants who would review the paperwork to ensure the arrest was lawful, the proper charges were filed, and the narrative justified each charge filed.

It appeared the city had enough faith in my knowledge of the Crimes Code, the Vehicle Code, Criminal Procedures, and other sources to transfer me to the Warrant Office to perform those duties. However, most sergeants did not want to work in the Warrant Office. One of the Warrant Office sergeants asked me while I was awaiting promotion if I would be interested in working in the Warrant Office. I was not going to say no since I was primarily interested in getting the promotion.

The Warrant Office was not an assignment that had sergeants waiting in line to take because it entailed no supervision on the street and little to no interaction with the public. It was a first-floor, corner office, with a sole window that was covered for security reasons. One sergeant and two to three officers sat in desks nearly abutting each other for an entire eight-hour shift.

The Warrant Office during the AM shift was busy as the central repository for warrants obtained by officers and detectives. It also served for the processing of paperwork for every arrest occurring throughout the city. Within a few hours of starting the PM shift, a line of officers would form to have their paperwork reviewed and approved by the Warrant Office sergeant. That line of officers generally did not end until nearly the end of the night shift, at five-thirty in the morning. Most night shifts had me eating my lunch with one hand while in the other hand I reviewed police incident and arrest reports so we could move the identification and arraignment of prisoners along and get the hard-working officers back into the street to continue doing police work.

For those who enjoy sitting behind a desk for eight hours reading another person's documents while never seeing the light of day, this would be an enjoyable assignment. For those who became police officers to be mobile, to anticipate different situations every few minutes, and to feel fulfilled when apprehending some of the most despicable and dangerous elements of our society, this was more of a job than an adventure. However, I learned in the Marine Corps to be thankful for any assignment. I knew I was there because someone somewhere trusted me to perform those duties well. I decided to concentrate on the positives rather than on all the negatives this assignment held. I knew that eventually all things shall pass.

The positive aspects of the assignment included (1) getting to know all the officers making arrests throughout the city, (2) working lots of overtime, and (3) getting a thorough understanding of each of the elements of every crime, understanding criminal procedures, and learning the police procedures most officers seldom encountered.

For nearly two years I got to see the hardest-working police officers throughout the city since they were the ones consistently coming through the office with good arrests. Within each department they were the top 20 percent who did 80 percent of the work. Those were the officers I could relate to and could provide positive reinforcement for the jobs they were doing.

★★★★

While I had been a sergeant in the Warrant Office for two years, I was able to take the lieutenant's test. My time in the Warrant Office was invaluable because I had learned enough in that assignment and been prepared enough to take the test for a lieutenant's position. I tied for second on that test and ended up in third place on the list since the person I tied with was more senior to me.

I knew the city would eventually make at least three lieutenants over the next three years and felt I would be promoted. Just as I was on the sergeant's list for two years, I sat on the lieutenant's list for another two years. Two ahead of me had been promoted to lieutenant which left me the next available person to be promoted to lieutenant.

I got to learn much more than the various legal codes while working in the Warrant Office and in its Communications Section. I started to see how some officers used their prior working relationship with me or their higher rank to take shortcuts.

The department created the Warrant Office to ensure that a responsible sergeant reviewed the arrest reports, that all charges filed were appropriate and supported by the narrative documenting the actor's actions, and that it was clear how those actions violated specific laws. To ensure this was accomplished, the officer knowing all the information regarding the incident, making the arrest, and filing the charges had to be the person to bring the paperwork to the Warrant Office.

I learned how important this was while I was working as a plain-clothes officer. I had a stolen car arrest and failed to properly document my arrest. The sergeant working in the Warrant Office asked me where in the report I had written that the car was stolen. I had documented how we spotted the car, how we followed it, and how we made the arrest. But when I reviewed my paperwork, I realized I had failed to document where and when the car was stolen. Everyone makes mistakes, and the Warrant Office worked the way it was supposed to work by catching my omission.

On more than one occasion, as a sergeant, I found that procedure was not followed. After reviewing the paperwork and asking an officer a question regarding any charge, I inevitably heard, "I don't know, that's not my arrest." My response always was, "Take the paperwork back to the station and have the arresting officer bring the paperwork here as regulations require."

I knew this would upset another supervisor somewhere in the city since he or she had apparently told the transporting officers to take someone else's prisoner and paperwork to the Warrant Office even though it violated policy. Although there were many instances, the one which disappointed me the most was when transporting officers from #8 Station brought in some paperwork and a prisoner. They were uniformed officers and the arrest had been made by plainclothes officers. I sent the paperwork back with the transporting officers, and the plainclothes officer eventually came to my office.

The plainclothes officer worked in #8 Station when I worked plainclothes in #7 Station. We had backed each other up on occasion when we worked the streets. I will never forget his comment to me when he entered the office. He said, "I thought we were friends." I told him, "I thought we were friends too." He never spoke to me again. One of the plainclothes officers working with him at #8 Station was Officer Kevin Massey. His revenge was to make untruthful statements about me, accusing me of domestic violence when I was the chief of police. He would eventually have to testify in federal court that he had claimed I had physically abused my wife because he thought it would be funny.

★★★★

My most eye-opening experiences as a sergeant were yet to come. In 1985, a sergeant vacancy arose in the Special Operations Division (SOD). The SOD at that time consisted of officers assigned the duties of bomb disposal, Tactical, river patrol, and the patrol of large urban parks. ("Tactical" refers to units sometimes called either SWAT [Special Weapons and Tactics] or SERT [Special Emergency Response Team].)

The chief of police issued a memo instructing sergeants interested in a transfer to that division to submit a transfer request and a résumé. It was the first time I had witnessed a request for a résumé to accompany a transfer request. As things turned out, it would be the first and last time I would ever submit a transfer request. I thought this was my chance to volunteer for an assignment that would put me back out on the street. I submitted a transfer request with my résumé, which included experience with weapons I learned to use in the Marine Corps including rifles, machine guns, grenade launchers, and plastic explosives. The Tactical part of SOD used grenade launchers for tear gas and plastic explosives for Tactical entries.

I received the transfer to SOD in August 1985. When I reported for duty there, I met with the commanding officer of the division, Captain Robert Bentley. He was a tall, husky Irish cop in his early fifties, with white hair. He was eighteen years my senior and had nineteen more years of police experience.

I was left surprised by our ten-minute conversation. He was brutally direct and left no doubt regarding his dissatisfaction with my transfer to the division. He had requested another sergeant, Sergeant Drew Little. I had no idea why I was chosen since I definitely did not have anyone recommending me for the assignment. I was not politically connected within the department and had no outside political connections.

Captain Bentley explained his position. He was one of only two captains left in the department, which was phasing out the position.

They had been replaced with a commander rank. While captains previously were in charge of police stations, commanders now held those positions and they were equivalent to the rank of an army/marine/air force major, which outranked the captain.

SOD was the last refuge for a captain to be in charge of a unit working in the streets. The captain told me that since I was transferred to SOD and since I was the next person on the lieutenant's list, rumors swirled that I would be promoted to lieutenant and replace him after I learned all the duties in SOD. The rumor also indicated that Captain Bentley would be transferred to headquarters to oversee an administrative unit.

Captain Bentley advised me that he had been around too long in the department to allow that to happen. He informed me that for as long as I was in SOD, I should expect no training, and I was prohibited from participating in some of the specialized activities including going onto the boat assigned to river patrol. With my being unable to learn any of the responsibilities of SOD, he indicated I would be unable to take command of the unit. He advised me to consider transferring out of the unit. I felt I could not do that since someone somewhere had a reason to transfer me there and had faith in me that I would accept my assignment and make the most of it.

There are many rumors that circulate within a police department and the vast majority of them have no basis in any facts. However, I knew some officers who would start a rumor either to see how long it would take for it to come back to them and how much it would change by the time it did. Sometimes there may have been some hope that the substance of the rumor actually did occur. No one had ever informed me of anything similar to the rumor Captain Bentley had heard prior to or following my transfer.

I told him I understood his position. As a former Marine, I accepted my position and my superior officers without question. I would not go over his head even if I had actually known anyone in the department to go to.

Although I never did get any specialized training, I read as much as I could on police Tactical incidents and handling explosives. I depended upon the officers I supervised to do what they were required to do and to help me learn "unofficially" along the way.

Officers who reported to me grew to know me and trust me. Some eventually confided that Captain Bentley used to mock me and make obscene gestures toward me when I was unaware of it. In his effort to undercut my authority in the unit, he diminished himself in the eyes of those same officers.

Captain Bentley got his best chance to encourage me to transfer out of SOD within a month of my assignment there. The SOD sergeants always reported for duty one and a half hours prior to the start of their tour of duty. Our AM shift started at 7:00. However, the sergeants always reported for duty on the AM shift at 5:30 to prepare for the shift. The end of the shift, although officially 3:00 PM, actually occurred at 1:30 PM since the PM shift sergeant relieved the AM sergeant one and one-half hours early.

My maternal grandfather died on September 12, 1985, approximately one month after I was assigned to SOD. My family was to meet at 2:00 PM on the first day he was laid out at the funeral home. The SOD officers were assisting with Traffic division officers during a small parade in a downtown park. I was scheduled to work the AM shift and planned to be relieved from duty at 1:30 in order to make it to the funeral home in time for the family viewing. I wanted to be there for my mother who had just lost her father.

I worked the event with Captain Bentley and a few subordinate officers. I mentioned to the captain I would appreciate leaving the event at the end of my tour of duty in order to arrive at the funeral home in time. Also, my relief had actually shown up prior to 1:30. I asked Captain Bentley for permission to leave since my relief was on site.

He informed me that although the sergeants relieved each other early every day, I was "officially" on duty until 3:00. He directed me to a more remote portion of the park even though no one was in that area; all officers were at the entrance of the park. I stood at the location as instructed until 3:00. At 3:00 he sent an officer to inform me I was officially relieved. I was unable to make it to the funeral home in time for the family viewing.

Working for him was extremely difficult but did not last long. Within seven months, Captain Bentley's fear of being transferred to an administrative position was realized. In March 1986, a person jumped into one of Pittsburgh's three rivers from a bridge. The River Patrol, staffed by Officers Richard Alexander and Donald Hoover, took the boat through the cold, wintry water to the location where the man was last seen.

They found his body floating but had difficulty retrieving him because the water current had washed him under a docked barge. Retrieving him from the quick current was dangerous since the current was attempting to push the riverboat under the barge. They eventually used a boat hook and a rope to pull him to the boat. The man had been in the water, and underwater, for approximately an hour. They viewed this as a recovery of a body instead of a rescue of a drowned person. They tied a rope around his feet and pulled the body in tow to the location where EMS was staged to attempt what they believed would be a cold-water rescue.

EMS personnel knew people could be resuscitated even though they had been under water for an extended period if the water was cold enough. Police had never been trained in cold-water rescues. The sight of the man being towed with river water flowing over his head was captured by the media, which staged nearby to photograph and record the "rescue." This incident created a stir with the media, community, and inside the department.

As a result of the "towing" incident, the Public Safety director had the Emergency Medical Services Bureau take over the duties of the Police River Patrol and renamed it River Rescue. The duties of the sole officer left to serve on the River Rescue boat was to operate the boat while two paramedics handled the rescues. Part of the fallout from this media disaster was that Captain Bentley was transferred out of SOD following the incident and Lieutenant Declan Mulligan was transferred in to take command of SOD.

When I later spoke with the officers who operated the riverboat during the heart-breaking incident that caused Captain Bentley's transfer, they informed me that he had told the officers it wasn't their fault for what occurred that day. Instead, he told the two officers it was my fault since I should have been on the boat with them. The officers did not know then that Captain Bentley had specifically directed me never to be on the boat.

Once Lieutenant Mulligan took command, tactical training was at least initiated as we trained with the Allegheny County Police Tactical Unit. During that training program other deficiencies in equipment and training were exposed. For example, we still used revolvers on the tactical team as we trained with county police who used pistols. We were not able to keep up with the speed maneuvers during training since we continually had to stop and reload our six-shooters while the county police had three times the amount of ammunition in their weapons and could easily reload.

During my slightly more than two years working in SOD, I saw firsthand the lack of equipment and training for officers who were expected to handle calls on the river and tactical calls, and safely handle bomb calls. The lack of current policy, the lack of operational training for officers assigned to specialty units, the lack of training for supervisors, and the purposeful obstruction of supervisors' attempts to perform their duties created an enormous liability to the department and all personnel involved.

During 1986 and 1987 I was able to learn considerably under Lieutenant Declan Mulligan's leadership. This was the first of two occasions when I would work for Declan Mulligan. Outside learning began to occur more often. When I reflected back on Captain Bentley's control of SOD, I realized that when he attempted to stifle my career for fear of it outshining his, he did a disservice to me, to all of SOD, to the department, to the community we served, and even to himself. Had I been permitted to learn and lead, I may have been in a position to achieve a different outcome on the river that cold, wintry day.

Even with its dysfunctions, the department continued to move on. By the end of 1987 there were many more promotions and reassignments within the department. Captain Bentley was promoted to commander and placed in charge of Traffic Division. Lieutenant Mulligan was promoted to commander and placed in charge of a patrol zone. I was promoted to lieutenant and transferred to supervise a shift in Zone 1 on the North Side. Department rumors that I would take charge of SOD were proven to be false, as were most department rumors.

Even though Captain Bentley's efforts were to destabilize my capacity to perform and lead within SOD, I always treated him with the respect a superior officer should expect from a subordinate. When all was said and done, he realized I never had any intentions of undermining, harming, or replacing him.

Years later (1990), I was transferred to Traffic Division when all lieutenants in the department were transferred. Traffic Division was considered a choice assignment. I had no idea how I rated that assignment, but when I reported to Commander Bentley, who was in charge there, he told me he had specifically asked for me to work under him. Commander Bentley treated me well and even had me assigned as the acting commander when he was absent.

It was interesting that our careers would cross paths three different times, including the time I relieved him when he retired from Zone 2. I had been promoted to commander in mid-1990 and was better prepared to accept command of Zone 2 in mid-1994 because of Commander Bentley's coaching. Commander Bentley was supportive in the transition. He died of emphysema in 2000 at the age of sixty-seven.

LESSONS LEARNED

1) Many departments fail to provide adequate training or any training when assigning personnel to new positions. This may be due to a lack of understanding of the importance of training or a lack of funding. Generally, the first budget cuts during lean years reduce or eliminate training funds. Once those funds are gone, it is difficult to have future budgets with reasonable training funds.

2) It is better to have fewer, better-trained officers than a larger number of poorly trained officers.

3) Accepting what appears to be a less desirable position can have its benefits. It positioned me for future assignments. It also provided evidence to superior officers that I was willing to accept any assignment without complaint.

4) Some officers, who claimed to be "friends," used their prior working relationship with me in an attempt to avoid their adherence to the rules. It would have been beneficial to have received training to know how to contend with the situations a new sergeant would encounter.

5) Some officers and supervisors are difficult to supervise since they are being protected by higher ranking supervisors.

6) In a supervisory capacity, insisting that others adhere to regulations may alienate some officers and supervisors, but it is often possible to do so in a way that leaves a path open for good working relationships and even later friendships.

7) After being assigned to work in the Warrant Office and as the supervisor in 911, I learned that additional supervisory training is essential for sergeants working specialized positions. A sergeant promoted

only two months before being assigned to supervise all 911 call-takers and dispatchers is not trained enough to handle the personnel working those critical positions.

8) After being assigned to Special Operations, I realized how deficient the department was due to the lack of equipment and training for Tactical calls and bomb calls. Officers and supervisors assigned to those units needed far more training.

9) Some supervisors actually prevented other supervisors from learning their jobs since they feared subordinates would be able to do their jobs better than they could. All supervisors should be evaluated on how well they prepare their subordinates for the jobs they have.

10) The multitude of a department's failures eventually leads to lost careers, costly lawsuits, and outside intervention through lawsuits, memorandums of understanding, and consent decrees to correct inadequacies. In the long run, departments that do not correct their own deficiencies will find others who will come in to make the changes for them. And those working in the department generally will not like how the changes are made or the outcome of the changes.

CHAPTER FIVE

The Good, the Bad, and the Ugly

"The single biggest way to impact an organization is to focus on leadership development. There is almost no limit to the potential of an organization that recruits good people, raises them up as leaders and continually develops them."

—JOHN MAXWELL,
The 21 Irrefutable Laws of Leadership

ZONE 1

The date 10/9/87 is easily remembered and significant to me for personal and professional reasons. On that day I was one of five to be promoted to lieutenant and I stood next to the first woman to achieve the rank of lieutenant in the Pittsburgh Police. Although only knowing her by name as Cathy Vallone at the time, changes in my personal life over the next five years would result in her becoming my wife. Professionally, I would supervise a shift of officers and find myself in a position to arrest an officer for the first time in my career. Unfortunately, it would be far from my last time.

The department saw changes in May of 1987 when Richard D'Angelo took charge of the department as the new chief of police. He had spent years in the department and left in 1986 to head a university police department. Now the Pittsburgh Police had a chief of police who had a master's degree and understood the value of training. This was exhibited when his first class of supervisors attended a week-long mandatory training course.

The course, Police Officer Supervisory In-service Training (POSIT), provided by the Justice and Safety Institute of the Pennsylvania State University, was designed for first-level supervision. The course was extremely valuable. I remember saying that if I had only received that training four years earlier, I would have been a far better sergeant. It was that course that cemented the idea that I needed to document as much as possible including the good, the bad, and the ugly of policing. I differentiate bad and ugly as the bad being honest mistakes officers make doing their jobs and the ugly as acts purposely done that are illegal, unnecessary, or unethical.

In light of the fact that new lieutenants who had never received prior supervisory training and those promoted to sergeant on 10/9/87 benefitted from the training, POSIT should have been one of the courses provided to the lieutenants. POSIT was a good start, but the Justice and Safety Institute also had a police executive (POLEX) course designed for mid-level supervisors. That level of training would have benefitted those of us promoted to lieutenant.

Although the one-week training was beneficial, additional subjects should have been included in the training for both sergeants and lieutenants. These subjects could have addressed the challenges of supervising, including how to deal with the lack of information related to prior grievances, how to initiate awards for good performance, how to initiate a request for an internal affairs investigation or, especially, how to initiate disciplinary charges against an officer. Problems were bound to arise in trying to lead a group of officers without training in how to use all the necessary tools of the rank.

I assumed my duties as a shift lieutenant the week following our training. To assist with supervision of the shift, I had three sergeants. Two of those sergeants had just been promoted to their ranks the same day I was promoted to lieutenant. The three of us had attended the same training session. I only had one sergeant with any supervisory experience.

I was fortunate to have a good commander as a mentor. Commander Anthony Wright had been the Night Watch commander (in charge of the city on the night shift) before being assigned to command Zone 1. Whenever I encountered problems that I was not sure how to address, I was always able to speak to him and I always received knowledgeable guidance. Having a superior I could turn to for advice made my job easier. I learned methods for addressing lesser performance deficiencies rather than resorting to discipline.

Over the next two years, I would be confronted with what was the good, the bad, and the ugly on a department level. The good resulted from conscientious, trained, and experienced police supervisors laboring to ensure the department had responsible and effective policy, training, supervision, and discipline. The bad was lack of or insufficient policy, training, supervision, and discipline. The ugly was corrupt police officers and the department's failure to take meaningful action to weed those officers out.

THE GOOD: FIELD TRAINING OFFICER PROGRAM

Not only did Chief D'Angelo ensure new supervisors received training prior to assuming their new duties, he created the field training program for officers graduating from the police academy. The program was led by Commander Mark Nelson. Stocky, muscular, and square-jawed, Commander Nelson looked as though he belonged on a recruiting poster for a police officer or for the USMC. His appearance ensured he was taken seriously. He was also a member of Mensa, which indicated he was capable of creating a training unit from scratch.

Commander Nelson developed a process whereby new officers would receive training from experienced field training officers (FTO). When a class of recruits graduated from the academy, Nelson drafted experienced officers and supervisors to assist with the field training portion of the recruits' development.

I only knew Commander Nelson from my initial recruit training at the police academy where he served as a firearms instructor. I had not imagined he would draft me as his first choice as the lieutenant to supervise the shift of recruit officers and FTOs. Nelson drafted me for three recruit classes during 1988-1989. The field training for those three classes lasted three months each. The program involved constant oversight of the new officers, daily and weekly evaluations, and a comprehensive training manual. Each new officer worked with one of three different FTOs during the three months of training. To ensure they received all required training, the dates of specific tasks had to be documented along with the recruits' initials and the initials of the field training officers.

I benefitted from my experience with training as much as I was able to provide leadership. The recruits were able to work alongside experienced and motivated officers who could help kickstart their careers. I thought back on my lack of a formal field training program when I graduated from the academy and was grateful that I had one officer, Ryan Green, who provided me with so much to start my career. I was thankful the new officers would be trained properly. Knowing how training should be done, I would always value the benefit of training and insist that training budgets be increased and maintained even during financially difficult times.

THE BAD: CITIZENS' COMPLAINT INVESTIGATIONS

While I was working at Zone 1 as a lieutenant, the zone commander assigned me to investigate a citizen's complaint. It was customary for a district lieutenant to receive a citizen complaint from Internal Investigations when the complaint was considered minor. Many times, the complaints were of officer rudeness. The commander had handed down those duties as commanders did in any duty location.

The assignment did not come with any training or explanation as to how to do the investigation, any equipment such as recording devices to capture statements during an interview, any forms to be completed during the investigation, how to properly assess and document credibility of the complainants and officers, or how to prepare a final report.

Even though new lieutenants received one week of formal training when promoted, it didn't cover enough subject matter to help them do the jobs that were expected of them. The report on the first investigation would have to be done the hard way—by muddling through both the investigation and the completion of the report. The first investigation would have to serve as the format for later investigations. However, there was no way all investigations throughout the city were as thorough as they should have been or as consistent. Each investigation and its outcome would only be as good as the lieutenant completing it.

The public was definitely not getting what they expected or what they paid for with their taxes. The lack of training in this critical area reduced the effectiveness of the department, left the investigating lieutenant exposed to criticism for conducting a poor investigation, and left the department vulnerable to liability.

As previously mentioned, I considered officers who made mistakes while trying to do their jobs as an example of the bad in policing. I did have some officers whose hearts and minds were in the right place but made mistakes along the way.

Carl Watts was a police officer assigned to my shift in Zone 1 during December 1989. On December 8 he was operating a police wagon with a partner, Al Ferrara. Officer David Foster, working another car, saw a white car used in a purse-snatching incident fleeing from him. He pursued the car and learned it had been stolen.

Officers Watts and Ferrara were using emergency lights and siren to assist when the police wagon Watts was driving failed to negotiate a bend in the road and struck a steel-reinforced, wooden telephone pole. The police vehicle was towed and both officers had to be transported to the hospital for medical care. Officer Ferrara was treated and released, but Officer Watts was admitted due to his injuries.

At the hospital, the doctor in charge requested that I speak with him. When I did, the doctor said Officer Watts had been in the hospital many times and he had suspected each time that Officer Watts had been drinking. The doctor said there was no doubt Officer Watts had been drinking prior to this crash and the doctor wanted to know what I was going to do about it.

I summoned the Breathalyzer operator, Officer Drew Anderson, who came to the hospital for a blood draw so the Crime Lab could do an analysis of Watts's blood alcohol level. The results indicated the officer had alcohol in his system but not exceeding the level that would categorize him as driving under the influence. Watts later said he did not drink before coming to work that day but that he had been drinking after his shift the night before.

The bad in this incident was that an officer was trying to do the best job that he could, but he wasn't performing as expected because of the alcohol in his system. A second and more important bad aspect of policing was that the department didn't have a system to identify officers who were struggling with alcohol abuse even though the department's own counselor knew that 25 percent of the department was struggling.

It became clear that too many officers used alcohol to self-medicate to relieve the stress from their work. The abuse of alcohol can lead to health problems, relationship problems, and financial problems. Some statistics indicate that for every officer killed feloniously in the line of duty, two will commit suicide and ten will be terminated from their employment. Over the coming years, I realized the need for an early warning system to save police officers' jobs and their lives.

THE UGLY: FIRST ARREST OF A POLICE OFFICER

Towards the end of 1989, I had returned to my duties as a shift lieutenant in Zone 1. For the first time in my career, I would be forced to initiate disciplinary actions against two off-duty officers. I would also be forced to arrest one of the officers. Although my reputation as a disciplinarian meant that troubled officers would bid on shifts other than mine, off-duty officers I encountered would be from other districts and shifts. And they would include dark-blue and midnight-blue officers.

On December 6, 1989, a call came over the police radio about a disturbance at a local tavern. This tavern was the favorite watering hole for officers finishing their afternoon-shift tour of duty. It was only blocks away from the station and a nice place where officers could find food, beverage, and live entertainment (jazz) without much chance of having to become involved in policing when off duty and consuming alcoholic beverages. It was known as a cop's bar. And it was much classier than the typical cop's bar.

In two years of working Zone 1, I had not received a call from this restaurant/bar before, so I started towards the bar. Officers were arriving while others appeared to be leaving as I got out of my police car. The owner of the establishment approached me and said he had everything under control. He added that he was grateful for a quick police response but said the problem was gone.

I later learned that a patron and his wife had been in line near the bar to be seated for dinner when they overheard a woman sitting at the bar using profanity. The man asked the woman, who was off-duty police officer Mary Anne Cook, to refrain from using vulgarity. Cook became abusive towards him and vulgar, and at one point opened her purse where he could observe her firearm.

The owner of the tavern interceded to control the situation but Cook responded by threatening to shut his business down for drug sales. Cook had been assigned to Narcotics but was subsequently reassigned to a light-duty position in the record room due to an injury she claimed she had sustained during her annual firearms qualification.

The tavern owner did not want her to be disruptive to his business. He had worked long and hard to maintain the restaurant's reputation as a comfortable retreat in the middle of a struggling business section. However, he recognized Cook as a police officer, and he did not want to jeopardize his relationship with loyal police clientele by involving Cook's superior officers in her drunken rant. When I came to the front door, my identity was unmistakable. Although officers and sergeants wore a navy-blue uniform shirt, lieutenants and higher ranks wore a white shirt to distinguish their position in the department. The owner of a cop's bar was well aware of the significance of the white shirt.

Since the tavern owner had informed me that the problem was resolved and that he did not want to explain any further, I accepted that and began to leave. While I was leaving, I stood in front of the tavern speaking with a sergeant who had just arrived. The owner came back outside and apologized, saying he had tried to cover for the intoxicated woman officer seated at the bar but that when he went back inside, she started her vulgar tirade again. He realized he could not control the situation and needed police involvement.

He pointed the woman out to me. She was seated on one of the first seats at the bar. Those waiting for dinner would be standing or seated nearby. I approached her and asked her to accompany me to the rear of the bar. I knew there was a back door at the rear of the bar and had intended to escort her out of the bar where she could be transported home by another officer. Cook looked at me and said, "I'm not going anywhere with you, I don't know who you are." I was speechless. While it was true that I had never met Cook, it was obvious by my uniform that I had the rank of lieutenant. Two other officers and a sergeant surrounded me.

To handle the situation with as little attention as possible, I asked to see her identification. She refused. I explained that she appeared to be intoxicated and if she refused to be escorted from the bar, or at least show identification, she would be arrested for public intoxication. She refused again. She was putting on a show for those around her and should have known that I was not about to turn around and leave. She forced the need for some action. I arrested her, escorted her outside, cuffed her, and directed a police officer to take her to Traffic Division where we conducted a Breathalyzer examination.

While at Traffic Division, Cook claimed she was not on compensation for her alleged injury. She told Commander Chuck Noonan, who was in charge of the city on the night shift, that she had been returned to duty in Narcotics and was on an undercover assignment. She refused to tell anyone the nature of her assignment. It was true she had been returned to duty, but it was to a light-duty assignment in the record room. Light-duty personnel did not wear a uniform, did not answer calls for service, and did not conduct investigations. They performed only administrative duties.

The tavern owner was reluctant to pursue any other charges in response to her threats to use her position to shut down his establishment on false charges of drug sales. The patron and his wife who had been subjected to Cook's vulgarity and intimidation by showing her weapon also refused to pursue any charges.

I reported to Traffic Division to complete the paperwork for mandatory testing of officers who appear to be intoxicated. Cook was being charged departmentally with conduct unbecoming an officer. When she refused to take the Breathalyzer examination, she also became subject to the departmental charges of failure to obey orders and insubordination.

Now, my biggest challenge with this was in trying to figure out how to initiate disciplinary action. Since I had never received training regarding disciplining officers and had not initiated disciplinary action previously, I was unfamiliar with the forms or how to complete the forms. I spent part of the night giving myself a crash course by studying the procedural manual along with the Disciplinary Action Report to document the incident.

During late 1989, the Zone 1 lockup was being used as the city's lockup. After Cook's Breathalyzer test, she was transported to Zone 1 to await arraignment. Within an hour of her arrest, Cook was being held in a cell directly behind the lieutenant's desk. While I was preparing my report on the incident, she continued making vulgar remarks, only this time they were directed toward me. She threatened, as did many other people who were arrested over the years, to sue me and to make sure she had my badge. She kicked at the cell bars while screaming profanities. She put on a real show for the people who had to come into the station and for the officers working there.

While she was in the midst of her outburst, her drinking partner from the tavern walked into the station. Officer Alice Mills was also a Pittsburgh Police officer and had been assigned to Zone 2 but was on compensation for an injury she claimed. Mills wanted us to release Cook to her. She was advised to speak with the night court magistrate since Cook could not be released before seeing the magistrate.

When Mills persisted that I release her friend, I gave her a direct order to leave the station and to not come back or she also would be charged with departmental violations. I had to walk with her to the door to get her to leave. As she left, she said I had a "fucking piss-poor attitude." I also charged her departmentally with insubordination and failure to obey an order. Although I completed the disciplinary paper-work, I did not testify at her disciplinary hearing and did not learn what corrective action, if any, was taken.

While I was finishing the paperwork related to this incident, an officer who had been on the scene was completing the paperwork related to Cook's weapon, which was seized upon her arrest. The officer asked me what he should do with her firearm. I asked him rhetorically what he did with the weapon of anyone else who was arrested. He replied he would send it to the Crime Lab as directed by regulation. Obviously, most officers do not encounter a situation when they would have to send another police officer's firearm to the Crime Lab. Sending the firearm to the Crime Lab meant it would remain at the Crime Lab for a period of time to be tested.

It was interesting to see how one drunken moment in a bar could create so many problems for an officer. If she had cooperated with the patron, the owner would not have gotten involved. If she had cooper-ated with the owner, the police would not have been involved. If the police had not been involved, the shift lieutenant would not have been involved. If she had cooperated with the lieutenant, she would have been driven home to sleep it off.

Instead, she went to jail, her gun went to the Crime Lab, and her friend charged with departmental violations. Cook dug a deep hole for herself. But what was to prove most remarkable about this matter was the result from the testing done on Cook's firearm at the Crime Lab.

About a week after this incident, Commander Wright called me into his office when I arrived for work. I knew, and trusted, Com-mander Wright so I knew he would support me for arresting this officer. What he was to tell me was quite surprising. The Crime Lab results showed that Cook's gun had been used in two crimes reported by the county police. The owners of two houses and cars that were the targets of shootings on July 21 were relatives of a man convicted of sexually assaulting Cook's five-year-old niece. Cook's firearm had been used in both shootings just months before her gun was seized during her arrest at the tavern.

On June 14, 1991, the *Pittsburgh Post-Gazette* reported that Mary Anne Cook, who had been an officer since 1983, was convicted of reckless endangerment and criminal mischief for shooting into the two houses and cars. She received two years of probation from Judge Peter Leonard.

What was even more noteworthy about this court case was what Judge Leonard did and said during the trial. The *Post-Gazette* article said that Judge Leonard ordered Mary Anne Cook to attend an alcohol treatment program. It also quoted him as saying, "It appears to me that there was an alcohol problem that led to this problem." However, Cook's attorney told the *Post-Gazette* reporter that he was not aware of any evidence showing that Cook had problems with alcohol. Her attorney was quoted as saying, "The only evidence about alcohol was that she was arrested at a bar." Her attorney said Cook would face a departmental disciplinary hearing and could lose her job because of the conviction.

I did learn years later that officers often were able to receive alcohol and/or drug treatment counseling in lieu of losing their jobs as the outcome of a disciplinary hearing.

Many elected officials sought the support of various unions, including the local police union. It may have been a coincidence that Judge Leonard determined, without evidence provided during testimony, that the officer had an alcohol problem. There could be no doubt that the judge's words would be valuable during a disciplinary hearing since arbitrators always opted to provide treatment in lieu of termination whenever an officer claimed to have an alcohol or drug problem.

Officer Cook received a five-day suspension for her conduct. The city had a five-step disciplinary process that included: 1) oral reprimand, 2) written reprimand, 3) one-day suspension, 4) three-day suspension, and 5) five-day suspension pending termination. Although she received the maximum 5-day suspension, there was no indication from the news articles that she had been terminated. One was left to wonder if the judge's comments led to the officer maintaining her job as a police officer.

I was stunned to learn that both officers blamed me for the action taken against them. According to one of them, I was the one with the "fucking piss-poor attitude." Although I had not thought about the various groups of officers that I identified in groups of blue at that point in my career, I was able to see where both of these officers fit. Officer Mills was, at best, in the dark-blue group and, at worst, in the midnight-blue group. The midnight-blue group are those who should be weeded out of a department. Mary Anne Cook was definitely one of the midnight-blue officers due to her criminal acts of shooting into homes, her criminal threats to shut down a legitimate business on trumped-up drug charges, her untruthfulness toward Commander Noonan, and her outrageous behavior at the tavern.

In any other job in the real world, both officers would have been terminated. In policing, the bottom group of officers is difficult to get rid of due to tolerant civil service commissions, lenient arbitrators, politicians who back them due to their campaign or financial support, business or community leaders who are friends or relatives of the officers and exert pressure for leniency, members in the command staff who are reluctant to wrangle with the union representing the officers, insufficiently trained supervisors, or supervisors lacking the fortitude to make the difficult decisions.

TRAFFIC DIVISION, PART I

On January 1, 1990, all the department lieutenants were transferred to different duty stations. I believed it was good for personnel to be transferred regularly. It was an opportunity to learn so much more about the department, other department personnel, the various neighborhoods, and the different problems affecting each neighborhood.

I was surprised to see that I had been transferred to Traffic Division since it was considered a desirable position for a lieutenant and I had only been a lieutenant for little more than two years. I reported to Commander Bentley who told me he had requested that I be one of his lieutenants.

I found that to be odd since he previously did not want me working for him when he was a captain in Special Operations. However, this time I was no threat to his position. I felt he believed I would perform well for him as I had in our previous assignments. My conscientious performance years before was reaping benefits, including additional overtime pay.

I worked hard to learn the responsibilities of Traffic. Nearly all the officers there were experienced and reliable. They knew their duties, accepted them willingly, and avoided any problems since they did not want to be transferred from the division. I began to understand the concept of a laissez-faire style of leadership in that position even though I was not to receive leadership training until years later.

Traffic Division was one of the easier assignments I had in the department, but it wasn't to last long. After working there for five months, I was interviewed for the rank of commander and was promoted in early June 1990. I would have been a much better supervisor if I had received the training that we all needed to perform the duties of our ranks and assignments. I believe I was considered for the rank of commander because I would work hard at learning how to improve my performance in each assignment I worked and how to make the best choices even if they weren't the easy choices. In addition, I demonstrated I would do what needed to be done to ensure proper supervision even if it wasn't popular with all officers.

I realized that what the dark-blue and midnight-blue officers thought and said about me was unimportant. My supervisory actions that caused discontent among the dark-blue officers must have brought me to the attention of my supervisors and the public we served. I cared more about what the good officers thought even though they rarely expressed their opinions publicly. Any supervisor waiting to hear the thoughts of the officers in the light-blue categories would have to wait a long time.

LESSONS LEARNED

1) Formal training in all aspects of supervision is essential to be an effective supervisor, including how to submit officers for awards, how to conduct investigations into citizens' complaints, and how to recommend both non-disciplinary corrective action and disciplinary action. A department's failure to provide training in all these areas leaves supervisors ill-equipped to perform their duties, to ensure that officers perform as expected, and to increase the department's effectiveness in serving the community that deserves and should expect more.

2) Having a supportive, experienced mentor greatly increases a supervisor's effectiveness and success.

3) On many occasions, a police officer can be his/her own worst enemy. Failure to comply with simple instructions can sometimes lead to departmental discipline and criminal charges.

4) When supervisors directly address officer misconduct, they earn the respect of the good officers in the sky-blue and light-blue categories even if the matter is not commonly discussed; the same supervisors will be demeaned by the dark-blue officers who will prefer to blame the supervisor for the end result rather than accept the blame for the officer's own dishonorable conduct.

CHAPTER SIX

Watch Commander

"How people treat you is their karma; how you react is yours."

—Wayne Dyer

In June 1990, Chief Dean Silverman replaced Chief Richard D'Angelo as the chief of Pittsburgh Police. Other changes came along since many members of the command staff opted to take a one-time offering of ¾ retirement rather than the typical ½ retirement. This meant that those retiring increased their retirement pay by 50% if they accepted the early retirement. Many ranking officials retired, creating commander promotional opportunities. Although I had less than three years in the rank of lieutenant, I was one of three promoted to the rank of commander.

I was assigned as a watch commander. My week would generally begin on a Friday afternoon and end at 7:00 AM on Wednesday morning. I would work the PM shift on Fridays and Saturdays and the night shift from Sunday through Tuesday. The night watch commander oversees the entire police department during the evening and night hours and on weekends when other commanders and the assistant chiefs are not actively working. The watch commander's office was next to the 911 call center. My shift started there before moving on to another part of the city as emergency calls arose.

It had become clear to department leadership that the rank of commander was necessary on each shift to supervise the lieutenants since sergeants and lieutenants belonged to the same union as the officers. Some sergeants and lieutenants were not strong leaders, which meant that some of the officers working in those zones weren't properly supervised. One example of inadequate leadership was Lieutenant James Brady. When he was a lieutenant working the night shift on Tuesdays and Wednesdays, he would tell half of the officers to go home at roll call one night and the other half to go home the following night. Although he had minimum staffing levels to ensure officer safety, the officers worked at half-staffing just so they could each have a night off with pay each week.

Of course, Lieutenant Brady would take off one of those nights also, meaning the lieutenant worked four days and was paid for five days each week. Each police report had to have a lieutenant's signature so he had a hand stamp made with his name on it so that a sergeant left working could stamp the lieutenant's signature on each report. One night, a sergeant stamping the reports used the stamp upside down on each police report. Although the sergeant would later say it was unintentional, his explanation was astonishing. The lieutenant was called to answer for that. He eventually was caught, disciplined, and transferred when an officer anonymously called an assistant chief and reported what he was doing. The assistant chief came out in the middle of the night to stop the practice.

Fortunately, the leadership in the Coast Guard Reserves permitted me to complete my monthly drill duty on consecutive Thursdays. The Coast Guard Reserves would provide the administrative experience I would need in the coming years with the police department. I attended their leadership training for all enlisted personnel of the rank E-5 and above, observed annual training in many subjects, experienced the qualification checklists required prior to authorization to complete many duties, completed documented training manuals, submitted to hours-long oral board examinations to achieve specific job qualifications, and participated in performance evaluations.

I benefitted more from my connection with the Coast Guard than I would have been able to pay to receive. I was able to see how an organization provided policy, training, and supervision for each specific job prior to anyone being assigned to do that job. Although I had only been in the USCG for three years at this point in my career, I was to complete twenty-three years there before my military retirement.

As with most other promotions and assignments, I did not receive any police training before being promoted to the rank of commander or being assigned as a Night Watch commander. I had to self-determine what a commander should be doing as the ranking officer-of-the-day. I had heard about Lieutenant Brady relieving officers at the beginning of their shift so I checked in with each duty location a couple of times each week to review daily assignment sheets listing all the officers working and I also monitored the radio for officer activity. I called in service as soon as I began my shift. I wanted the shift supervisors to know I was out there somewhere in the city and would be checking in with them eventually. I made sure I stopped at each station several times per week and backed up officers on calls to hear firsthand of their concerns.

There were many times the sergeants and lieutenants were happy to see I was working. This was true especially when there were exceedingly difficult decisions to make. One of the first was the arrest of an off-duty city police officer, Officer Dwight Stevens. Almost everyone in the department knew Dwight Stevens. He was a large man who was well over six feet tall and close to three hundred pounds. He was an outspoken person who wasn't hesitant to let others know how he felt. His size and demeanor meant that virtually no one opposed him or challenged him.

One night, off duty, he was involved in a traffic collision and was arrested for driving under the influence. He was arrogant, abusive, and threatening during the entire process. The lieutenant on duty in that district was Lieutenant Cliff Perkins. Perkins was an African American promoted to lieutenant the same day I was promoted to lieutenant in 1987. Officer Stevens had used racial slurs when referring to Perkins. When they transported Stevens to the cellblock downtown, as they did with everyone arrested, he refused to go inside.

Obviously, none of the officers wanted to fight with another officer who could do considerable damage to a group of them. Stevens was a Goliath even when not drinking. No one knew what he was capable of doing when he was drinking. The supervisors, including Perkins, were perplexed as to how to get him to go into the cellblock without many people being hurt. This was one of the times officers and supervisors were glad to see a watch commander who would be responsible for the decisions made in handling this challenging matter.

After being briefed, I approached Stevens and told him he would have to go into the cell inside the cellblock. As he did with everyone else, he made derogatory remarks to everyone around him and racist remarks to Lieutenant Perkins before informing me that he definitely was not going into the cellblock to be locked up. I think what he sensed from me was that I was not intimidated by his threats or his bullying nature.

I explained to him that he was going into the cellblock just like his prisoners did and he could walk in there and only face the DUI charges that were already being filed or he could fight with all the officers and supervisors present to avoid going into the cellblock and subsequently be charged with resisting arrest and assaulting officers. I suggested several times that he could be known as an officer arrested for DUI, which happens occasionally, or he could have the reputation of a cop fighter, but the choice was his. After he had time to think about what I had said, he voluntarily walked into the cellblock.

Although I had known Officer Stevens for years, I knew he would be one of the officers who would never speak to me again. An officer so intoxicated that he threatened to fight other officers obviously had a problem that he couldn't control or admit to. If he could not admit a problem, he'd never admit that what happened to him the night of his arrest was of his own doing. It would be easier to blame the supervisors for what happened to him. Sometimes officers are so arrogant that they believe they are above the law and should not be placed under arrest for anything they have done.

Dwight Stevens never apologized or thanked me for spending as much time as I did, trying to talk him out of being angry. Although he would face criminal and departmental charges, they were not anywhere as serious as they could have been.

As a watch commander, I could always tell when a district lieutenant encountered a difficult situation. The call would come over police radio that a lieutenant needed to see me at a specific location. There generally was not any additional information relayed until I got on the scene.

I had the occasion to be called to an accident one night by a district shift lieutenant. Watch commanders were not usually summoned to a call for an accident. I knew when I was called there by the lieutenant that a difficult decision was needed, and that that decision would be forced up to my level.

When I arrived on the scene, I learned that a car belonging to off-duty Officer David Flecker had been involved in a serious single-vehicle collision with a pole. Obviously, there was excessive speed involved as well as alcohol since there was the aroma of intoxicating beverages on the breath of all three people who had been in the vehicle. None of the officers on the scene observed the collision or could determine who had been operating the vehicle.

David had been an excellent officer who sometimes seemed to be as dedicated to policing as he was to his off-duty weightlifting. He was respected by his supervisors who appreciated his work ethic, and he was well liked by his peers. However, with every superhero, there is some weakness.

Once on the scene of the accident, I learned David was injured seriously. It appeared he may have broken his arm or elbow. He also had other injuries, including a head injury, that required medical treatment. He was insistent he would not go with the paramedics and that he was going to walk home. I thought his life could be in jeopardy if we were to allow him to leave on his own with a head injury. His behavior was erratic, abusive, and threatening if anyone attempted to treat him or prevent him from leaving. I knew he had to be transported for a Breathalyzer examination since his conduct violated department policy, which included off-duty conduct. He agreed to go to the hospital rather than be transported to Traffic Division for a Breathalyzer examination. There was no question the other two people would be going to the hospital since they were lying on the ground suffering from their injuries.

Once we arrived at the hospital, three things occurred. First, I ordered Officer Flecker to submit to a blood alcohol test which officers could not refuse, even off duty, if they were suspected of being intoxicated. I had to inform him that failure to submit to a blood alcohol test would result in disciplinary action.

Secondly, the other two people transported to the hospital were able to speak and both confirmed they were passengers in the car while it was being driven by Officer Flecker. Once officers had been told that Officer Flecker was the driver, they had evidence that he was driving and apparently driving under the influence due to his conduct.

This bit of information led to the third occurrence which changed the nature of the incident from conduct unbecoming an officer and public intoxication to a criminal offense of driving while intoxicated. Since the event was now considered a criminal case, I had to advise Officer Flecker that instead of being ordered to submit to a blood alcohol test, he now had the option to submit to testing as any other DUI suspect would have. Although he was advised he had the option, he was also advised that if he refused, he would automatically have his license suspended for one year—and officers without a driver's license were not permitted to work. This would have turned his refusal into at least a one-year suspension of his ability to work. Officer Flecker opted to submit to testing, which would prove he was operating under the influence.

The irony of Officer Flecker's situation was that if he had cooperated with officers on the scene, he probably would have been transported to the hospital and treated. The sergeant would not have needed to call the lieutenant to the scene who then realized this situation could be handed off to me as the watch commander. Officer Flecker's conduct at the scene made the situation much more complex and serious than it needed to be.

The criminal charges filed during this incident would continue for seven years as the case was appealed. The defense argued that since Officer Flecker was ordered initially to submit to alcohol testing, he did not believe he had the option of refusing the blood alcohol test that would prove he had been driving under the influence. The defense prevailed and Officer Flecker was cleared of the charges filed against him.

Although the officer's attorney and the union representing the officer appeared to win, they won the skirmish but lost the battle. The real battle should have been to ensure that Officer Flecker received the help he needed. In any event, his erratic behavior would continue for many years. When I became the chief of police many years in the future, Officer Flecker was involved in another incident, this one related to what we have come to know as road rage.

This incident occurred when Officer Flecker was driving behind another motorist. He would later say the operator of the car in front got out of his car and attacked him, resulting in Officer Flecker needing to defend himself. What Officer Flecker did not know was that the driveway of the apartment building he had followed the other driver into had a camera and recorded the entire incident. The recording clearly showed Officer Flecker exiting his vehicle, approaching the other driver who was still in his vehicle, and pulling the driver out of his car. Officer Flecker then beat the man.

By the time this incident occurred, I had been the chief for four or five months. Officer Flecker had his initial disciplinary hearing in July 1996. He would lose his job over this assault. It was extremely disappointing to see someone who had so much potential in the law enforcement field end up losing his job for things that happened while he was off duty. When I first met Officer Flecker during his recruit field training, I believed he would eventually become the chief of police in our department. He was that good. The only ones who really helped Officer Flecker were the supervisors who attempted corrective action.

Those who fought so hard to ensure that Officer Flecker evaded any consequences for his missteps failed to get him the help he needed to avoid further problems. The future problems would end up destroying his career. Even if he had not lost his job, he didn't live long enough to have retired. Officer Flecker would die in 2004, many years before he would have completed twenty years of service.

TRAFFIC DIVISION, PART II

Around March of 1992, Police Chief Dean Silverman assigned me to fill in as the commander in charge of Traffic Division since Commander Chuck Noonan was scheduled to attend the FBI National Academy for approximately three months. Chief Silverman had me work alongside Commander Noonan for one week to understand the duties of that position. I heard Commander Noonan would have preferred to make his second in charge, Lieutenant Sam Stanton, the acting commander instead.

Noonan did not have much time to spend with me before he left for the FBI Academy. I met with others in Traffic Division and knew many of them since I had served as a lieutenant there just two years before. One person I needed to meet with was Stanton, Commander Noonan's choice to be second in command. I could sense the same type of resentment I had received when transferred to SOD as a sergeant.

Stanton's jobs in Traffic consisted of making the plans for the special events and overseeing vehicle collision reconstructions. Both of those jobs were important to the division and to the bureau. Stanton had managed to ensure that he was trained at the highest level of collision reconstruction. From what I understood, he had some officers trained at lower levels of reconstruction to assist with on-scene evidence-gathering but trained at the highest level for himself. He must have realized his skills were critical to the department and that he could not be replaced since other officers weren't trained to his level.

In a meeting with Stanton in Traffic Division, he made clear his disdain for Homicide detectives investigating fatal car crashes. He believed the Homicide detectives lacked the technical reconstruction skills needed to investigate those cases.

Outspoken in his beliefs, Stanton was in turn not held in high regard by Homicide detectives or the commander in charge of Major Crimes who oversaw the Homicide Unit. Some of the Homicide detectives reported incidents when uniformed officers, trained in vehicle reconstruction but not trained in conducting interviews, would interview a witness at the front desk of a district station. The front desk was the busiest site in any police station and not the appropriate location to conduct any interview.

This made it impossible for both vehicle crash reconstruction officers and Homicide detectives to work together as they should have. The department decided that Homicide detectives would be in charge of the investigation and that reconstruction officers would capture the evidence to determine the cause of the collision. This strained working relationship would lead to an incomplete homicide investigation years later in the Armstrong tunnels.

I had only been in charge of Traffic for a week when Stanton came into my office and gave me an overtime card for eight hours worked on his day off that weekend. The eight hours of pay was to compensate him for changing one intersection of the Pittsburgh Marathon route that was planned every year. I questioned him as to who authorized him to work the eight hours. He said Commander Noonan permitted him to work whatever hours he believed he needed to work to plan special events. I told Stanton he was not authorized to work any additional overtime unless I first approved it. I could see how Stanton would benefit since he was the only person capable of planning special events. My temporary assignment in Traffic Division was the first time I would see what I deemed unnecessary overtime paid. I was to learn that getting rid of it would be the most sensitive issue, creating hostility when a supervisor attempted to control the amount of overtime an officer could make. As some officers were to say, "Now he's taking money out of my pocket."

I was to get my payback from Stanton and Noonan within months of my temporary assignment to Traffic Division. Another Traffic Division lieutenant informed me that Commander Noonan was in town over one weekend during the FBI Academy training and was saying he would be promoted to an assistant chief's position when he completed the training. He also said that I would get my payback for having made changes while he was gone. Curtailing the overtime of his friend Stanton did not go over well with Noonan.

When I heard these comments, I called Noonan at the FBI Academy and asked him if he had made the comment that he'd pay me back when he returned to Pittsburgh and assumed the assistant chief position. Noonan said, "No, Bobby, me and you are okay." I was to learn that was untruthful when following Noonan being promoted to assistant chief, I was moved back to my watch commander position. Noonan knew he would be promoted when he returned from the FBI Academy because Mayor Sarah Abrams, who had promoted Chief Dean Silverman, planned to replace Silverman with Wilbur Amos. Sure enough, in June 1992, Chief Amos took the department helm and named two assistant chiefs. Assistant Chief Chuck Noonan was to be in charge of detectives and Assistant Chief Declan Mulligan was to be in charge of operations (patrol division).

I was called into Assistant Chief Mulligan's office to be informed of my reassignment from Traffic Division back to a watch commander position. Mulligan informed me that I had done such a good job there that they were returning me to my position. How he could keep a straight face telling me that was incredible.

While Mulligan was informing me of my "new" assignment, Public Safety Director Rivera walked into Mulligan's office. He saw that I was calm and that I had accepted my assignment diplomatically. He said, "You're making this easy on us." I appreciated his acknowledgement that I was getting someone's payback but taking it without creating any problems for anyone else in the department. As I returned to my position as the Night Watch commander, Mayor Sarah Abrams promoted my wife, Catherine McNeilly, to the rank of commander. Cathy and I had only been married for six months. Cathy was given the PM watch commander position. Her hours of work would be 3:00 PM to 11:00 PM and my hours of work would be 11:00 PM to 7:00 AM. In addition, they gave her Tuesdays and Wednesdays as her days off and they gave me Wednesdays and Thursdays as my days off.

We would only have one day off together each week. I learned from my Traffic Division source, given that Chuck Noonan liked to brag about his paybacks, that Chief Wilbur Amos commented, "We'll see how long that marriage lasts."

There were a couple of remarkable developments over the next couple of years. First, Cathy would be reassigned one year later (1993) to be in charge of the Police Training Academy. She saw a need for specialized training for supervisors in our department. She asked for command staff volunteers to attend the state training commission's courses for "train the trainers" to bring supervision training to our department. Since I was the only commander who volunteered, she and I attended the training and then began giving supervisory courses to our department for several years.

The second development was the election of Mayor Tom Murphy. Tom Murphy informed Cathy and me that he had asked about fifty city officers who should be the next chief of police. He said approximately thirty-five of them said one or the other McNeilly. After Mayor Murphy met with Cathy and me, I could tell the city would change dramatically under his leadership.

LESSONS LEARNED

1) Those promoted to command-level positions need training to prepare them for those assignments. At this point in their careers, outside training becomes critical.

2) Some officers complain about the supervisors who take corrective
   action when officers are disciplined. However, the good officers witnessing the conduct of the bad officers appreciate the strong and de-
   cisive actions taken by strong supervisors. A strong supervisor needs
   to be aware that the good officers will generally never comment on
   the actions of a strong supervisor. They will, however, comment on
   the inaction of a weak supervisor during critical times.

3) Having a command-level officer on duty at all times is necessary to
   ensure that the only supervisor available does not have conflicts if
   that supervisor was a union official who would eventually represent
   officers accused of misconduct. If all members of the police agency
   are union members, they should not belong to the same union.

4) Some of the officers who appear to have the most potential in police agencies damage their careers or end their careers because of
   unacceptable off-duty conduct. If only these officers could get the
   help they need in their personal lives, many would not hinder or ruin
   their careers, or even end their own lives. An early intervention system can save careers and lives.

5) Some police managers are capable of despicable acts to hurt those
   they believe to be their competition. The higher one goes within a
   police department, the more brutal the internal politics become.

CHAPTER SEVEN

District Commander, Zone 2

"Our greatest challenge may not be physical courage on the street, risking life and limb, but moral and ethical courage when standing up for what is fair and just. Courage is a special kind of knowledge. There are no awards or commendations for moral courage."

—LAWRENCE DUPREE, COMMANDER,
7th Police District, New Orleans Police Department

"Moral courage is the most valuable and usually the most absent characteristic in men."

—GENERAL GEORGE S. PATTON, JR.

W ilbur Amos became the chief of police in June 1992 and would remain as chief of police until December 1995. He was a large man with a commanding presence. He was a sergeant in Narcotics when I first met him while I worked plainclothes. I understood he was a Narcotics detective before he was promoted to sergeant in the Narcotics Unit. He never served as a lieutenant and was promoted from sergeant to commander and placed in command of the entire Narcotics Unit. Amos was eventually promoted to the rank of assistant chief and was left in charge of Narcotics. By the time Amos was promoted to the rank of chief of police, he had spent nearly his entire career in Narcotics.

The years Amos was chief was a critical time for the Pittsburgh Police. From 1992 to 1995, the city hired approximately 550 officers for a 1,200-officer department. The officers came from locations throughout the country. The majority of those officers were young white men with either no police experience, limited experience, or experience working in small police agencies. Many of those hired had never worked or lived in a diverse community. Most were ill prepared to work in a large agency consisting of a varied group of officers policing in a multicultural municipality. With proper and sufficient training, officers could have been better prepared for what they would encounter. That training never occurred.

This was a time the department needed clear direction and considerable resources to provide all new hires with guidance regarding department policies, enhanced training (including cultural diversity training), sufficient supervision, and immediate corrective action when officers failed to adhere to policies or training. Corrective action could include counseling, training, transfer, or one of the five disciplinary steps available to supervisors.

Many decisions were made from 1992 to 1995 that would leave the department vulnerable to future liability. I was convinced the mistakes had been made due to Amos's limited experience and his unwillingness to accept input from his commanders. In fact, during his three and a half years as the chief of police, he never had one command staff meeting. He relied upon Assistant Chief Mulligan to meet with commanders if there was any direction to be provided for any events.

Some of the department deficiencies included the following:

1. The first and most glaring ongoing mistake was lack of regular command staff meetings. The commanders never had the ability to provide input into any direction the department was headed. An autocratic style of leadership is good in crisis situations, when subordinates lack experience or ability, or are poorly motivated or lack discipline. Since none of these deficiencies existed among the command staff, the agency needed a participative style of leadership among its top ranks.

2. Chief Amos decided he would implement community policing since considerable federal funds had become available to hire officers. The only direction provided to district commanders regarding community policing came through the chief's dissemination of magazine articles related to the topic. Unfortunately, community policing meant different things to different departments. The magazine articles didn't suffice for meaningful direction.

3. With few exceptions, the department hired straight down the police officer eligibility list rather than using the civil service guidelines for choosing the best one of the top three candidates. Many times, all three would have been acceptable and should have been hired. On the other hand, many candidates who should not have been hired were hired.

4. The department provided only two weeks of training to all candidates who had already received basic police-recruit training. The training was specific to city police operations such as completion of police reports, city traffic citations, introduction to city police forms, radio call signs, chain of command, and other matters specifically related to Pittsburgh Police.

    After the city failed to provide all recruits with complete academy training, some officers expressed that they did not believe they had been trained sufficiently and requested additional training from supervisors and commanders.

5.   The department disbanded recruit field training. Officers, some with only two weeks of academy training, were assigned directly to districts to work patrol.

6.   No experienced officers were trained as field training officers.

7.   Policies were changed under Chief D'Angelo (1987-1990) and under Chief Silverman (1990-1992). No policies were issued after 1992. If any were, commanders were not privy to changes.

8.   The Narcotics Unit was working with groups of about eight to ten officers travelling in multiple vehicles that would swarm an intersection and force anyone loitering in the area to lie on the ground and be subjected to searches. Those holding drugs or weapons were arrested. Others were released. The apparent lack of probable cause and the way residents were treated during these encounters created considerable ill will. District officers were left to contend with the residents' rage after the Narcotics officers left the area.

9.   The city was short of supervisors. When I assumed command of Zone 2, I was budgeted for four lieutenants and nine sergeants. I had one lieutenant and six sergeants.

10. Sergeants and lieutenants who were being promoted were not provided with supervision training.

11. Commanders were not provided with any information regarding lawsuits filed against the Pittsburgh Bureau of Police, grievances filed by the union, or arbitration decisions regarding the grievances or discipline. Without that information, the mistakes made in one district could be made in another.

12. Internal Investigation findings into citizens' complaints that had been sustained (meaning the investigation findings proved the officer had violated policies) following an investigation were changed by the chief with just the stroke of a pen and no explanation.

13. Officers did not complete use-of-force forms. Most police reports had a statement simply indicating the officer had used sufficient force to effect the arrest. In the absence of widespread use-of-force reports, the number of times that force was used by officers could not be determined. If the supervisor signed the police report indicating

"sufficient" force was used, the supervisor would approve the use of force without a full accounting of the type of force used.

14. Officers did not complete a search/seizure report when they seized someone's property on the street. Every department needs to know which officers are seizing property, how often, and determine if it adheres to law and policy.

15. Supervisors and commanders did not have access to their subordinates' information regarding the number of times complaints were registered, how many times they used force, the number of times they were disciplined, the extent of training they received due to deficient performance, or the levels of discipline they received.

16. The department failed to conduct performance evaluations for any officers or supervisors.

17. The department terminated the employment of its only attorney who had been hired to serve as a legal advisor to officers and supervisors. The legal advisor had been with the bureau for many years and was almost always available for critical advice. Now, with the influx of new, inexperienced officers, the lack of sufficient training, and the lack of enough supervisors, the department needed a legal advisor more than ever.

ASSIGNMENT TO ZONES 1 AND 2

In July 1994, Commander Cathy McNeilly assumed command of Zone 1 on the North Side of Pittsburgh. Zone 1 included all parts of the City of Pittsburgh north of the Allegheny and Ohio Rivers. At the same time, I assumed command of Zone 2 in the Hill District. The police station was situated in the Hill District, but the district included Downtown, several public housing units, and several other neighborhoods. The police series *Hill Street Blues* of the 1970s got its name from the Hill District station. This district was also approximately one-sixth the size of the city.

The Hill District had once been a busy business district and a night-life attraction. Over the years, the buildings and roadways had degraded and the area had become financially depressed. I was to learn that three of the four poorest census tracts in Pennsylvania were located in the Hill District. Some of the public housing areas were high-crime areas with considerable drug trafficking and violence.

The Hill District was a short distance from Downtown. Attempting to address the street crime would be a difficult undertaking without well-trained, well-equipped, and motivated personnel. I devoted a considerable amount of my time when first assigned to command Zone 2 to addressing the personnel problems. It would be difficult to make improvements due to few resources.

One problem for the bureau arose when the city terminated the employment of the only legal advisor. I was informed that if I needed legal assistance now, there was an assistant city solicitor assigned to work with the police bureau. I learned quickly that assistance was no longer always accessible and certainly not quick to respond.

There was a protest planned one Saturday at the abortion center downtown. I sent a request to the Law Department for advice on how we should address the rights of both protestors and those patronizing the center. I received my reply two weeks later. Fortunately, we managed to wrangle our way through that volatile situation.

The 550 officers who were hired between 1992 and 1995 were recruited from across the country. Many were not provided with sufficient academy training. None received field training that would have included evaluations and completion of training manuals, and none had enough supervision. With newer officers, more supervision is required rather than less supervision.

Commander Cathy McNeilly reported that 90 percent of her patrol officers in Zone 1 had fewer than three years of experience. In Zone 2, the rule that permitted an officer having four years of service to work the front desk as an acting sergeant was abandoned since entire shifts were working without any officers having four years of service. The acting desk sergeants were not even eligible to take a sergeant's promotional test until they had four years of service.

Right after being assigned to Zone 2, Assistant Chief Declan Mulligan informed me that I would be receiving fourteen new officers from the next graduating academy class. He said they would all be assigned to walk beats in the Downtown area. This instruction was absurd since they would not know what to do once they got downtown. Since many of my shifts had only one or two supervisors, I was forced to receive calls from new officers asking what they should do for routine calls such as how they should handle an illegally parked car or someone detained for retail theft.

While I was commanding Zone 2 from 1994 to 1996, several commanders worked extremely hard to ensure proper policing was provided. Many of us were concerned that the number of vehicle collisions (although it was difficult to determine precisely since the department wasn't tracking any data), the number of citizens' complaints, and the number of lawsuits were increasing.

Since the department failed to conduct regular command staff meetings for commanders and chiefs, Cathy and I began organizing monthly lunches with the six district commanders so we could address some of the department's emerging problems. Eventually the commanders in the other branches (Special Operations, Traffic, Academy, etc.) learned of our meetings and joined us. We eventually had our own informal command staff meetings even if the chief did not conduct any.

My wife and I attempted to fix some of the problems the department had due to limited resources. Some of our efforts were: (1) to get officers the equipment they needed for their safety and to reduce the level of force needed on the street, (2) to instruct officers who were not prepared to work diverse communities, (3) to set up computerization, (4) to provide additional training, (5) to hold staff meetings, (6) to recognize good policing, and (7) to address substandard policing.

EQUIPMENT

I knew officers who had been injured by being bitten on the hand or who had been stuck with needles during searches. The chief had issued an order that officers were forbidden to wear gloves with the summer uniform. I wrote a memo to Chief Amos requesting authorization for officers to wear gloves for protection against bites and needles when they were conducting a search or making an arrest. I also requested authorization for officers to be equipped and trained with pepper spray, collapsible batons, and Tasers.

At that time, the officers only had hand techniques (such as a palm strike or punch), a wooden baton, a blackjack, or a firearm as a means of making an arrest when confronted with resistance or in self-defense. I never received a response from the chief. I did hear unofficially that the chief believed that providing less-lethal options to officers would increase the chances for use-of-force complaints. It appeared that the opposite was true.

TRAINING/COUNSELING–OFFICERS WORKING DIVERSE COMMUNITIES

Cathy met a doctor with a degree in social work who worked with the Pittsburgh Public Schools. Cathy and I scheduled meetings with the doctor either in her zone or in mine. We required several of our officers to attend each of the meetings, which were designed to address cultural diversity. We believed the open discourse among younger and older officers, white and minority officers, and men and women officers helped our officers understand the views of others during the discussions. Many misperceptions were confronted, challenged, and corrected.

COMPUTERIZATION

Since the police bureau was not computerized, Cathy wrote to a company in her zone requesting the donation of a computer they were discarding as they upgraded. Within weeks, her personnel were entering and tracking all crime reports. Her personnel had immediate information available to answer nearly all questions related to criminal activity in her zone.

I followed her lead and requested a computer from a downtown business. Cathy came to Zone 2, installed the program she was using in Zone 1, and trained some of my personnel to do the same. Having the computers saved hundreds of hours of work each week by ridding the station of cross-reference books listing detailed information regarding a) those arrested, b) vehicles, c) weapons, d) drugs, e) associates, and other related information.

ADDITIONAL TRAINING

Due to insufficient training provided to new officers, officers with only one or two years of training were used as field training officers. Ongoing training was provided by monthly training questionnaires I created from assessing deficiencies. Monthly training questions covered areas related to use of force, searches, citizens' complaints, vehicle operations, and other critical subjects.

STAFF MEETINGS

Cathy and I both met with shift supervisors regularly. In order to do so without paying overtime, we scheduled the meetings for the last two hours of the night shift so we could proceed to the AM shift after they began work, and then meet with the PM shift after they started work that day. It meant long workdays some days, but we needed to expend the time to ensure our supervisors were on the same page we were.

RECOGNITION OF GOOD POLICING

To recognize good police work, we began recognizing an officer, or a pair of officers if they shared the workload as partners, as an officer or officers of the month. I am certain the effort was appreciated. My first officer of the month in Zone 2, Stanley Ingram, eventually rose to the rank of deputy chief.

ADDRESSING SUBSTANDARD POLICING

Unfortunately, in police work not all officers perform as required or expected. The medium-blue, dark-blue, and midnight-blue officers occupy a considerable portion of a supervisor's time and attention. In order to address substandard performance, supervisors need to have the courage to act decisively when necessary. I recognized the difficulty supervisors face when confronting an officer's poor performance or outright defiance.

I have always said supervisors demonstrate considerable physical courage in responding to calls for shots fired, bar fights, violent domestics, and other rapidly evolving and violent incidents. Although those supervisors have the courage to do so, having the courage to sit across the table from an officer and tell him/her that their performance is not cutting it is much more difficult.

As I rose through the ranks, I had more officers reporting to me and had to use discipline more often. During my command of 150 officers in Zone 2, about a dozen officers were disciplined during those two years. One of those officers would be terminated, and actions were initiated against a handful of other officers who would eventually be suspended or terminated, or would resign in lieu of termination.

I learned later that Assistant Chief Chuck Noonan had said there were four in the command staff who used discipline too much. He listed those as Assistant Chief Mulligan, Commander Edgar Wyman (who would eventually serve as an assistant chief and deputy chief), my wife, and me. I was amazed at the irony of his comments. He would later be sued for not taking any action when a detective reported to him that she was being sexually harassed by Commander Roy Davidson, a close friend of Chief Amos.

What made his comments even more absurd was that the department would, in less than twenty months, be sued by more than sixty complainants and joined in the lawsuit by the NAACP and the ACLU. The department would also be investigated by the United States Department of Justice, Civil Rights Division, for many deficiencies, including lack of discipline in the department.

PERSONNEL PROBLEMS

The city had hired many officers with questionable work histories. I knew of two in my zone who had been under investigation or had been terminated from another department.

One officer working for me who I believed should not have been hired was Ted Moore. I knew him from my Judo and Tae Kwon Do workouts and heard he had been terminated by another local police agency. Ted was a physically fit, high-strung person, whose ramblings appeared to amuse some in the dojo. I searched to see how he had been hired given his history. When he was being hired by the Pittsburgh Police, he explained the reason he left his prior employer as, "I'd like to talk to you about that." Apparently, he was hired by the Pittsburgh Police without anyone ever questioning him. He would prove to be extremely troublesome and would self-destruct over the coming years.

My first encounter with Officer Moore was when he was working the AM shift at Zone 2. I had received complaints from businesspeople downtown that an officer was walking his beat in the central part of town with a short-sleeved shirt exposing a tattoo that read "Kill by Profession." I attended roll call every morning at 7:00 and 8:00 AM to personally inspect the officers going on duty. I could not detect anyone with that type of tattoo. I was surprised when I received a call one morning from a businesswoman downtown who said she could see the officer walking by as we spoke. I immediately drove to the location and saw Officer Moore.

Although no tattoo was visible when he stood roll call, he would roll up his sleeves once he left the station, exposing the bottom portion of his tattoo. The full tattoo read "Love by Chance, Kill by Profession." I had to issue an order that officers were prohibited from rolling up their shirt sleeves while on duty. Officer Moore complied, but apparently continued his melt-down over the years. After I disciplined him for not logging all his calls, he secured a transfer to another station. He was sent to Zone 5. He knew he would continue to face disciplinary action for his transgressions, but he was the type of person who just had to keep flaunting his antics in front of his superiors.

The next complaint regarding Moore came years later when I was the chief of police. It came from Commander Lorena Billings, an African American woman who was the commander of Zone 5 that had many African American residents and businesses. I had assigned Lorena to Zone 5 since it was the busiest of the patrol zones with the largest number of calls for service and the largest number of violent calls for service.

The complaint Lorena brought to me was that Moore was parking his personal pickup truck, which displayed a Confederate flag in its rear window, in the police lot. Lorena asked what action she should take. I told her to tell him he could not park in the lot if the flag was displayed. She had clearly talked to someone about it already since she informed me his defense was his freedom of speech. I acknowledged we could not stop the expression of his rights but that did not extend into a city-owned parking lot. I told her to inform him that he would have to park his pickup on the street. She did mention her concern that a vehicle with a Confederate flag would be destroyed in that neighborhood. I responded that it was a decision he would have to make.

Officer Moore obviously removed the flag from the truck window since I never heard his truck was vandalized. But he just could not help himself. He decided to get a tattoo on his lower arm of a naked woman draped in a Confederate flag covering intimate parts of her body. When Lorena brought that to my attention, I had to order Moore to wear long-sleeved shirts. He initially refused and was disciplined. I planned to fire him for insubordination.

The union president, Mickey Hughes, complained that Moore had to wear a long-sleeved shirt year-round and had lost forty pounds as a result. Deputy Chief Declan Mulligan displayed his regular dry wit when he asked the union president if he could borrow Officer Moore's shirt so he could lose forty pounds. The arbitrator suspended Moore, who realized he would have to wear the long-sleeved shirt year-round or face additional disciplinary action leading to his termination.

That still was not enough for Moore. He was the type that if he lost, he had to prove something. He was like that on the mat in Judo class just as he was in the workplace. Since he was having a string of failures with his antics, he obviously believed a transfer to another district would give him opportunities to test his new supervisors.

He informed Commander Billings that he could not work in Zone 5 any longer since the community was largely African American and many of the officers in that district were African American. Moore said he was experiencing anger from African Americans and he felt he was going to hurt someone. He told Commander Billings that he could only work in Zone 4 which was mostly white middle class, or in the Warrant Office, which was mostly administrative.

When Commander Billings informed me of his "demands," I explained to her that there were African Americans who lived in and drove through Zone 4 and there were African Americans who went to the Warrant Office to turn themselves in on outstanding warrants. It was obvious that anyone working as a police officer would encounter people of all backgrounds regardless of their duty location.

When Commander Billings asked me what I should tell Moore, I told her to tell him he was fired. Moore did lose his job over his ceaseless troublemaking, poor decisions, and volatility. It took many years, many citizens' complaints, and considerable supervisory actions to correct a problem that should never have been created for the department. When he wrote "I'd like to talk to you about that" when he was being hired, someone should have talked to him at that time and completed a thorough background investigation.

★★★★

During the late 1980s and early 1990s the City of Pittsburgh experienced many of the same problems that other cities across the nation were attempting to address, including the crack cocaine epidemic. It not only led to a surge in gangs, gang violence, shattered families, and destroyed lives but it led to officer temptations and addictions.

Officer Edward Watson was another officer who was extremely troubled. Watson was a young, physically fit, well-dressed officer who provided a good picture of what an officer should be. He was assigned to Zone 2. I assumed that's why Chief Amos ordered him to be detailed to provide security to City Council. I was informed when I took command of Zone 2 that Watson had reported his firearm stolen in a burglary of his residence. Commander Bentley informed me Chief Amos ordered Watson's stolen gun to be replaced with a city-issued firearm.

After being assigned to Zone 2 a short period of time, Officer Watson reported losing another gun to yet another residence burglary. Officer Watson approached me about being issued another city-issued firearm. I refused and informed him he would have to purchase his own firearm in order to return to work. Obviously, he went to Chief Amos instead. Chief Amos ordered Officer Watson be issued a second city weapon to replace his second "stolen" firearm. By the time I was the chief of police, he had reported the third firearm as stolen from his residence. He approached me to obtain yet another firearm. I refused and told him he could not return to work until he had his own weapon.

Later that day, we received a complaint from a firearms dealer that Officer Watson had come into his business establishment with a friend and that they both appeared high on drugs. When he refused to sell Watson a firearm, Watson and his friend became hostile toward the businessman. Edward Watson never did return to work following that incident.

Just as Edward Watson had reported several guns stolen, Narcotics detectives advised me that Officer Joe Federici had sold his firearm for crack cocaine. They could prove he sold it since they had his firearm. Federici sold the firearm to an informant while they were investigating Federici. They had been investigating him from the time they reported that Officer Federici, off duty, had been pointing them out to the very dealers the detectives were investigating. Officer Federici was arrested.

I served Federici with his copy of the disciplinary paperwork at the County Jail where he was an inmate. Officer Federici never returned to the job.

CAN GANG MEMBERS BE POLICE OFFICERS?

Not all the hiring was strictly down the eligibility list. Two candidates were rejected. They were Calvin Fox and Raphael Avila. Since we did not have staff meetings, and communication among the brass in the department was nearly nonexistent, we only had rumors that they were passed over because they were gang members. A judge ordered the city to hire both candidates. Calvin Fox was sent to Zone 5 where one of the commanders, Commander Edgar Wyman, worked. Wyman was one of the commanders Assistant Chief Noonan identified as using "too much discipline." Raphael Avila was sent to my zone, Zone 2.

Although the city failed to provide any field training that could have been beneficial with the continued training of these two officers, I had created my own field training program in the zone. I assigned an officer to be Avila's field training officer. That officer, Andrew Winters, would later be promoted to lieutenant and then accept the chief of police position in a suburban department. I provided instructions that Officer Avila was prohibited from working unless he was with his field training officer.

Officer Avila's training officer informed me that when they worked the July 4th festivities at a large park downtown, Avila greeted obvious gang members with handshakes and hugs commonly exchanged among gang members. The gang members were dressed in red which indicated they were associated with the "Bloods." During one of the field training sessions, Officer Avila requested that his training officer drive him home. When they got there, he invited his training officer into the house where there were photos on the walls of apparent gang members all dressed in red attire and holding various weapons. Avila seemed proud enough of his affiliations to share it with his training officer.

Officer Avila's performance was poor and within a few months he had been disciplined several times. The final disciplinary action involved him and his partner, Calvin Fox. They went, off duty, to a local university and identified themselves as police officers investigating two women who attended that university. University officials refused to provide the personal information of the two women and notified the bureau. I completed disciplinary paperwork for Officer Avila that would eventually lead to his termination.

Avila appealed his termination until he had exhausted every level of appeal. He then had the audacity to come to my office one evening when I was the chief of police to work out some way of returning to the department. Officer Avila never returned to the Pittsburgh Police. I learned years later that Judge John Matthews had sworn Avila in as a state constable.

MEETING WITH THE FBI

Shortly after I took command of Zone 2, two Narcotics detectives approached me in the parking lot of the station. I knew both well and had worked with them in the past. They explained they wanted to pass on sensitive information regarding one of the officers working in Zone 2.

They had received information from a confidential informant that Officer Tony Cooper was stopping various drug dealers, taking the drugs they had for sale, and letting them go. Cooper was working plainclothes in Zone 2. The detectives also explained that the informant told them the officer then gave the drugs to another drug dealer who had an arrangement with Cooper that the drug dealer would sell the confiscated drugs and they would split the proceeds.

I know how difficult it is for officers to bring that information to a superior officer. There was always the risk that the officers' confidence would be betrayed if the information resulted in revealing their identity. I knew they came to me for two reasons. The first was that I would protect their identity and not expose them to the dangers of midnight-blue officers. The second was that I would take the information they provided and make sure something was done about it.

I requested a meeting with my assistant chief and the chief of police. I explained to them what the Narcotics detectives told me and requested an investigation of the officer. Not only did the chief indicate he was not going to follow up the accusation, but he told me they had been hearing about that for quite some time. When I left the chief's office, I was dismayed that nothing would be done to investigate allegations of a corrupt officer.

I struggled for some time with how to handle the department's lack of action. I knew a corrupt officer working with a drug dealer could be a danger to any officer who responded to a call for drugs being sold on the street. The officer getting the call would think that his or her backup was coming, but the backup might be coming to protect his own interests in the drug dealer and the money coming from the dealer.

I decided, on my own, to meet with FBI agents to see if they could initiate an investigation. I realized I jeopardized my position in the department by going to an outside agency without having the authorization of my superior officers. I was convinced any harm that would come to me would be less than the harm that could come to one of my officers by not ensuring some action was taken. I met with the FBI for hours as they grilled me about various officers and supervisors within the Pittsburgh Police. I was at Zone 2 for twenty months. During this entire time, I was hoping the FBI investigation would provide some results.

During those months, Officer Cooper stopped in my office to talk to me. I knew Cooper and Officer Fred Morris, who had worked plainclothes together in #5 Station when I worked in plainclothes in #7 Station. Cooper told me two things that I would always reflect upon. The first thing he told me was that he wanted me to know many people confused him with Officer Morris. That seemed strange. I wondered if that were just a coincidence that he would tell me that or if word of my meeting with the chief of police had leaked out to Cooper.

The second comment he made to me was that there were two officers in the zone that he insisted I should not trust. He identified them as Officer Bobbie Newman and Officer Jan Forrester. I had worked with Bobbie's father-in-law in the old #3 Station and knew him to be a good person. I had backed up Jan during a call when she and another officer were struggling to handcuff a man on a downtown street. Their location was just around the corner from the cellblock. I heard their radio transmission and was just passing their location and stopped to help. Jan would later remind me that I grabbed their subject by the shirt and lifted him off the ground. I quickly walked him around the corner to the cell block before his feet touched the ground.

I realized from Cooper's words that I now had two officers I could trust. After being promoted to chief of police, I moved Officer Newman to headquarters where she would eventually work in Criminal Intelligence, and I moved Officer Forrester into the Integrity Squad where she would be involved in investigations of allegations of corrupt officers. A sign over Officer Forrester's desk displayed NYPD Officer Frank Serpico's words when he testified to the Knapp Commission: "We must create an atmosphere where the crooked cop fears the honest cop, and not the other way around."

It was known throughout the department that Chief Amos tried to keep officers in the Community Oriented Policing Division (COP). He formed the unit when federal funds were available to hire officers through the Community Oriented Police Services (COPS) Office. The unit had over one hundred officers scattered throughout every neighborhood in the city. However, they had only a few supervisors and a few vehicles, and many officers complained there was little direction. Many officers requested a transfer from that division to work in one of the zones where officers worked in police cars and responded to calls. I was to witness the strong measures taken to discourage officers from requesting transfers out of the community-oriented division.

Assistant Chief Mulligan called to inform me that I would be receiving an officer who had requested a transfer to a district. Officer Gillian Marsh had worked in the COP Division but wanted to work in a patrol zone. This would have diminished the number of officers in the

Community Oriented division since Chief Amos was trying to satisfy each community's desire for more beat officers in its neighborhood.

Assistant Chief Mulligan explained that the chief wanted me to give Officer Marsh a poor assignment with an undesirable shift and days off in the middle of the week. I found that amusing since the chief ensured that my wife and I got the same treatment when he assigned us to the watch commander positions. I did the exact opposite for Officer Marsh. I gave her the shift she requested with better days off. Because she had more time than most officers in my zone and because she expressed an interest in working a zone to gain policing experience, I made her one of my field training officers.

By the time my wife retired from the Pittsburgh Police, Gillian Marsh was one of her shift lieutenants. I found it amazing that some supervisors and police managers would try to punish subordinates like Officer Marsh for wanting to advance in their career while ignoring officers like Tony Cooper who needed to be investigated.

Looking back on my twenty months in command of Zone 2, I had to take disciplinary action that would eventually result in the termination of a handful of officers. Most of those officers were terminated after I became chief of police. The terminations were for a variety of infractions including drug use, selling a firearm for drugs, identifying Narcotics officers to drug dealers, racist comments, and gang activity. I had not set out to establish a reputation as a disciplinarian. I had to wonder if the four of us commanders were the only ones with disciplinary problems since Assistant Chief Noonan singled out only the four of us for using "too much discipline."

ARMSTRONG TUNNELS SHOOTING

In April 1995, a pursuit was initiated by a Zone 2 officer when Jimmy Atkins was observed driving the wrong way on a one-way street. The high-speed pursuit stretched five miles, passing into Zone 3 before returning to Zone 2 with a housing authority officer directly behind the vehicle. The chase continued inside the Armstrong Tunnels, where the officer, Troy Denman, fired his weapon at the car. Reportedly, four officers fired at least fifty-one rounds at Atkins, with Atkins being shot fourteen times. Atkins died in his car.

Since the fatal shooting was in my zone and involved some of my officers, I was notified and drove to the tunnels. Once inside the tunnels, I approached two of my officers and asked them how they were doing. I could see they were not shot but I couldn't tell how they were handling the stress of the shooting.

I was approached by Homicide Commander Robert Bradford who informed me I could not speak with my officers. They were standing by to be taken to headquarters to be interviewed and they were prohibited from speaking with anyone until they were interviewed.

I knew the procedures for any homicide investigation. The Homicide commander was in complete charge of the scene. Since I was not permitted to speak with my officers and there was no other place to be in the tunnels since it was crime scene, I went to my station.

I was upset that I could not somehow be involved in the investigation since they were my officers and the shooting was in my zone. That morning I called Assistant Chief Mulligan to express my displeasure. Of course, there was nothing he could do either since Commander Bradford was solely in charge. I was surprised and disappointed that neither one of the assistant chiefs nor the chief of police came to the scene for a police-involved shooting that included multiple Pittsburgh officers and the death of a motorist.

I never thought any more about the shooting until I learned years later that Atkins's mother had obtained videotapes in 1999 that provided evidence the incident did not occur as Officer Denman said it had.

Troy Denman was arrested and tried for murder. After a hung jury, the DA's office accepted a plea agreement from Denman for involuntary manslaughter and sentenced him to 11½ to 23 months in jail. The DA accepted the plea to avoid further hung juries and to ensure Denman never worked as a police officer again.

District Attorney Christopher Abrams hired an independent investigator to determine why the evidence had not been introduced to the coroner's jury. The video evidence probably would have altered the decision of the jury. Deputy District Attorney Carter Davis had presented the evidence during the coroner's inquest but failed to introduce the videotape. The special investigator from Philadelphia, Attorney George Peters, completed his report, faulting Davis for withholding the evidence. A second investigation was completed that came to the same results.

After that, I was told that if the vehicle crash investigators had been called to the scene, their measurements and recordings and their testimony at the coroner's inquest may have resulted in all the evidence being presented. The bad working relationship between Traffic Lieutenant Sam Stanton and the Homicide Unit apparently created a situation where the traffic personnel were not summoned to the scene. It appeared personalities got in the way of good police work.

If either of the assistant chiefs or the chief of police had gone to the scene that night, there would have been someone with the rank to ensure that everyone who was necessary for the investigation had been there. When I became the chief of police, assistant chiefs and I came out on all police-involved critical incidents.

Years later, Henry Baker, a former Pittsburgh Police officer who was a critic of the police, attempted to fault me for this botched incident, saying I was the chief when a white officer shot and killed a black motorist and that I should have been held accountable. I had to remind him, and the media, that I wasn't the chief then. Assistant Chief Chuck Noonan, who oversaw the Homicide Unit, and Chief of Police Wilbur Amos were in charge then and they were both African American.

LESSONS LEARNED

1) Mass hiring should be avoided. If it is unavoidable, screening of candidates is imperative in conjunction with additional training, enhanced field training, adequate and accountable supervision, immediate and appropriate discipline for violations of policy and training, and tracking of employee performance.

2) The first step to avoiding hiring officers who would prove to be bad for the department should be to conduct thorough screening of candidates that would serve to exclude the hiring of those who should not be officers.

3) Staff meetings are critical to any agency. They not only give the chief the opportunity to provide direction but they give ranking officers a forum in which to keep the chief informed of problems in the department, to let him/her know how officers are feeling, and whether the needs of the community are being served. Every department should have regular staff meetings.

4) Training of personnel for new assignments or promotions should be conducted prior to their working those jobs.

5) Those assigned to new positions should complete a check-off list to be assured that they know how to perform all the duties of the position they are assuming.

6) It is beneficial for workers to have varied assignments during their career in order to ensure that they are better rounded and that the department has personnel that can be moved into other assignments quickly if needed. There are times a learning curve for training may not be available.

7) All departments should conduct performance evaluations of all officers and supervisors.

8) All supervisors should be apprised of any lawsuits filed against the department, grievances filed by the union, or arbitration decisions regarding the grievances or discipline.

9) A department should have quick access to a legal advisor.

CHAPTER EIGHT

Taking the Helm

"The pessimist complains about the wind. The optimist expects it to change. The leader adjusts the sails."

—JOHN MAXWELL

C hief Amos retired at the end of December in 1995. It was the last day he could retire and receive the ¾ retirement. In the interim, Commander Todd Beacham took charge of the bureau until a nationwide search was conducted for the next police chief.

Mayor Murphy obtained a foundation grant to hire the Police Executive Research Forum (PERF) to conduct a nationwide search for a police chief. Those who wanted to be considered were required to apply. I applied as did a half-dozen commanders and Assistant Chief Declan Mulligan. I did not expect to be seriously considered for the position but believed I might be able to obtain a promotion to an assistant chief position. Cathy and I had discussed the problems with the bureau and realized that whoever accepted the position would have the near-impossible job of correcting all that was broken in our bureau.

Some officers in the bureau believed all was well with the Pittsburgh Police. Some may not have known enough to know what the problems were, in which case they were naïve. If they truly did know the bureau well and claimed there were no problems, then they were less than forthright. Cathy and I had witnessed for years the deficiencies and knew the new chief would have a difficult time surviving in the position if s/he worked to fix all the problems. We believed the next chief would barely survive two or three years and would be forced out. That is the average amount of time a chief survives in a large city.

The problems included a conspicuously young, inexperienced group of officers who had been rushed through the academy, received no field training, and received little supervision. They would be entering what I thought of as the sophomore stage of development by having a few years on the job. Many in that stage of development believe they know how to run a department better than the chief does. And many of them are not reluctant to say so. This stage of development is fraught with diminished morale and, I believe, is the most troublesome time in an officer's career. We had 550 officers in that group. And there were many other problems that will be addressed in the next chapter.

Fortunately for the City of Pittsburgh, Mayor Murphy was well educated, experienced, intelligent, and extremely ethical. I was aware of and greatly respected the fact that he had attended a seminary. He received a lot of life experience in the Peace Corps. I would marvel that his Peace Corps experience and my Marine Corps experience worked so well together. Mayor Murphy was determined to ensure that each department performed professionally. He demonstrated his commitment to the Police Bureau in his hiring of the Police Executive Research Forum (PERF) to conduct the nationwide search for the next chief. It was the only time I had witnessed the city hire an outside professional organization to find the best chief available. It was also the only time I was interviewed for any position.

When I walked into the mayor's office for the interview, I was met by Tom Murphy; the prior police chief; Charlotte Lansinger, a representative from PERF; and several others serving on the interview panel. What I remember most about the interview were two questions I was asked. The first question was, "What would you do to change the bureau?" I had prepared for the interview by anticipating that very question. I retrieved my list from my coat pocket and began discussing changes I would make.

I was asked many questions about many of the items on my list. I would save that list. I did not know it at the time, but the list would become extremely important within the next few months when the United States Department of Justice began investigating the Pittsburgh Police for what they described as a pattern of violating citizens' civil rights.

The last question I was asked during the interview seemed to indicate I could predict the future. I was asked to identify the biggest problem facing the bureau. I immediately said it would be "officer morale." I said this because I knew the stages through which officers progressed as they developed.

The first stage consists of the first few years when new officers need a supervisor to provide instruction since they lacked experience. But they generally do not need a supervisor to provide motivation since newer officers tend to be highly motivated about the prospect of an exciting job they were hoping to attain. Most of the officers working in patrol were completing that phase after having obtained a few years of experience.

The officers hired in the mid-1990s were about to enter the second phase of their development. They would need supervisors who not only continued to provide direction as the officers developed, but their supervisors would need to address lower levels of motivation.

As officers encounter court cases lost, public complaints, supervisory corrective action, and negative media comments, motivation can be greatly impacted. Many years would need to pass, and officers would need considerable training and experience to gain skills and adjust their expectations to successfully move on to a third phase.

While all the candidates awaited a decision on who would be the next chief, other important issues began to unfold. On December 12, 1995, an African American motorist, died inside the city limits while interacting with five officers from three suburban departments. The motorist was the cousin of a Pittsburgh Steeler and was borrowing his car. On December 28, a judge ordered three of the five officers to stand trial. On May 16, 1996, the judge ordered the jury to be picked from outside of Allegheny County where Pittsburgh was located.

In addition, during the last days of March 1996, a lawsuit was filed against the Pittsburgh Police by the American Civil Liberties Union on behalf of the NAACP, Parents Against Violence, and sixty-six individuals. There was considerable tension among many community groups and the police.

On April 2, 1996, the week following the filing of the lawsuit, Mayor Murphy announced at a press conference that I would be the next chief of police. Although Cathy and I had earlier discussed my taking an assistant chief's position if one were offered, I had to accept the chief's position. I believed that a refusal to accept the position (which meant I'd be leaving all that the job entailed for someone else to struggle with) would demonstrate a lack of courage. I knew I could not pass on any hard job. I had never done that throughout my career nor had I ever demonstrated a willingness to let someone else do the hard job when I enlisted in the Marine Corps during the Vietnam War.

I did have concerns that I was only forty-five years old and needed to be fifty to obtain a pension. I realized I would also be the fifth chief in ten years. My only request to Mayor Murphy was that if I accepted the position, I needed reassurance that he would run for office again. Once I had that commitment, I felt that I would get through any turmoil.

When my appointment was announced on April 2, 1996, I was very conscious that it was the Tuesday of Holy Week. As difficult as things might get in my new position, I knew I could rely upon my faith to get me through. I was sure that every new ordeal would be a test of my resolve.

CONFIDENTIALITY

What is extremely critical for a chief is confidentiality. The secretary I inherited was friends with a Zone 6 sergeant, Phillip Wells. Every discussion held in the chief's office was somehow leaking out at Zone 6 via the rumor mill. We provided some information that was accurate and some that was false in order to determine the source of the leak. It did not take long for the friendship between the chief's secretary and Wells to be revealed. She was transferred and a trustworthy secretary was moved into the chief's office to replace the outgoing officers and supervisors. No other leaks emanated from the chief's office after those personnel moves. Two secretaries lasted the decade I served as chief and at least fifteen years after I was gone from the bureau. They served five different chiefs. We operated better with fewer and more trusted personnel. It is no exaggeration that some officers' lives depend upon maintaining a confidence.

I took additional steps to ensure enhanced confidentiality. It was going to be important to know who was trustworthy since we were going to be investigating our own officers, some of whom may have been involved in criminal conduct.

One of my first moves, once the bureau was restructured, was to move members of the command staff. I realized that some members might have loyalties to others they had worked with before. I was interested to know who had friends inside or outside of the bureau, who was connected to a politician, and who was interested in ousting me as chief to take my place.

To determine whom to trust, my wife and I developed some methods to determine trustworthiness. For the first step, we embedded one encoded symbol into each of the command staff's memos. This created additional work for us since fifteen separate confidential memos needed to be prepared—one for each member. If any confidential memos were leaked, we would know from the embedded character who had leaked the memo.

Another security measure we used following the command staff restructuring was to notify each member of the command staff days in advance of their new assignment. The first round of assignments resulted in only one name being leaked. The bureau seemed to know that Commander Joe Morgan was going to Narcotics since he was the only person I told where he was going—to the Narcotics Division. When his name was leaked, I transferred another commander to Narcotics. He was disgruntled for the rest of his time with the bureau, but I believed I could not trust him.

I had announced I would commit to regular rotations of command staff in 1996. By 2000, rotations were due. I wanted to prevent chiefs from working in only one duty location during their entire career. I wanted each commander to experience operations, investigations, and administration.

Just before I made the announcements publicly, I called each commander into my office and explained which duty location they would be transferred to. I also provided information regarding two or three other commanders. No one received the same information. When the newspapers identified some of the commanders being transferred, all I had to do was compare the news article with the names provided to each commander. It was obvious Commander Dean Romano was the leak.

THE FIVE C'S

Some issues discussed in management training are the reasons many police chiefs lose their jobs. They include five categories. I refer to these as the five C's. They include (1) **Cops**—providing for officer needs, (2) **Corruption** within the ranks, (3) **Community** dissatisfaction, (4) **Costs**—inability to remain under budget, and (5) **Crime** rates—inability to reduce crime or to reduce it fast enough.

What I found to be difficult is that some of these five issues can be in conflict with some of the others or even all the others at times. For example, if emerging crime requires a proactive police presence in certain neighborhoods, this need could conflict with what the community expects from their police. Similarly, remaining within a fiscal budget is important to the chief and department, but officers do not want a budget so limited that it interferes with their ability to supplement their income with overtime pay. When a chief attempts to reduce overtime in order to stay under budget, this move may not sit well with the officers who will receive less overtime in their pay.

THE FIRST "C"–COPS

Although the prior chief prohibited officers from wearing certain safety equipment, I was determined to provide officers with updated equipment to reduce injuries to themselves and to the public, and lawsuits. When I served as the commander in Zone 2, I recognized that officers needed additional equipment. I wrote a memo to the chief requesting that our officers (1) be permitted to wear ballcaps while working patrol, (2) be permitted to wear protective gloves when conducting a search or making an arrest, (3) be equipped with collapsible batons, (4) be equipped with pepper spray, and (5) be equipped with Tasers. I never received a reply to my memo.

Once I took the helm, Commander Catherine McNeilly and I researched the many benefits to upgrades in equipment. Each piece of equipment was reviewed to determine its benefit before it was introduced to the bureau. Officers were permitted to wear ballcaps to prevent loss or damage of the bulky official dress cap during foot pursuits and arrests and to wear protective gloves to prevent injuries. Other equipment introduced to the bureau included collapsible batons, pepper spray, Tasers, and a choice of the 9mm firearms carried in 1996 or an upgrade to .40-caliber firearms. Bicycles were eventually introduced as another means of patrol.

Although I believed the new equipment was being introduced as quickly as possible, some officers complained they were not introduced sooner. It was even more disappointing that the same officers who complained never spoke a word about the lack of, or even the consideration for providing, that equipment during the prior three and a half years under the past chief. It was obvious that the officers who complained belonged to the dark-blue group of police officers. They would find some reason to be dissatisfied with changes that were going to benefit officers.

I had to ensure that any change I made would not be criticized and then overruled by council ordinances. For example, I needed to demonstrate that changing to the .40-caliber weapons was acceptable since the county police and the state police were already using those weapons. It was more time-consuming to research pepper spray, which I believed could be even more controversial since the prior chief claimed it had the potential for abuse.

The research into pepper spray led to studies providing evidence that using pepper spray instead of other force measures actually reduced the number of injuries to officers, the number of injuries to subjects being arrested, and the number of citizens' complaints. Even after the study's findings justified purchasing the equipment, funding it in a cash-strapped bureau needed to be budgeted for the following year and training had to be developed. I knew if I introduced any changes in equipment without being able to defend their use and provide for the proper policies and training, the officers would lose the ability to keep them.

The good jobs being done by officers in the sky-blue and light-blue groups were not recognized or made known to the public. In an effort to recognize the officers, regular awards ceremonies were scheduled in City Council chambers. The ceremonies were attended by the mayor, the entire command staff, and the media. Media coverage of the awards and the dramatic efforts of exceptional policing during lifesaving, perilous arrests, and excellent crime solving were regularly made public.

In addition, the types of awards were expanded to provide for recognition of safe driving and good conduct, and to acknowledge officers-of-the-month and officers-of-the year. Most of the awards were accompanied by a ribbon to be worn on the officer's uniform as a display of the officer's distinction in policing. It seemed like a small matter, but officers were upset if they failed to receive an award when they believed it was due.

THE JACK LYONS INCIDENT

As I neared the end of the three weeks of SMIP training in Boston, I was notified of an incident that nearly cost the life of one of our officers. Officer Jack Lyons was informed by a motorist that a driver of a car might need medical attention. Officer Lyons, working the night shift, pulled in behind the car in question that was sitting at a green light and got out to investigate.

He noticed that the three men in the car were sleeping. Two men were in the front and one was in the rear seat. When he knocked on the window to awaken the driver, the rear-seat passenger awoke, noticed the officer outside of his car, and quickly threw some small, sealed balloons into his mouth. Officers knew this was a method to carry cocaine and heroin and swallowing them was a way to get rid of the evidence.

Officer Lyons immediately opened the back door and attempted to retrieve the drugs from the suspect's mouth. The driver then woke up, hit the gas pedal, and sped around another police car which had parked in front of it. The door slammed shut on Officer Lyons's hand and he was dragged down a main street at speeds up to 70 mph. Officer Lyons jumped onto the trunk of the car to avoid being dragged. When he did so, he saw the rear-seat passenger and the front passenger pointing guns at him.

What the officers on the scene didn't know was that this car was stolen, it had just been used during an armed robbery, and the stolen wallet of the victim was in the car. What they quickly learned was that the occupants possessed drugs and were armed.

When Officer Lyons saw firearms pointed at him, he pulled his weapon and fired at the occupants of the car. With one hand still caught in the door, Officer Lyons pulled off an incredible feat. He killed both passengers and wounded the driver. As the car made a sharp right turn, Officer Lyons's hand slid out of the car door because the force of the turn had caused his wedding ring to peel the skin back on his ring finger like a banana peel, which freed him. Officer Lyons was rushed to a hospital with serious injuries from being dragged by the car.

The wounded driver abandoned the car shortly afterward and was arrested. When officers opened the door that had trapped Officer Lyons's hand, Lyons's wedding ring fell from the door jamb. The ring had held him firmly attached to the car until it peeled his finger.

When I heard this, I left SMIP training early and drove the ten hours straight back to Pittsburgh. I immediately went to the hospital in the early morning hours to meet with Officer Lyons. I spoke with his wife and friends while he was in surgery. I assured them we would help him and his family with his needs.

I made sure to activate the Critical Incident Stress Debriefing team for all personnel involved and to provide counseling to the officer, his family, and other officers. I had an officer posted at his house for security and in the event the family needed anything from the bureau.

The negative attention the police bureau had received in the past was revived during this event. A councilman, Solomon Unger, accused Officer Lyons of shooting the men first. Of course, Councilman Unger had no way of knowing what happened that day but was making accusations before the case was even investigated. I obtained a copy of the recordings and permitted the media to hear the incident unfold for themselves. I knew we needed to get out in front of this matter right away rather than allow those who did not know anything to make accusations that could influence people's perceptions.

Within months, there was a coroner's inquest regarding this incident. The jury was made up of six people. I advised duty locations that they had authorization to send officers to the inquest. I sat next to Officer Lyons the entire two days of the inquest, even when he testified. He did a great job of explaining exactly what happened. Other officers who were there or who witnessed Officer Lyons being dragged also supported his testimony.

I was disappointed when three of the six jurors voted to try the officer for manslaughter, and one voted to try him for murder. The other two voted that the officer should not face any charges. The coroner did not recommend any charges against the officer and the district attorney announced there would be no charges filed against Officer Lyons.

When members of the public demanded action be taken against Officer Lyons and the media made inquiries as to why disciplinary action would not be taken, I insisted that Officer Lyons had done what he was trained to do and what any officer would have done in that position. I stressed that all his actions were necessary to survive the incident.

I could have said more about the incident but there was still a pending trial for the driver who had been captured and charged with aggravated assault. The bureau and the district attorney's office needed to ensure that nothing was said to prevent a fair trial for the driver.

When Officer Lyons did return to work, I placed him in a light-duty detective position. When he recovered, I moved him to a full-duty detective position.

Nearly three years later, in February 1999, a family member of one of the occupants of the car claimed he wanted the case reopened and accused the police of a coverup. The family was accusing Officer Lyons of violating bureau policy. I was quoted by Meredith Raine in the *Pittsburgh Tribune-Review* (2/19/1999) as saying that Lyons had violated no policies or procedures, and that "he did exactly what he needed to do to stay alive."

Our bureau needed a lot of work to avoid another horrendous incident like this. Three important issues came to the fore.

First, we needed a new policy to protect our officers from enduring a similar encounter during which the officer could be seriously injured or killed. A policy was instituted prohibiting an officer from reaching into a running vehicle.

Even with that policy and appropriate training in place, there was another incident, this time of an officer jumping into a truck to stop a DUI suspect from speeding off. The awards board believed the officer should receive an award for jumping into the passenger side of the truck and using his hand to depress the brake pedal while the officer on the driver's side of the vehicle physically arrested the driver.

When I became aware of this initiative, I realized that many in the bureau still did not get it. That officer had unnecessarily exposed himself to danger: if the officer's hand was on the brake pedal, his weapon had to have been exposed to the driver. Additionally, the incident occurred just before a tunnel. The officer's legs hanging out of the vehicle were prone to injury.

I knew of another incident when a drug dealer attempted to jump into a vehicle to retrieve drugs when the driver refused to pay for them. The car sped off with the dealer half in and half out of the car. When the car sideswiped a metal pole, the dealer's body was cut in half.

I told the awards board that not only would there not be an award, but the officer involved needed to be counseled for violating bureau policy. I considered it insane to award an officer for taking unnecessary risks to make an arrest.

The incident could just as easily have resulted in an on-duty death. It was obvious to me, but apparently not to some other officers, that unwise acts needed to be discouraged rather than encouraged. Not only was the act unsafe for the officer but it created an unnecessary deadly-force situation for the subject since it increased the officer's, or another officer's, need to use deadly force. Too often officers, believing they are acting courageously, put themselves into hazardous situations and then claim they needed to use deadly force to protect themselves.

The saying "The lack of prior planning on your part does not constitute an emergency on my part" should be interpreted in policing as "The lack of proper techniques or tactics on your part should not constitute a deadly-force situation for the public." I learned from the times I was injured due to poor tactics that I should never expose myself unnecessarily to danger. We had to change the culture of rewarding officers for being injured by providing training and supervision that would correct an officer's reckless acts, however well intentioned.

Second, we seldom ever saw the prior chief being interviewed during his three and a half years as the chief. When we built a new headquarters years later, I put the public information officer's office right inside the door to the police administration offices. I also insisted my office be located beside the public information officer's (PIO) office for transparency.

Having a PIO and my being present during critical incidents seemed to make a difference. During one shooting incident in the Strip District, a man pointed a weapon at two off-duty officers working a detail. The man was shot and killed. At the coroner's inquest I approached the young man's uncle and expressed my sympathy for the family's loss. I had learned to do this from the SMIP training. The uncle told me he did not believe it was the fault of the officers and said he thought his nephew had committed "suicide by cop." I was amazed at the dramatically different results of two shootings only years apart.

Third, the awards board recommended that the officers receive the bureau's highest medal for the shooting incident. The bureau was already in the process of revising the awards policy to triple the number of awards available for officers. Previously, officers didn't seem to receive the proper acknowledgement within the bureau.

I pointed out to the awards board that the incident did not conform with the criteria for the Medal of Valor, which was the highest medal the bureau could award. According to the policy description, that award "... shall be awarded to members who distinguish themselves by performing an act of exceptional courage and bravery above and beyond the call of duty."

All during the legal proceedings when so many were demanding that Officer Lyons be tried for murder and manslaughter, I argued against the charges because he "...did what he was trained to do, he did what any officer would have done in that position, and all his actions were to survive the incident." If those criteria were to be followed, it would be difficult to say his actions went above and beyond the call of duty.

Many officers were upset that Officer Lyons received the Purple Heart rather than the Medal of Valor. It was almost as if they believed the Purple Heart was less honorable. Many military veterans, including my cousin who was killed in Vietnam, received a Purple Heart for their injuries or death without also receiving the United States Medal of Honor.

THE SECOND "C"–CORRUPTION WITHIN THE RANKS

Police corruption has been described as misconduct involving the abuse of authority for personal gain. Other types of misconduct include (1) *procedural*, when officers fail to comply with department regulations, (2) *criminal*, when officers violate laws, and (3) *unconstitutional*, when officers violate a citizen's civil rights.

All these forms of misconduct lead to some type of corrective action. Significant increases in each of these areas were inevitable given the number of problems encountered by so many young, inexperienced officers in the Pittsburgh Police force who lacked sufficient training, supervision, and discipline.

It would be the number of disciplinary cases and the level of discipline imposed that would alarm officers not accustomed to witnessing many disciplinary measures and outrage the police union who had to defend each officer being disciplined. It was my responsibility as chief to oversee the first of three disciplinary hearings each officer had once disciplinary measures were initiated.

Although any officer not satisfied with my level of discipline could appeal my decision to the Public Safety director and subsequently appeal to a neutral arbitrator, the union aimed their guns in my direction in an effort to have me back down. They knew they could not pressure the neutral arbitrator's decision and would have less effect trying to pressure the Public Safety director than the chief of police.

The bureau needed to shoulder some of the responsibility for many of the officers disciplined. I am convinced that most disciplinary measures and terminations are due to a department's failure to address the proper recruitment, policies, training, supervision, discipline, and early intervention that could have prevented many of the failures.

Right after being named as chief, I made another trip to the Federal Bureau of Investigation. I inquired whether there was progress in any investigations from the time I visited there as a commander. I was informed there had not been any investigations since the FBI did not have authorization from the chief of police to conduct investigations. I told them they now had the chief's complete cooperation.

I chose three officers to form a new "Integrity Unit." The Integrity Unit would conduct internal investigations regarding complaints of police corruption and misconduct. They were to conduct these investigations with the assistance of the FBI. To ensure no one could claim that the chief targeted any one officer for investigation, I instructed the detectives to inform me of their cases only when they were prepared to make arrests.

The detectives chosen had worked Narcotics and were detectives I completely trusted. Although they were assigned to the FBI, I told the command staff they would be assigned to the Attorney General's (AG) office since officers assigned to that office worked Narcotics investigations. I wanted to take precautions so the investigations would not be compromised. I already knew there were some in the command staff who had leaked information either unintentionally or purposely for personal reasons. The Integrity Unit investigations continued for more than two years before their unit became known. They had other earlier arrests, but the arrests in December 1999 brought much attention to their work.

The Integrity Unit detectives worked the case I had brought to the attention of the FBI years earlier. That case involved two Narcotics detectives who informed me of an officer taking drugs from a drug dealer in the Hill District and turning them over to another drug dealer to sell, after which they would split the proceeds. What appeared to be an illegal gambling operation was established in the Hill District. The operation was conducted by the FBI. They recorded Detective

Tony Cooper during his many stops at the site to accept payments. He explained he would advise the operators of the "illegal" gambling operation if they were going to get raided since he was the detective working at Zone 2 in the Hill District. Cooper even sent his brother to accept a payment.

Another Integrity test involved an apartment in Zone 2 where Cooper and his partner, Detective Derek Higgins, worked. We circulated rumors that the resident of the apartment sold drugs from that location. A 911 call reported a burglary in progress at the apartment. When Officers Cooper and Higgins arrived, the front door was kicked in, the apartment was ransacked, and a safe was located in the bedroom. Detectives Cooper and Higgins found the safe to be closed but unlocked. Some of the money found was turned in and some was not. The apartment had been rented by the FBI and contained recording devices throughout.

On another occasion, a car had been reported stolen. Officers recovered the car and when Detective Higgins looked through the car, he found money in the glove compartment. The car had recording devices in it and recorded him looking at the money, leaving the location, and returning. On his third trip to the car, he took nine hundred dollars.

On yet another occasion, another car had been reported stolen. Officer Gerald Thompson, from Zone 5, recovered the stolen car. In the car were valuables and $165 in cash. The officer's actions were recorded. He turned in sixty dollars.

All these officers were arrested in December 1999. Detective Cooper retired rather than be terminated which could mean the loss of his pension. He was convicted of a felony and sentenced to prison. The commission of a felony prevented his ability to return to work as a police officer.

Officer Higgins had taken less than $1,000, which was the threshold for the crime to be categorized as a felony. Since it was a misdemeanor, he was entitled to a disciplinary hearing. His first hearing was in front of me as the chief and I fired him. The Public Safety director was the next appeal for the officer, and she upheld the termination. The third, and final, appeal was to a neutral arbitrator. He reduced the sentence and ordered the officer returned to his position.

Officer Thompson's first-level disciplinary hearing was in front of me as the chief. I fired him. Following his appeal to the Public Safety director, she upheld the termination. He appealed to a neutral arbitrator and the termination was upheld. One never knew what to expect from an arbitrator. Thompson had kept only about $100 and his firing was upheld while Detective Higgins kept $900 and his termination was overturned. Higgins would eventually be promoted to sergeant years after I retired.

Following those arrests, I believed the behavior of officers would change for the better since they realized Integrity testing was occurring. I was therefore surprised that there were more complaints, more investigations, and more arrests. The Integrity Unit established an e-mail address so officers in the bureau could send them information regarding corruption while maintaining their confidentiality. The Integrity Unit informed me that 70 percent of the complaints they received were originated by officers within the bureau. It was obvious good officers did not want to work with corrupt officers. All that was needed was a discrete method for officers to report the corruption.

Another case worked by the Integrity Unit involved Officer Sheila Buckley. Officer Buckley was one of the officers who constantly flouted policy and bureau direction. The first time she came to a disciplinary hearing in front of me she was charged with leaving her assignment, turning in her police radio, and going home before her shift was completed. Her defense during the hearing was that "everyone does it." She refused to provide the names of any officers who went home early.

The second time she came in front of me in a disciplinary hearing she was charged with violating a direct order. The Port Authority Transit (PAT) police complained that officers were driving their personal vehicles on the bus routes. Bus routes were open only to buses, PAT vehicles, and police vehicles. After the order was issued prohibiting personal vehicles on the busway, Buckley was stopped by PAT police for operating her personal vehicle on the busway. She later explained she used the busway as a shortcut to work and again claimed that "everyone does it."

The Integrity officers were investigating Buckley after two officers working her shift said they overheard her in another room giving a description of herself and providing prices. The officers suspected she was involved in prostitution. The Integrity officers discovered an ad in the *Pittsburgh City Paper* where she offered "Lunchtime treat, Mon & Tues." Mondays and Tuesdays happened to be her days off.

The Integrity officers enlisted the help of a district attorney's investigator so she would not recognize a "patron" as an officer investigating. According to the police report, the investigator offered her $120 for "sex services for one hour." Her initial disciplinary hearing was set, and I expected her to say for the third time, "Everyone does it." However, she did not appear for her hearing, apparently put off by the television cameras set up around police headquarters. Her attorney requested an appeal which went directly to the Public Safety director. The television crews walked the two blocks to the union office and filmed her leaving there. She never returned to the bureau.

Another of the Integrity investigations involved Officer Roy Clemmons. Detectives were investigating complaints he was selling drugs while on duty and in uniform. A DEA agent was used to make buys from the officer while he was on duty. At one point, Officer Clemmons appeared to realize he was being investigated. He told the agent that if he found out the agent was an officer, he would "Glock" him. Our officers wore Glock pistols. Clemmons was later found guilty in federal court and was sentenced to ten years in prison. I was surprised to see him years later when he walked into the high school in a suburban township that I just happened to be passing through that day. Clemmons told me he had only served between seven and eight years.

Following the initial arrests by the Integrity Unit, rumors surfaced throughout the bureau that tests were being conducted when they really were not. For example, officers who found a gun or drugs in a police car from the earlier shift were convinced they were being tested. They were reporting the found gun or drugs rather than take a chance that it was an Integrity test. One officer complained that a five-dollar bill had been lying on the floor in #4 Station for a week and everyone was afraid to touch it. Those were not tests of integrity, but the officers' suspicions that they were being tested had an impact on their behavior.

One officer called the Integrity officers asking them why he was being tested. The Integrity officers invited him to their office where he accused them of testing him because Officer Wayne Johnson had offered him money to ensure that a case of drunk driving was dismissed in Traffic Court. The Integrity officers wired the officer to record the encounter and Officer Johnson was arrested after he offered the bribe. Officer Johnson resigned.

The Integrity Unit, comprised of sky-blue officers, was extremely successful in identifying and investigating officers who were involved in criminal behavior. These were the officers belonging to the 1-2 percent of officers in the midnight-blue category. They were officers who used their position for illegal purposes and to benefit themselves.

TERMINATIONS

The working relationship between Union President Mickey Hughes and I was already difficult when Mickey told me in 1996 he would not negotiate with me about changes in the bureau over the next two years because he did not want anything to change until the next contract arbitration. Our ability to work together became more strained during a meeting when we discussed scheduling our first set of disciplinary hearings that could lead to some suspensions and some terminations. Many disciplinary hearings were all scheduled to happen on the same day since they all required attendance by the same command staff members, the union attorney, and union leadership.

At the conclusion of the meeting, I questioned the union attorney about the method used by the prior chief to schedule the officers' disciplinary hearings. Officers were entitled to a hearing for any proposed disciplinary measure that could result in a suspension or a termination. The disciplinary hearings were set within ten days following my signature on the disciplinary action report. I knew the union attorney had to be present for the hearing and so I wanted to ensure we scheduled the hearing for when he was available. That seemed to take priority over the ten-day deadline for scheduling hearings. Mickey told me they scheduled the hearings according to the union attorney's availability and not to worry about any contract timelines.

One of the first officers terminated was Kyle Rogers. He had reported his mother's car stolen and filed an insurance claim. Officers arrested Kyle Rogers on May 1, 1996. When Rogers had his hearing, the union defense was that the hearing was not held within ten days of my signature on the disciplinary form as required by contract. When I questioned Mickey Hughes about his earlier claim that timelines were not important, he told me it was not his place to disregard the timelines for officers being disciplined. An arbitrator ordered Rogers's position to be reinstated.

Although Rogers was returned to his position, there were three subsequent developments. The first was that I would never lose another disciplinary case after the arbitrator's decision due to timelines although the union could not say the same. The second was that I never took Mickey at his word again. I had to verify all his assertions. The third was that Kyle Rogers was terminated two more times before his termination became permanent.

The final termination followed his conviction that had a possible sentence of more than one year for the insurance fraud. The federal government considers a conviction with a one-year sentence to be a felony. Rogers's conviction prohibited him from owning or possessing a firearm, which meant he could not qualify with his firearm, which meant he could not achieve the required certification through the state Municipal Police Officers Education and Training Commission. Without certification, no one can serve as a police officer in the state. It took three years before the bureau charges resulted in a termination. Mickey continued to argue after Rogers's termination that Rogers should have been returned to work as a police officer without a firearm.

A March 18, 1997, *Pittsburgh Post-Gazette* article titled "Fired officers get back on force on technicalities" listed the names of ten officers who had been fired. Six of those officers returned to work on the "ten-day hearing" technicality. I was quoted as saying, "Even though the arbitrator tells us we have to take them back, they can come back in two ways—doing the best job they can for the citizens and the bureau and themselves, or they can come back with the attitude that they beat the city. If that's the case, we'll be seeing them again." Most of the officers were never disciplined again. They apparently came back with the attitude of just doing their job and did not need disciplinary action again. However, some did face additional disciplinary action and were eventually terminated.

★★★★

For nearly a decade, I served as Pittsburgh's chief of police. There were approximately one hundred disciplinary cases each year. Many officers had their charges dismissed, many cases were resolved through oral or written reprimands, many resulted in suspensions, and some resulted in terminations. Although one thousand disciplinary cases may seem like a lot for a bureau of one thousand officers (over a period of ten years), many of the cases involved minor infractions and many of the officers disciplined were "frequent fliers," meaning they appeared at many disciplinary hearings. For some of those officers the disciplinary hearings resulted in a termination that was upheld by an arbitrator.

At the beginning of my term as chief, I was confronted with officers charged with sexual assault, excessive force including pistol whipping subjects, using the confiscated drugs taken from a prisoner, selling drugs on duty, bribery, theft, insurance fraud, and prostitution. Many of these cases resulted in suspensions and terminations.

Toward the end of my ten years as the chief, there were not as many suspensions or terminations since the charges were not as severe. Many disciplinary cases involved not wearing seat belts, responsibility for vehicle collisions, and losing police equipment such as radios. If there was any indication that taking a strong stand against corruption provided significant results, the reduction in the number of severe disciplinary cases was testament to how much the bureau had changed for the better. The changes were due to the presence of many good people in the bureau and in the command staff, as well as the Public Safety director who supported the proper discipline, the members of the law department who assisted with disciplinary hearings, and Mayor Murphy who expected excellence in every department.

I offer the following examples of disciplinary cases that might never have happened under strong leadership in a culture that desired to do what was right. Instead, the officers involved were motivated by their personal survival instincts and the assumption that they would be successful in beating disciplinary efforts.

- Officer Damian Hendricks was charged with sexually assaulting a man who was drunk and had fallen asleep at Hendricks's residence. He was terminated and the termination was upheld. Years later, in December 2011, Hendricks was arrested for impersonating a Pittsburgh Police officer.

- Officer Glenn Wilson lost a civil suit for beating and pistol-whipping a person during an arrest. He also had five prior complaints for using excessive force during arrests. He was terminated.

- Officer Dennis McGovern was involved in a drug arrest with his partner. His partner transported the arrested person to the County Jail while McGovern was supposed to return to the station to package the drugs for delivery to the Crime Lab and complete the paperwork. It was reported that McGovern smoked all the crack evidence. A report stated he was found the next morning blurry eyed in a back room at the station. McGovern immediately left the station and checked himself into a drug rehabilitation facility. Officers knew that any first time use of drugs for which they were caught would be a free ticket to return to work following an arbitration hearing.

  The drug charges against the suspect had to be dismissed due to lack of evidence. The city was also liable for a false arrest. Following his termination, the arbitrator did return McGovern to work. He was assigned to the East End of Pittsburgh since he had been working the West End when he allegedly smoked up the evidence. McGovern eventually left the bureau and I was later advised he was arrested in a neighboring state for drug possession.

- In 1996, Officer Joseph Arnaz was charged with excessive use of force which had been witnessed by three officers from another department and a civilian witness. He was terminated but reinstated by an arbitrator with a 92-day suspension. After his termination but prior to his reinstatement, he entered a police facility and faxed a fake memo purportedly from me that said I was resigning my position as chief of police due to my involvement in domestic violence. Obviously, he was incensed that I fired him, and he apparently sent the memo as revenge.

  Lieutenant Tony Rossi, assigned to Zone 2, was smart and proactive. The lieutenant received the fax Arnaz sent, recognized it as fake, and went to the duty location from where the fax originated. There he learned Arnaz had just been there and left. Arnaz was not authorized to be in a police facility after he had been terminated. Rossi searched for evidence and located a copy of one of my memos with my signature on it, the text blocked out, and a false narrative of my resignation typed into the body of the memo. The memo was located in the copy machine. Arnaz's fingerprint was on the memo.

An investigation began when Arnaz returned following the arbitrator's decision to overturn his termination. When Arnaz returned from his suspension, he was ordered to submit to fingerprinting which he refused. Arnaz was terminated again, and this termination was upheld.

- Officer Gino Ricci was arrested for indecent assault, aggravated indecent assault, corrupting the morals of a minor, and official oppression. A fifteen-year-old girl accused him of detaining her and fondling her after he caught her swimming in a public pool after hours. She said he drove her to two locations before releasing her and giving her his pager number. Ricci was terminated.

- Officer Dylan White was a large, physically imposing man who played semi-professional hockey. At the end of a hockey game when players shook the hands of their opponents, White was accused of punching one of the other players, breaking his jaw. Although White was off duty and the alleged incident occurred in another county, bureau policy demanded that any arrest of an officer be reported to one's supervisors. White failed to notify anyone in the bureau when he had been charged with assault. One of his supervisors learned of the arrest and initiated disciplinary paperwork.

When White came in front of me for his first hearing, the recommendation was for a two-day suspension. I suspected White was using steroids due to his size and apparent emotional instability. I offered him a suspension if he agreed to a program referred to as Track III. (Track I was a self-referral for assistance with alcohol, drug, or anger management. Track II was a referral ordered by a police supervisor.) Track III was a written agreement the officer would sign which required him to receive counseling and drug testing if needed. Failure to comply with Track III meant termination. White said he would not agree to being drug-tested even if he were to lose his job. I informed him he was terminated.

White appealed my decision to the Public Safety director. She offered him the same deal to keep his job as long as he agreed to drug testing. He again refused. White appealed her decision to the neutral arbitrator who offered him the same deal that the Public Safety director and I had offered. He told the arbitrator he would not agree to drug testing. The arbitrator, who was the final decision maker in his case, fired him.

- Officer Fred LeVoy had been on one episode of the television series *COPS*. I was working as the Night Watch commander for the city when it aired. He came across so poorly that other departments were calling and leaving messages, ridiculing him for how he handled an interaction with a prostitute in one of the episodes. His many disciplinary cases led to his being placed in Track III. When officers went to his house to take him to his random alcohol/drug testing, he refused to go. He was terminated for his refusal.

  At an arbitration hearing on another matter, the arbitrator ejected LeVoy from the meeting due to his behavior. LeVoy stood in the hallway and shouted he wanted to engage in a fist fight outside with me. At the time, the arbitrator was deciding if all officers with fifteen years would be paid at the higher rate of master police officer or if a percentage of officers in patrol would be paid this higher rate. The arbitrator's decision would also affect the pay of retired officers like Fred LeVoy. The arbitrator, after witnessing Fred LeVoy's behavior, decided that every retired officer *except* Fred LeVoy would receive the higher pay or pension. His antics resulted in a lower pension for himself only.

- Officer Steve O'Reilly had been disciplined many times during his relatively short career with the bureau. O'Reilly failed to adhere to bureau policy prohibiting driving a police car over a charged fire hose. The hose parted, swung wildly, and knocked a man to the ground. The man suffered brain damage and would never be able to function on his own again. The city paid hundreds of thousands of dollars to assist with the man's care. O'Reilly was terminated. An arbitrator returned O'Reilly to the job. O'Reilly was eventually terminated for violating the city's residency requirement.

- Officer Alex Fetterman had been working an off-duty detail in 2003 when he attempted to arrest a man. The subject ran and Fetterman chased him and had to use force to handcuff him. Several other on-duty officers came to his assistance. I was advised when it dawned on Fetterman that city overtime pay for a court appearance would not be authorized for an arrest made while working an off-duty detail, Fetterman uncuffed the subject and let him go. Fetterman then obtained a warrant for the man he let go and, while on duty, arrested him for the charges he would have filed. This appeared to be an effort to ensure he was paid overtime for a court appearance related to the arrest. There was an internal investigation. Investigators stated he was untruthful, but the on-duty officers explained precisely what occurred. Fetterman was terminated. The termination was upheld.

  Five years later, Alex Fetterman was arrested for a shooting incident in a suburb. Witnesses told police that Fetterman was with a group of about fifteen to twenty men displaying the Pagans' motorcycle club insignia. The Pagans were known to law enforcement as an outlaw motorcycle club involved with drugs and violence. It was reported the Pagans were threatening three men in a bar. When the men left, news reports stated some of the Pagans followed them into the parking lot. Fetterman was accused of using a knife to slash a car tire when the men attempted to drive away. The reports also state he shot once into the ground and once into the car as the occupants drove away. Another Pagan reportedly shot once into the car. One man received a gunshot wound to the chest and died within two hours.

- Officer Fred Raymond worked many off-duty details. He was initially caught working a detail without the proper bureau authorization to do so. He was disciplined for that infraction, and part of the penalty for the infraction prohibited him from working any other off-duty details for six months. On the night before Thanksgiving, I drove into the train station in Downtown Pittsburgh and there was Raymond, working the off-duty detail. Since there was so much traffic, I had to drive past Raymond, park, and return to locate him. Of course, he spotted me driving past him. I learned he had run from the train station, abandoning his off-duty post rather than face me. He was disciplined again and suspended.

In another incident, Fred Raymond was working a two-officer unit and responded to a call at a home for a domestic. The woman was intoxicated, and the man with her said he was going to leave the house. After Raymond finished his shift a couple of hours later, he returned to the house and reportedly had sex with the woman. After Raymond left her house, she called the police to report that she had been raped. The woman was transported to the hospital and a rape test was conducted.

The woman's blood alcohol level was above a .40. Those familiar with BAC (blood alcohol content) know that a person will generally be on the brink of losing consciousness or in a coma with a BAC of .35 to .40. Above a .40 there is a strong likelihood of death. However, those with a high tolerance can manage to survive that level of intoxication.

An internal investigation was conducted and Raymond was interviewed. I was informed he initially denied any involvement with the woman but later during the interview acknowledged the woman performed a sex act, but he denied having intercourse with the woman. He was confronted with the fact that his DNA, her husband's DNA, and a third unknown man's DNA were found in the woman's vagina.

Raymond was charged criminally for the sexual assault and administratively for multiple charges including violations of the code of ethics and truthfulness, as well as incompetency. The district attorney opted not to pursue criminal charges due to the woman's history of incidents and unreliability. The rape conviction would have led to Raymond's termination. Without a criminal case, the disciplinary action would be for administrative charges only.

I still believed a termination was proper for several reasons. First, from what was reported, he took advantage of a woman who was not able to care for herself. Second, he also took advantage of a situation when he was summoned to help a family as a civil servant. Instead of helping the couple, he returned when the husband was gone and took advantage of the wife's vulnerability. Third, he lied during the internal investigation. I could only wonder how Raymond would have felt if another officer had done the same thing to *his* wife.

I testified at the disciplinary hearing in front of the arbitrator that this was the most despicable act I had ever witnessed by an officer. I said that although there were officers who stole property from victims, what Raymond took from this woman and her husband was more valuable than property. The couple had summoned officers for help and instead of helping them he made the situation worse for them. The arbitrator rewarded him by returning him to the job.

I knew I could not assign Raymond to work the district where he might victimize other women, so I assigned him to the mail car, which another officer charged with rape had worked for many years. The mail car delivered confidential police mail from one station to another. Officers throughout the bureau referred to the mail car as the "rape car." Fred Raymond is still a police officer at this writing and served as a trustee for the local lodge of the police union.

Although some officers referred to Raymond as "Raping Raymond," he had the audacity to tell the council president that what he did was merely "dating" another woman and he equated that to my dating my wife who was a police lieutenant when I was a police commander. I knew he was not foolish enough to believe there was any comparison.

Years after I was gone from the Pittsburgh Police, my wife disciplined him for calling off sick thirty-seven times to work secondary employment. By this time, David Bailey was the mayor and her disciplinary efforts were quashed by the assistant city solicitor with not a word being uttered by the assistant chief, deputy chief, or the chief of police.

SUSPENSIONS

Most disciplinary measures did not involve a termination. Most were oral or written reprimands. There were many suspensions for either serious violations of policies or for multiple infractions leading to progressive disciplinary measures that eventually resulted in suspensions.

It is interesting that some of those officers accepted responsibility for their mistakes or misconduct while others failed to take responsibility. Whether they did or not depended upon the group to which the officers belonged. Any officer who accepted responsibility for a reprimand was evidence the officer belonged in the blue group or higher. Those not accepting responsibility were in the medium blue to midnight-blue groups. They generally blamed someone else such as the commander or chief for being too strict, were angry for being disciplined, and sometimes participated in activities to strike back at those they blamed for the disciplinary action taken against them.

- For example, several officers were drinking at one of their homes one weekend and thought it would be a good idea to conduct target practice in the backyard. It was something one would expect to read in a book like Joseph Wambaugh's *The Choirboys.*

  Each officer offered to take a one-day suspension to accept responsibility for his actions with the promise not to appeal the disciplinary action. I agreed. It resolved several separate disciplinary cases, permitted the officers to return to work to further their careers, did not tie up the command staff and the assistant city solicitors preparing for appeals, and saved the union and the city the costs of arbitration. However, not all suspensions were that easy or that easily accepted.

- Officer Jason Keene was accused in 1998 of failure to conduct a proper search of a subject. He arrested a man for DUI, transported him to Traffic Division for a Breathalyzer examination, waited for his testing to be done in the police facility, and then transported him to the County Jail. At the County Jail the corrections officers seized a gun the subject had been carrying since his arrest.

  I had already informed union president Mickey Hughes that I could not accept anything less than a one-day suspension for any officer failing to search a subject to remove a firearm before transporting the subject. Keene had jeopardized his own life, the lives of all officers in Traffic Division, and the lives of the corrections officers. Policy required officers to thoroughly search a prisoner prior to transporting even if the prisoner had been searched by other officers.

Some officers have been killed by a prisoner being transported in the back of a police car. Policing is dangerous enough without being careless and inattentive.

Keene harbored such bitterness that in 2003, five years after he was suspended, he wrote a letter to the editor of a newspaper in which he said that before the hundred officers in our bureau were furloughed due to a budget crisis, my wife should be the one to quit the force. Apparently, his bitterness festered for so long that it emerged in the form of disparaging comments about my wife. He may have been proud of himself for having his article printed, but I think he offered himself up to the community as one of the officers in the dark-blue category. Jason Keene is still a police officer and serves as an elected official of a local lodge of the police union.

- Sergeant Gregory Thomas was involved in a violent domestic assault incident in which he broke his wife's nose. He fled the scene and was arrested for driving under the influence. The union immediately asked my intentions regarding discipline. I informed them it appeared to be a termination offense but that if Thomas accepted several other disciplinary measures including a suspension and a reduction in rank to officer, I could foresee accepting an agreement. He was suspended and demoted to officer. He did perform well as an officer and years later was put into a detective position by the zone commander and eventually transferred to the Detective Division as a Robbery detective.

About a year after I left the bureau, Jake Matthews was chosen as chief of police. Jake and Gregory had been friends and worked Traffic Division as motorcycle officers. When Jake became the chief, he requested the city change its current policy that only sergeants and lieutenants could be considered for promotion to commander.

Once Jake Matthews had the rules changed, he promoted Gregory Thomas to the rank of commander. Thomas was promoted with three others. According to news reports, of the four, three had histories or were under investigation for domestic violence. Those promotions caused a considerable number of negative news reports, outrage from groups concerned with domestic violence, and City Council's intervention to prevent future similar promotions.

Years later, Matthews would promote Thomas to assistant chief of police. Politics *runs* everything. Bad politics *ruins* everything.

UNDERSTANDING DISCIPLINE

All the above disciplinary cases are offered to make a point. First, strong leaders use discipline when needed. Although the Pittsburgh Bureau of Police had not been accustomed to imposing serious disciplinary measures for many years, a review of some of the listed cases provides evidence that discipline is one of the tools needed to steer the bureau in the right direction.

It also sheds light on how discipline affected future incidents of misconduct and the serious nature of the misconduct. One way to reduce the amount of times discipline is imposed and to lower the level of disciplinary measures employed would be for supervisors to understand the types of officers under their commands. All officers are not "good guys" and they definitely are not all equal. Once supervisors realize the types of officers they have, they can provide the proper type of supervision.

What became apparent throughout the bureau was that most officers were never disciplined. In fact, those officers regularly received bureau awards. Some officers had minor violations and never faced discipline again. Other officers had more serious violations but never faced discipline again. Unfortunately, some officers became "frequent fliers" and were disciplined regularly. Inevitably, some officers were disciplined so many times that progressive disciplinary measures led to their termination, or the seriousness of the misconduct was so severe it warranted termination.

I was left to wonder why some officers were terminated and returned by arbitrators to never again be involved in misconduct while other officers were returned only to find their way back to my office for another disciplinary action that resulted in termination. Due to arbitration decisions, some officers were fired three times before termination was final. Many officers in the dark-blue group and all officers in the midnight-blue group would definitely be back. They either couldn't help themselves and/or they received no effective supervisory oversight.

The number of disciplinary cases and the results of those cases clarified several principles for me. The first was that the need for discipline can be reduced if a department ensures: (1) proper selection of recruits, (2) policies that conformed to best practices, (3) suitable training, (4) close and effective supervision, (5) meaningful disciplinary action for incidents of misconduct, (6) timely early intervention, (7) responsible internal investigations, and (8) Integrity testing.

Another principle was understanding how officers fell into groupings that explained why some officers were never disciplined while others were regularly disciplined and even terminated. If a supervisor understands the nature of each group of their subordinate officers, the proper supervision can be applied to help an officer to obtain assistance when necessary and to avoid further misconduct. Early intervention may result in lowering the number and level of disciplinary incidents, saving a career, and possibly saving an officer's life.

Statistics show that more officers will commit suicide than will be killed in the line of duty. Some of the pressure officers face may be the result of their experiences at work. While most supervisors claim the health and welfare of their subordinates is a prime responsibility, those supervisors who fail to address misconduct tend to help their subordinates down the path to poor work, failed careers, and more serious personal problems. Understanding the groups of officers and where each of the supervisors' subordinates fit in should help supervisors know how to lead their officers to success.

REASSIGNMENTS: WORKHORSES
AND SHOW HORSES

When I worked as a watch commander, I reported to Assistant Chief David Faust. He was a gruff straight talker who opened my eyes to the inner workings of decision making in the police bureau. Since my wife and I were not politically connected, I had never expected to rise above the rank of lieutenant, which was a competitive civil service position. We were both promoted to lieutenant and later to commander even though we avoided those connected to politicians. I will never forget how he explained some promotions and assignments.

Chief Faust said some people use political connections to obtain a desirable position or a detective position, or to be promoted to the commander's rank. Many commanders were promoted from an officer or detective position to commander. They had never supervised anyone since they had never served as a sergeant or lieutenant. Everyone knew their political connections when they took those positions. Faust referred to those people as the show horses because they were all show and little action. They did not know enough about policing to make sound decisions for the bureau.

Chief Faust explained that although those less competent people filled those positions, the bureau still needed people who could do the work that needed to be done within the bureau. He referred to those other officers, detectives, supervisors, and commanders as the workhorses. They were the ones working the hard jobs and were knowledgeable since they had "worked in the trenches." They seldom got the glory, but they were the ones who did the bulk of the work.

Once I was the chief, I intended to move unproductive show horses aside and replace them with the workhorses the bureau needed. I was convinced the bureau could do more work of a higher quality with fewer personnel if only the right people were in the right positions.

I knew from nearly two decades working with the bureau that there were some detectives who did little to no work but remained in their position for political reasons. They may have been related to someone or a neighbor of someone, worked on a political campaign, or used some other connection with an elected official or influential businessperson to obtain and maintain their positions. While they tied up those positions doing nothing, cases were either not solved or the bureau had to pad the department with more detectives to ensure the police work got done.

After reviewing the statistics of the four detectives and one sergeant assigned to the Auto Squad, it was apparent they had done little work. There were only eight arrests during the first ten months of 1997.

I knew I was going to have difficulty removing these detectives since one of them, Jerry Peters, used to brag that he did not have to do any work since he had political connections. Everyone seemed to know his connection was City Council President David Bailey. What I did not know was that another detective, Al Ferrara, was the nephew of State Representative Dominic Ferrara.

What I will most remember and respect Mayor Tom Murphy for was his reply when I told him I needed to transfer unproductive detectives who were politically connected. He said he put me in charge of the bureau to operate it the way it should be operated. He said he would deal with the political fallout when it occurred. As good as his word, Mayor Murphy fielded all the complaints from politicians and permitted me to make personnel decisions based on productivity rather than politics.

The minutes from our command staff meeting in November 1997 documented my discussion with all commanders and chiefs in which I told them about my plans to make changes in the Auto Squad. The detectives were transferred in February 1998. Detective Peters claimed he was a whistleblower in an effort to prevent his move from the detective branch.

Peters claimed he met with Council President Bailey to discuss the grant funds the unit had access to during December 1997 and January 1998. Those meetings were held, if they were held at all, months after I announced changes in the Auto Squad. The union provided funding for Peters to file a lawsuit claiming grant money had not been spent and that Peters was transferred because of his supposed whistleblowing.

During the trial, Peters testified he never used politics to obtain or maintain a detective position. Prior Public Safety Director Anthony Rivera testified during the trial that Peters had been transferred out of the detective branch prior to Mayor Murphy taking office. Rivera testified he subsequently received a phone call from the mayor's office, while he was the Public Safety director, directing him to return Peters to his position as a detective.

That trial provided evidence that Peters had been returned previously to a detective position due to political connections even though he hadn't performed at acceptable levels. It also proved I had notified the command staff of their pending transfers before he approached Councilman Bailey, and that there was no misappropriation of grant funds. When the media questioned Peters following his loss in court, he made an inane comment about the flag still flying over the federal courthouse. He knew his unproductive work record had caught up to him, but he was not concerned since he wasn't out anything, the union having paid thousands of dollars for his lawsuit.

After the lumps were replaced, the newly assigned Auto Squad detectives made over eighty arrests the next year. The officers assigned to the Auto Squad were each chosen due to their excellent work performance as sky-blue officers and proved their work ethic. Under Mayor Murphy, the crime rate continued to drop in Pittsburgh and clearance rates for solved cases remained high even though the number of officers was reduced from nearly 1,200 officers to fewer than 900 officers. This was primarily due to removing politically connected lumps from important positions and replacing them with workhorses.

THE THIRD "C"–COMMUNITY

Even efforts to strengthen bonds with the community come with the potential for some officers to use those relationships for their own advantage. When I was sworn in as the chief, part of my presentation discussed the creation of a citizen/police academy so city residents could receive training on police operations. The citizen police academy is designed so that city residents can learn and understand police procedures to enable them to work with officers to help keep their neighborhoods safe. Many departments had citizen academies to enhance community relations.

After the announcement, Detective Olivia Caldwell approached me explaining she already had an interest in, and had done some work toward, the creation of a citizen/police academy. She requested that she be involved in getting the academy started. I accepted her offer.

Although she was assigned to the Robbery Squad in the Investigations Branch, she was detailed to the Training Academy in the Administration Branch. It seemed as though the academy had started well and had already had two or three successful classes in its first few years.

Olivia Caldwell did a good job of ingratiating herself with many active community members. It appeared no one was questioning her activities for the first few years. That changed once the bureau began conducting annual performance evaluations.

I was eventually advised none of the supervisors at the academy wanted to do her performance evaluation since they said they never had the opportunity to observe her work. Her supervisors said she was at the Investigations Branch when she wasn't at the academy. We then learned that no supervisor in the Investigations Branch would complete her performance evaluation since she wasn't there long enough for anyone to observe her work. Each duty location believed she was spending most of her time at the other duty location.

It became clear she needed to make a choice about her duty location so everyone would know where she was assigned and who would be responsible for her supervision and evaluations. I notified her of her choice. She immediately went to City Council and to the newspapers and television stations to pressure me to allow her to have her way.

A *Pittsburgh Tribune-Review* article titled "Transfer perplexes police detective, City Council" reported that City Council had stepped in and asked me to explain my rationale. Council was advised she was being paid as a detective and none of the other officers at the academy were paid the higher detective rate. Caldwell was quoted as saying, "I should be paid more money because across the country you can be a commander and do this job."

Caldwell claimed she faced a no-win situation and was quoted as saying, "That's like standing there and putting a gun to my head and saying there's a burning inferno in that room. You can go in there or the other room where there's a guillotine."

It was obvious that Caldwell had a penchant for melodrama. Either job, as a robbery detective or as an academy instructor, was one that many officers could only wish they would have the opportunity to work. She used her connections with council and the media to create a firestorm.

When Caldwell left the bureau, she took a job as the chief of police in a nearby suburb, Braxton. She often called me for advice.

An article titled "…police union criticizes chief in wake of officer's discipline" appeared in the *Pittsburgh Post*-Gazette, reporting that "…an unsigned letter was delivered on behalf of some officers to council that was highly critical of Police Chief Olivia Caldwell." It also said, "The three-page letter alleged unprofessional conduct, poor treatment of officers and a hostile work environment filled with 'fear and uncertainty.'"

Charlie Walsh, the secretary/treasurer and principal officer of the Teamsters Local, said, "We're prepared to go to war with Braxton…" He also said, "I think we have a bad chief who does not look after her people, who does not do a good job running her department…", and "It's a huge mess. I think it's only going to get worse." The article stated, "Mr. Walsh, a former police officer in Bedford Hills, described a toxic environment at the Braxton Department with some officers worrying about not getting backup, fearing retaliation and being concerned over falling out of favor with the chief."

Those officers who eventually accepted a position as a chief of police were able to see the difficulties of leadership during difficult times. It's certainly a different perspective.

THE FOURTH "C"—COSTS

Pittsburgh had been struggling financially for decades. It seemed pretty evident to anyone paying attention. Pittsburgh officers were not making as much as other similarly sized cities and were making much less than many of the suburban departments surrounding the city. Many officers left the Pittsburgh Police during my career to take jobs with federal agencies, the Pennsylvania State Police, suburban departments, and private businesses.

I understood the necessity to operate within our budget and was determined we would do so every year. I knew it would be difficult since some expenses were beyond our control, such as mandated overtime for those officers subpoenaed to be in various courtrooms, homicide and narcotics investigations, and emergency operations. From the excesses I found in the chief's office alone, I believed we had to cut any unnecessary overtime to remain within our budget. If there is anything that will raise the ire of many officers, it is when someone makes the decision to save the city money at the expense of officers' paychecks that are no longer bolstered by the overtime they hoped to make.

A major overtime expense was the annual regatta, which was expanding from one to two weekends during the summer. The city was going to have to double the overtime for officers for security during the scheduled events. The bureau had previously provided hundreds of officers over the weekend for the regatta at no cost to those operating the regatta. Doing so for two weekends was going to strain the overtime budget. The collective bargaining agreement required that officers working on their days off had to be paid double their regular wage for a minimum of eight hours.

Instead of paying officers double-time pay to work both weekends, I opted to adjust their schedules so they could work the regatta during their regular tour of duty instead of overtime. Some officers still made overtime pay when they worked extra hours, but many of the officers made regular pay and none of the officers worked for double-time pay. The amount saved over the weekends was estimated at about $180,000. I believed this would be regarded as a responsible decision by city taxpayers, but it drew the ire of many officers and union officials since officers would not have a considerable amount of overtime in their pay.

It surprised me that the officers were so outraged because they were due to have many extra days off to work the regatta. The collective bargaining agreement with the union required officers to receive overtime pay if they had a schedule change without having two days off. In order to have the number of officers needed to ensure safety at the regatta at the lowest cost, approximately one hundred officers assigned to community policing had their schedules changed so that they only worked twenty-four hours of work for two weeks while still being paid for forty hours of work. This had been done by previous administrations but not one that oversaw so many officers.

Unfortunately, the schedule change meant that officers would not be working on the National Night Out that is held on the first

Tuesday in August. The regatta had been the last weekend in July and the first weekend in August. If officers were to work the regatta on Sunday, they had to have the following two days off during the first week of August.

For the National Night Out, community groups gathered outside while others had block parties to build community spirit. Officers generally attended the block parties. We planned to have district officers attend the block parties. The officers assigned to the regatta wanted to be paid double-time pay for eight hours to attend the block parties which generally last two or three hours. This made poor financial sense so it could not be accomplished. Many officers told the organizers of the block parties they could not attend. However, my position was they were welcome to attend any function off duty, but the city could not afford to pay them two days of pay to attend a block party.

★★★★

Another large waste of taxpayer money spent on overtime was in Traffic Division. When I was assigned to Traffic Division as a commander, I had originally stopped Lieutenant Sam Stanton from working unauthorized overtime whenever he wanted to do so. However, when I was moved out of Traffic Division when Chief Amos took the helm of the bureau, Stanton was permitted to work a considerable amount of overtime since he oversaw two sections of Traffic Division that were critical to the unit. For some reason, he was considered the only person knowledgeable enough to work the positions associated with these sections.

One of those positions placed him in charge of special events. Special events included all parades, races on the street, and city-held festivities. There were more than three hundred events each year. He had the documents for all prior special events held throughout the city on his computer where he could make minor adjustments to upcoming annual events. He was able to self-determine how much overtime was needed for him to complete the orders for the events. He could also schedule himself to work overtime during the event.

He was also in charge of the accident reconstruction unit. Again, for some reason, he was one of the limited personnel possessing the training needed for the highest level of accident reconstruction. He ensured he was needed, many times on overtime, to do the reconstruction of vehicle collisions. Efforts to reduce overtime to only-when-necessary didn't sit well with some officers.

When the nephew of State Representative Tony Russo was involved in a fatal collision that appeared to be due to his reckless driving, Lieutenant Stanton was supposed to complete the investigation. A considerable amount of time elapsed and he still had not completed the investigation. He claimed he was too busy, and overtime was not authorized for his special events duties so he decided to perform the special events duties during his regular workday instead of the vehicle reconstruction duties. The delays went on long enough that the family of the deceased and many in the public were claiming there was a coverup due to the reckless driver's uncle being a state representative.

I moved the special events responsibilities to the Administrative Branch and those duties would be assigned to an officer reporting to my wife. Cathy had worked with Stanton when they were both officers. She said Stanton claimed if the special events were transferred from under his control he would know how to "Format C," meaning he would erase all the special events files.

He did just that. She opted not to discipline him but made sure this would not happen again by requiring the new officer assigned to those duties to save all new special events orders in the city computer system rather than on a personal computer system. I saw Lieutenant Stanton later and asked him how he was doing. He said he had a lot of idle time since he did not have special events duties any longer. If he had not played the system so long, he would have made some overtime without it being excessive.

OFFICER'S EXTRA-DUTY PAY

One of my decisions provided 50 percent more overtime for officers working extra-duty employment without any extra cost to city taxpayers. The extra-duty pay was referred to as off-duty employment or secondary employment. The off-duty job involved officers working in plainclothes or in uniform providing police services to businesses who opted to have police officers present instead of security guards.

For example, many bars on the South Side of Pittsburgh opted to hire officers off duty to prevent disturbances. Generally, when customers saw officers instead of security guards, the number of fights and other disturbances was reduced. Having officers on site benefitted the business and the community but also benefitted the bureau because: (1) officers provided a deterrent, (2) officers are required to respond to a 911 call at the location if off-duty officers are not there, and (3) there were more officers working off-duty details on the South Side than there were on-duty officers working.

Officers throughout my career had worked off-duty overtime that had been managed by one of many officers or supervisors, including a sergeant working in the office of the assistant chief of operations. The officers managing those off-duty details ensured that officers were paid at their base rate of pay while the managing officers collected another 10 percent fee from the employing company. This seemed to work fairly well for the officers and exceptionally well for the officers working as schedulers since they received 10 percent pay for each dollar paid to the officers working the detail.

The city was on the losing end of this deal. The city lost money in several ways including: (1) the officers used city equipment including vehicles, gasoline, radios, and uniforms; (2) when people filed complaints against officers working details, they had to be investigated by on-duty personnel; (3) when officers were sued for off-duty work, the city had to pay attorneys to defend the officer and city; (4) any lawsuits or claims settled or awarded to plaintiffs were paid by the city; (5) when officers were injured working details, the city paid compensation; 6) officers who became disabled due to injuries and were retired were paid a disability pension; and 7) the employers had officers working for them but paid nothing toward their training or supervision while the city was still required to supervise the officers.

Changes were necessary regarding how off-duty work was scheduled, performed, and reimbursed. What brought this to the forefront was the reconstruction of the Fort Pitt Bridge which typically handled an enormous amount of traffic into, out from, and through the city. When the contract was being negotiated to have off-duty officers work traffic corners throughout the Downtown for many months that turned into two years, it was determined the contractors would need approximately one hundred officers per day working at least four-hour shifts primarily during the morning and afternoon rush hours.

I doubted we could have a hundred volunteers daily but knew we had to find a way to provide them so that traffic and business in the city would not come to a grinding halt. I informed the contractors they would have to provide an overtime rate of time and one-half so we could continue to provide the needed officers even if we had to mandate officers working overtime. And I informed them the city would add a 10 percent fee for managing the scheduling and for recouping other expenses the city incurred.

The contractors understood and did not balk at paying that rate. While we established how that detail would work, I informed the union that we were going to incorporate other details throughout the city and insisted that the officers working any details anywhere in the city should be receiving the overtime rate of time and one-half their base rate of pay. Union President Mickey Hughes complained publicly and to Councilman Unger that many of the businesses, like the bars on the South Side, would not hire off-duty officers because they could not afford to pay officers an overtime rate of pay.

I was incredulous that the union would suggest officers receive a lower rate of pay if they worked more than forty hours a week at a business while the union would have been outraged if the city attempted to only pay officers their base rate of pay for anything over forty hours. Some of the officers representing the union at one of the meetings agreed with me that all officers should receive the overtime rate for all off-duty details. That is eventually what occurred. I was successful in getting all off-duty officers a 50 percent pay raise for the hours they worked those details. Since details paid a minimum of four hours of pay, each detail they worked went from a minimum of $100 pay to $150 pay.

I would have thought I would be thanked. I'm certain many officers appreciated a 50% raise for their off-duty details. Some officers complained that the city was making 22 ½ percent on top of their overtime rate of pay and believed they, too, should be making the extra 22 ½ percent.

THE FIFTH "C"–CRIME RATES

The crime rate in Pittsburgh was in near freefall for many years. The union struggled to find any issue that would enable them to register a complaint due to their displeasure at having to defend multiple officers during disciplinary hearings and the city agreeing to a consent decree with the U. S. Department of Justice. Going from 1996 crime rates to 1997 crime rates, the union complained that even when we were one of the top ten safest cities in the nation (when comparing crime rates to population), they noted that Pittsburgh had slipped one place, going from sixth to seventh place.

The crime rate had been regularly falling each year from 1989. There are many reasons why crime rates fluctuate. Many people view crime rates as the responsibility of the police. Actually, the police play only one role in relation to the rise or fall of crime rates. There were other factors affecting the crime rates and I always made a point of discussing those to prevent the public from thinking it was the sole responsibility of the police to control crime rates. Taking credit for reducing crime rates means one must take responsibility for increasing crime rates.

In Pittsburgh, we were being faced with a declining population. However, the decrease in number of residents did not necessarily equate to a reduced number of calls for service or to a reduction in crime since many of those residents moving out were moving to the suburbs. Our calls for service continued steady from year to year.

Police officers do of course play a significant role in the reduction in crime. Even though the number of officers in the bureau fell from 1,200 to 900 in ten years, investigations continued to arrest those responsible for crimes, to get drugs and guns off the street, and to arrest gang members by the dozens, disrupting their efforts to instill fear in their communities.

Good police work was able to be accomplished despite fewer officers because supervisors identified the officers who performed well, practiced early intervention when they thought it was necessary, replaced show horses with workhorses, and either disciplined or terminated disruptive officers, weeding out the dark-blue and midnight-blue groups of officers and replacing them with officers who wanted to do real police work. Additionally, all officers were given clearer direction and understanding of policy, received better training, were more closely supervised, and were recognized regularly in awards ceremonies for their excellent service.

Another important reason for the reduction in crime was the urban redevelopment that resulted from Mayor Murphy's initiatives. As the number of large public housing complexes was reduced and vouchers for housing were issued, the locations where many violent crimes had occurred now experienced less crime. It is true that many just relocated to other sections of the city, which affected their crime rate. However, many of the residents of the housing developments moved beyond the city limits. With all the changes, overall crime trends continued to drop for seven years before I became the chief, and for two decades afterwards.

While Mayor Murphy credited the police with reductions in the crime rates in Pittsburgh, the policies enacted by the mayor to rebuild the city had considerable impact on crime rates. Mayor Murphy was a true leader who, instead of taking the credit himself, gave the credit to those reporting to him but also took responsibility for the decisions that did not achieve good results.

Anyone who tries to lead any organization through difficult times will be faced with some projects that do not work out and some that do. The successes of Mayor Murphy far outnumbered the projects that did not work as well. His critics would gloss over the vast number of successes, which were so impressive, just to try to sell themselves as better candidates for the mayor's office.

CONCLUSION

The Pittsburgh Bureau of Police had significant problems between 1992 and 1995. The problems included intense community dissatisfaction, dramatic increases in the number of citizens' complaints, substandard recruitment of officers, insufficient training, an inadequate number of supervisors, a dearth of meaningful discipline, huge increases in the number and severity of police vehicle crashes leading to an increase in the number and severity of officer injuries as well as a shortage of operable police vehicles, a waste of resources due to unnecessary overtime payments, and officer complaints of internal corruption going unchecked.

There was no way of tracking such variables as how many times officers were using force and the levels of force being used or how many searches and seizures were being conducted and by which officers. Police managers didn't know which officers were having collisions and why no actions were taken to reduce the number and severity of collisions (except on the commander level), and which officers were receiving the largest number of citizens' complaints along with the nature of the complaints and how they were resolved.

What could go wrong? Who wouldn't want to lead this bureau? The fallout from leading this bureau would be wonderful for one's career, right?

I knew taking the helm and setting a new course for the bureau was going to be a rough ride. It was time to batten down the hatches. Studies show that it takes at least five years to change the culture of an organization. A department does not develop problems overnight and will not work through them overnight either.

Jim Collins's book *From Good to Great* describes a level-five leader's need to apply a constant, unyielding pressure on a flywheel to start it moving and to keep it headed in the right direction. Backing off or buckling under pressure is sure to disrupt the constant effort at progress in changing any agency.

Mayor Murphy discussed some of the reasons he chose me to serve as his chief of police, including my commitment to computerization and training, and my determination to run a bureau that was effective and well disciplined. I was considered a disciplinarian by the small number of officers I disciplined or arrested as a lieutenant or as a commander.

As chief, I did not initiate disciplinary reports. Generally, sergeants and lieutenants initiated the reports for misconduct they observed and forwarded the discipline through the chain of command. The chief is responsible for only the decision at the first disciplinary hearing. I chose to support my sergeants and lieutenants in the field. They, in turn, helped change the course of the bureau.

Many officers and supervisors may not have voiced it publicly, but they were glad to see unethical officers weeded out of the bureau and other officers held accountable for their actions. I received many notes and e-mails from officers and supervisors expressing their appreciation at the improved working environment.

Of one principle I was certain: I was not going to avoid my responsibility as a change agent for a bureau in dire need of change. If I had to be known as a disciplinarian, then I would accept that label. It certainly would have been easier for me if the officers and supervisors had followed policy, treated people respectfully, and avoided criminal activities. The citizens of the City of Pittsburgh and Mayor Tom Murphy deserved an efficient and respectful police force known for its quality of service and I was going to ensure I delivered.

LESSONS LEARNED

1) A professional organization like the Police Executive Research Forum, the International Association of Chiefs of Police, or state level chiefs of police associations should be used to conduct searches for new chiefs of police. Internal candidates should apply for a chief's position.

2) Every learning organization should carefully review every critical incident to determine how to avoid a similar situation in the future.

3) Officers should not receive awards for an incident if they violated any policies that endangered themselves or others.

4) Attempting to improve morale by providing officers with more equipment has limited effect. For some officers, the equipment either doesn't come fast enough or it isn't the equipment they expect.

5) Attempting to improve morale by providing a 50 percent increase in pay for off-duty work will not satisfy some officers. Increasing pay doesn't necessarily improve morale.

6) No officer/supervisor should be irreplaceable to the point they can control any section of the department and dictate the amount of overtime they will work to produce their product.

7) Limiting an officer's overtime will often result in rumors of officer complaints about loss of motivation.

8) Taking disciplinary action can result in officer complaints of loss of motivation.

9) Departments consist of show horses and workhorses.

10) I learned the hard way to always abide by the strict guidelines of the collective bargaining agreement .

11) Researching the pros and cons and using a test period for any new equipment introduced to the department can prevent future criticism.

12) Departments need to demonstrate transparency, especially regarding critical incidents. It does not take much effort to inform the public that an investigation is being conducted and the results will be relayed as soon as possible.

13) Officers need a method to report corruption while maintaining their anonymity. Once officers know it is safe for them to report corruption, they will use the system.

CHAPTER NINE

The Country's First "Pattern or Practice" Consent Decree

"A leader takes people where they want to go. A great leader takes people where they don't necessarily want to go but ought to be."

—ROSALYNN CARTER

O n March 3, 1991, I was working as a commander overseeing police operations on the night shift in Pittsburgh. I had less than ten months in that position and fourteen years with the Pittsburgh Police. I did not know it then but what was happening in Los Angeles that night would have a great impact on my career.

That night a camera recorded some Los Angeles Police Department officers beating Rodney King for approximately fifteen minutes. The recording provided evidence of police abuse, which enraged people throughout the country. Some officers were disciplined and four were criminally charged. Of those four officers, three were acquitted and the jury was unable to reach a verdict for the fourth officer in 1992. Riots erupted, leaving more than fifty dead, thousands injured, and thousands arrested. Rodney King received an award of $3.8 million. Two officers were later convicted of civil rights violations and sentenced to jail.

This incident would have a significant effect on law enforcement throughout the country. There were congressional hearings on police misconduct. President Clinton signed a crime bill in 1994 which included the Law Enforcement Misconduct Statute 42 U.S.C. §14141. The Department of Justice was authorized to investigate and sue departments engaged in a "pattern or practice" of depriving people of their constitutional rights.

THE TINDERBOX

Taking the helm of the Pittsburgh Bureau of Police in the mid-1990s was going to be a difficult undertaking due to the massive hiring from 1992 through 1995. Many of us in the police bureau knew that some officers should never have been hired. We were also aware that morale issues would be the biggest problem a new chief would address. But it was not the only obstacle that needed to be addressed.

Those who failed to understand the necessity for change in the bureau fell into one of three categories. They were either (1) inexperienced officers who didn't know much about policing, or (2) experienced officers who were naïve as to what a good law enforcement agency should be doing, or (3) they were less than forthright because they knew what changes needed to be made but denied that those changes were necessary. All these failures created a tinderbox.

THE SPARK

Many police officials understand the implications of a consent decree. When a department is sued, it is expensive and time consuming for the department and police officials, and the outcome can render an unfavorable decision that would have an impact on police operations. To avoid court proceedings, it is common for both parties to come to an agreement as to the changes the department will make and to formalize them in a written document referred to as a consent decree. Before 1994, police agencies dealt with consent decrees on single issues such as hiring and promotions. Pattern or practice consent decrees generally involved a wide variety of issues.

What led to a United States Department of Justice (DOJ) investigation and eventual consent decree was the widespread dissatisfaction of citizens with their police. Evidence of this dissatisfaction was collected in Pittsburgh when a judge authorized Attorney Timothy O'Brien's access to some police internal investigative files. The information from those files provided the material to file a suit against the city. During the last days of March 1996, a lawsuit was filed by the American Civil Liberties Union on behalf of the NAACP, Parents Against Violence, and sixty-six individuals. ACLU Executive Director, Attorney Witold Walczak, notified the Department of Justice of a "pattern or practice" of violations of citizens' civil rights.

The March 27, 1996, *Pittsburgh Post-Gazette*'s headline "Rights suit targeting city police" reported that the lead attorney in the suit, Timothy P. O'Brien, described the Pittsburgh Police as having "...engaged in misconduct for so long, without fear of any meaningful discipline, that those officers who choose to violate citizen's rights know that they can do so with impunity."

The same article quoted ACLU Executive Director Walczak as saying the city's personnel policy "...contains neither a stick to deter officers from violating people's constitutional rights nor a carrot to induce respect for citizens' rights." He added that the relationship between police and the public, especially African Americans, "will only continue to deteriorate."

The Justice Department initiated a "pattern or practice" investigation following this lawsuit. The Civil Rights Division of the Justice Department had been authorized to investigate "pattern or practice" cases since 1994. The information contained in this lawsuit was exactly what the DOJ had been authorized to initiate an investigation.

CHANGING WINDS

The week following the ACLU lawsuit, Mayor Tom Murphy announced that I would be the next Pittsburgh Police chief. I initially announced to the police bureau and the media that some changes would be occurring over the next five years. Once in office, I realized the extent of the changes needed and how complicated each change was going to be. When union President Mickey Hughes told me that he did not want to see any changes for the next two years, I knew each change would become an ordeal with the union.

Mickey's overarching desire to avoid criticism from the union membership explained his hesitancy to make decisions. He opted to take every decision back to the membership for a vote. This meant months would pass before he could make any decision and the union's decision might mean that they had decided not to make a decision.

I found it exhausting to cope with someone who seemed to fear making a decision. As Theodore Roosevelt said, "In any moment of decision, the best thing you can do is the right thing, the next best thing is the wrong thing, and the worst thing you can do is nothing." Knowing the disconnect our bureau had with many segments of our community, some of the dysfunctions within our bureau, the pending DOJ investigation, and the short term in office experienced by most chiefs, I did not have time to procrastinate.

DOJ attorneys appeared to swarm the city. They met with members of the public, the Pittsburgh Law Department, the Police Bureau, the Office of Municipal Investigations, and others. I was a new chief when I met with the DOJ attorneys. My only reservation was that these knowledgeable and committed attorneys were young and lacked practical police experience. I believe they were feeling their way through all their interactions just as we were in our response. Their approach seemed aggressive and threatening at first. Without their initial inclusion of police experts on their team of investigators, there would have been a gap in understanding between the highly educated civil rights attorneys and those with an appreciation of the dangers from having policed in the streets.

At the same time, I recognized that their goals for the police bureau were not much different from mine. I provided them the list of the changes I planned for the bureau that were drawn from the list I used during my selection interview with Mayor Murphy and the Police Executive Research Forum. I advised them the list was my roadmap for bureau change.

As difficult as it was going to be, I was going to have to make sound decisions with my command staff and members of the Law Department since the union leadership demonstrated reluctance to participate. Their failure to participate would result in their exclusion during most decision-making. I realized this was easier for Mickey since instead of being criticized for his involvement in any change in policy or practice, he could easily criticize the change and use his displeasure to rally some of his membership.

I was determined that the needed changes would bring the Pittsburgh Police up to law enforcement's standards of "best practices." Best practices in policing have been determined by police for achieving public safety while maintaining citizens' civil rights and reducing potential liability. Police practices have evolved over time, due to studies, to determine the best method to perform any task.

An example of a common practice as opposed to a "best practice" is when police departments show photographic lineups to a citizen in an effort to have them identify a suspect. Some departments will have officers obtain a photograph of the suspect, locate several more similar photographs, and present them to the witness for identification.

A best practice would have the detective locate a photograph of the subject and include it with at least five other photographs of subjects with similar identifying features such as shape of face, facial hair, or distinguishing characteristics such as tattoos, scars, and birthmarks. The detective would then give the lineup to another officer who was not involved in the investigation and who would present it to the witness in order to rule out any intentional or unintentional influence in the witness's identification. In addition, the detective showing the lineup would advise the witness that the subject may or may not be in the lineup to prevent the witness from thinking s/he had to make a choice that could lead to a false identification. All identifications are maintained in a case file along with all photographs. The police report and case file should also include any statements made by the witness and a list of those present during the procedure. There are additional steps used for best practices in photographic lineup identifications, but those steps are efforts to prevent influencing the witness or obtaining false identifications that could send the wrong person to jail and allow the guilty to evade identification and apprehension.

In order to ensure best practices were achieved throughout the bureau, I reorganized the bureau and moved command personnel to make full use of their talents. Mulligan was the first person in the command staff I met with since he had always outranked me until my promotion to chief. There were four assistant chief positions available. I conferred with Mayor Murphy and explained my need to create a command structure similar to the military where there was a commanding officer and an executive officer who was the second in command. I offered Mulligan the deputy chief position as second in command, and he and I then considered who would fill the three assistant chief positions.

I recognized the dire need for changes to policy and knew that my wife, Commander Catherine McNeilly, to be the person in the bureau who had categorized all policies and orders issued by prior chiefs. She was unmatched in her ability to use computers and was extremely well-organized in both her professional life and in her personal life, a trait that would protect us later as explained in chapter 11. I needed her in the newly created Administrative Branch to oversee policy development, creation of all the forms the bureau needed, and a computerized system to track officer performance. Many of these areas had been neglected since the bureau only had two branches—Investigations and Operations.

The new forms would include use of force, searches/seizures, performance evaluations, police vehicle collisions, traffic stops, field contact search and seizure, awards, counseling, disciplinary reports, secondary employment, travel/training requests, all field training forms, policy review, annual transfers, and dozens of others.

Cathy would also be responsible for the development of new processes including a vehicle collision review board, a critical incident review board, COMSTAT (monthly meetings to address crime throughout the city via review of computerized crime statistics), and COMSTAR (quarterly command staff meetings to discuss the personnel data provided by the computerized officer-performance system).

The computerized system to track officers' performance was to be the method to track and address the increasing number of their complaints, uses of force, searches/seizures, vehicle collisions, lawsuits, missed court appearances, criminal investigations into officer conduct, and sick leave. Cathy was to name that system PARS for Performance Assessment and Review System.

Another command staff move was transferring Commander Faith Jones, who had a master's degree in education, to take command of the Training Academy. The development of new policies required a robust system to deliver the training that would follow. Other training would expand to include better recruit training, in-service training, field training, supervisor training, and management training.

The bureau's failure to investigate internal corruption would be addressed with the creation of the Integrity Unit. Those officers were chosen and assigned right after my swearing-in. Other measures introduced to the bureau included: command staff ride-alongs with officers four hours per month, a monthly officer ride-along with the chief, suggestion boxes in stations, a citizen's police academy, more officers attending community meetings, increased hiring standards requiring sixty college credits, introduction of additional equipment (such as pepper spray, collapsible batons, and Tasers), and introduction of computers.

A *Pittsburgh Post-Gazette* article by Michael Fuoco (11/20/96) discussed the disciplinary changes already underway in the bureau. He pointed out that during my first seven months nine officers were terminated, which was more than the number terminated during the prior decade.

ADDING HEAT

The foundation for my change was the early warning system. As a commander, I regularly read of other departments' initiatives to learn the best practices being employed in law enforcement agencies throughout the county. I understood that some police departments developed an early warning system to identify troubled officers. Some were simple systems that tracked only citizens' complaints and attempted to prevent additional complaints by counseling an officer who had reached a specific threshold. Some systems were more complex. One that included officers' credit ratings was eventually abandoned due to complaints it contained officers' personal information.

I realized the great benefit of an early warning system. The bureau needed to track officer performance to know which officers were (1) using force more often than others, (2) conducting more searches, (3) subject to criminal investigations, (4) making more arrests, (5) conducting more traffic stops, (6) having more traffic collisions, (7) facing lawsuits, (8) missing court, (9) receiving more complaints, 10) firing a weapon, (12) being counseled by supervisors, (13) being disciplined, and (14) using excessive sick leave.

Tracking officer performance would be essential to understanding which officers were involved in many of these activities to ensure that not only each one of these was proper but to identify trends among certain officers.

Some performance issues were necessary or expected at times including uses of force, firing a weapon, complaints, lawsuits, counseling, and sick leave. However, excessive activity in these same areas could be problematic.

Other performance factors were always troubling, including traffic collisions, being investigated for a criminal offense, missing court, and being disciplined. Operating a responsible law enforcement agency should require all available officer data to be immediately accessible to police supervisors and to allow those supervisors to take the appropriate action when trends were identified.

Tracking the statistics of officers' activities serves more purpose than ensuring bureau accountability. It identifies the best-performing officers and assists them with obtaining assignments and promotions when they may have been overlooked in the past. The information also can identify officers experiencing problems and possibly provide them the assistance they need to save their careers and their lives. One might ask how that would be possible.

While I served as commander in Zone 2, Detective Johnny Walker approached me. He led the Signal 13, which was the Pittsburgh Police version of Alcoholics Anonymous. Although I knew some officers struggled with substance abuse, I did not know the extent of the problem. Detective Walker informed me that 25 percent of our bureau, including the 150 officers I led in Zone 2, had problems with alcohol. I expressed skepticism about the percentage since he was telling me that three hundred of our bureau's officers, including about thirty-five of my officers, were experiencing alcohol-related problems. He assured me his numbers were correct but that most officers having those problems were also good at concealing them.

I researched the subject and learned that some studies indicated as many as 25 percent of officers had substance abuse problems. That partly explained the disciplinary action including terminations that I was forced to take while the commander at Zone 2.

Other studies indicated many officers suffer from post-traumatic stress disorder due to the nature of their work. Many of those officers and their supervisors fail to recognize PTSD and would not know how to get help for themselves or their subordinates even if they did recognize it.

A Pew Research Center survey of officers published on March 9, 2017, found that nearly one in five officers (21 percent) were frequently angry and frustrated on the job. It also found those officers more likely to support more physical or aggressive policing. The anger, the frustration, the prospect of policing more physically and aggressively, and the excessive use of alcohol dramatically decrease the likelihood that an officer will have a successful career.

Substance abuse issues left unaddressed can lead to agency liability, and officer performance failures, terminations, and even suicides. Statistics provide evidence that more officers will commit suicide than be killed on duty. Some studies suggest it can be twice the number. I knew more Pittsburgh Police officers who committed suicide than those killed on duty. And terminations can be ten times the number of on-duty deaths.

This was true in the 1990s and remains true today. Indra Cidambi, M.D., writing for *Psychology Today* (3/30/2018), discussed the seriousness of the issue. She wrote that between 7 percent to 19 percent of officers have symptoms of PTSD as opposed to 3.5 percent of the population, and that the number of police suicides is 2.3 times more than homicides. She also wrote, "One out of four police officers on the street has an alcohol or drug abuse issue, and substance use disorders among police officers are estimated to range between 20% and 30% … as compared to under 10% in the general population."

There are enough studies reporting on the number of officers suffering from alcohol abuse and the underlying causes to consider it a serious matter, not only for the bureau but for the officers' coworkers, their families, and the officers themselves. All too often in my career I have heard supervisors and officers say that their main concern is for their officers, their partners, and themselves to arrive home safely at the end of the shift.

But, for the most part, they fail to identify the alcohol abuse in terms of what is going to hurt them the most, slowly eroding their family relationships, their finances, their health, their work performance, their careers, and potentially even their lives. I had to wonder where their coworkers, their partners, and their immediate supervisors were when officers were struggling right in front of them.

It doesn't take much thought for a supervisor to recognize that an officer has alcohol problems because the officer will be identified through any one or combination of: (1) being late for work often; (2) receiving a citizen complaint(s); (3) using more force than usual or necessary; (4) having a vehicle collision(s); (5) having an intentional or accidental weapons discharge(s); (6) being subject to a lawsuit(s); (7) being the subject of a criminal investigation; (8) having been disciplined; (9) demonstrating a decrease in productive police activity such as searches, traffic stops, and arrests; (10) missing court appearance(s); and (11) using excessive sick leave.

Although any of these behaviors may occur from time to time, there is little doubt that an officer abusing alcohol will provide the evidence through his/her behavior. Having an early warning system gives supervisors the opportunity to identify the officer in trouble and to reach out in an effort to provide assistance.

Some supervisors and officers claim that an early warning system is not necessary to notice such changed behavior. If that were true, I must wonder why so many officers continue to struggle with alcohol abuse, relationship problems, and financial problems, which have led to higher percentages of divorce and suicide.

First, even the best of supervisors would be hard-pressed to cite the number of complaints received about an officer without a computerized system to track those performance measures, such as the number of vehicle collisions or the frequency of sick days used. Second, poor supervisors either do not know how to address the addiction problems their officers are struggling with or they do not have the courage to intercede. Third, even if a good supervisor has an inkling that an officer is struggling, one has to wonder why that supervisor would make so little effort to get the officer the help that is needed.

The chief of police in Pittsburgh is the only person in the bureau authorized to order an officer to get drug and/or alcohol treatment, anger management counseling, or psychological help. For a decade, with a few exceptions, those referrals were rarely made except following a disciplinary hearing in front of the chief or a critical incident. An early warning system, used appropriately, forces the supervisor to evaluate and document the officer's performance and to provide a written explanation of the supervisor's actions taken in response.

Early warning systems in law enforcement were not well known in the 1990s. They are much more common today. I believed we were on the forefront of providing responsible supervision by using an early warning system. I predicted in 1996 that a time would come when any agency not having an early warning system would be deemed neglectful. Many chiefs I met while attending Major Cities Chiefs meetings in the 1990s were not as convinced as I was about the effectiveness of early warning systems. But within ten years many of these same chiefs were developing or already using an early warning system. According to a National Institute of Justice report in July 2001, "By

1999, 39 percent of all municipal and county law enforcement agencies that serve populations greater than 50,000 people either had an early warning system in place or were planning to implement one."

GROWING WINDS

After many months of investigation, the DOJ indicated their intent to file a lawsuit to force policing changes in Pittsburgh. Anyone who has ever sued someone or been sued by someone knows that the outcome of a trial depends upon many factors. Even when a party believes they are completely in the right, the outcome does not always vindicate them. With the Pittsburgh Police being deficient in many management areas such as failure to properly report and track use-of-force incidents, searches, and seizures or to complete performance evaluations, there was a strong likelihood a court would mandate changes. And the changes might not be as good as those we could have made ourselves.

The Law Department explained that we had three choices: to go to court, to enter into a consent decree with the Department of Justice, or to enter into a consent decree with the American Civil Liberties Union. Attorneys in the Law Department explained that going to court would entail our spending a considerable amount of money and it would be a long and difficult path to challenge the federal government with its resources, including the large number of attorneys at its disposal, and the prestige it might have with the court.

Going to court wasn't a viable option because I was well aware of the city's financial situation and believed that the money spent in court would be better spent providing our bureau with the equipment, policy development, training, and supervision to make needed reforms. I also believed that a consent decree with the ACLU might be difficult since they were involved in the lawsuit filed in March 1996. A consent decree with the DOJ struck me as the best option.

My wife, Commander McNeilly, and I viewed the first draft of a consent decree in February 1997 while attending a Major Cities Chiefs meeting. We were partially pleased and partially alarmed at some of what we read. I realized that 90 percent of what I read in the consent decree included everything on the list I had prepared for my interview for the chief's position and the same list I had provided to the DOJ during their investigation.

Members of the police command staff, the Law Department, and the Office of Municipal Investigations met on Saturday mornings to negotiate changes in what would end up as consent-decree mandated changes. There was a benefit to negotiations.

Those meetings continued to just before the consent decree was announced in April 1997. Pittsburgh would be the first of many agencies to enter into a consent decree with the Department of Justice. Each of the required changes were considered best practices in policing and were already being done in some police agencies throughout the country. These changes ensured that officers avoided being placed in unnecessarily dangerous situations and were not given overly complicated forms to complete. Officers saw only four changes affecting them.

The first was that they would have to document each traffic stop. I learned from an experienced officer to always document the traffic stop information in case we were injured or killed so other officers would have the information and could identify and apprehend those responsible.

The second was that officers would have to document each use of force. This documentation was a basic expectation in policing that our bureau had neglected.

The third was to document each search and seizure. This documentation was also a basic expectation in policing that our bureau had neglected.

The fourth was annual performance evaluations. As part of the Pennsylvania Training Commission courses that my wife and I offered while we served as commanders, we taught "Effectively

Managing Personnel" to all bureau supervisors. The course explained the need to conduct performance evaluations. I was later to teach a two-day seminar called "Managing Liability" as part of a Police Executive course offered by the University of Pennsylvania Justice and Safety Institute. That seminar also stressed the need to conduct performance evaluations.

It was obvious to anyone who read the decree that there were few changes for officers. The vast majority of changes were going to be shouldered by supervisors and command staff, and by the internal investigations conducted by the Office of Municipal Investigations (OMI). Even though these changes brought the bureau into an era of modern policing, certain union officials and the dark-blue group of officers would resist those changes.

The union president would oppose a consent decree since he failed to negotiate the changes I had sought in April 1996. The changes were now going to be mandated in April 1997. The dark-blue officers would oppose because that is what they do; it is their nature. They resist work, complain if they have to do any more work than they had to do in the past, and just because it would require any change. What would shock the union and the dark-blue group of officers was not only the extent of changes ordered but that they would all begin to happen at the same time.

THE COUNTRY'S FIRST "PATTERN OR PRACTICE" CONSENT DECREE

On February 27, 1997, after the ten-month inquiry by the Department of Justice, Mayor Tom Murphy announced an agreement with the DOJ to ensure that police reforms were completed without long and expensive litigation. The consent decree contained good police practices.

The first paragraph of the agreement stated that the DOJ had found a pattern or practice that violated citizens' constitutional rights. In the fourth paragraph, the city denied the allegations but agreed to the consent decree because it concurred with obtaining the best practices and procedures for police management. City Solicitor Jacqueline Morrow summed it up best when she said, "This is not a corrupt police force. It was a young police force with inconsistent management."

Although there were some officers who should never have been hired and despite all the deficiencies in the bureau, the vast majority of officers were good people who were trying hard to provide for the safety of residents, businesses, and visitors. If we had had better management in the preceding years, we would not have been in the position we found ourselves.

The union president said he supported portions of the consent decree including those requiring more training for officers and better counseling services. He said he was not in agreement with internal investigation procedures that he said would permit unsubstantiated allegations to be used against the officer in disciplinary hearings. I have no idea where he came to believe that, but it was not true. Officers never could be disciplined, and never were, for unsubstantiated allegations. That just does not make sense to believe it could. I believed his emotions clouded his logic in making that comment.

REQUIRED TRAINING

Some of the main changes in the consent decree involved training. There would be mandatory supervisor training for all supervisors and mandatory management training for all command staff members. All officers would receive training in cultural diversity, ethics, and communications skills.

Cultural diversity training would be important since hundreds of officers hired in the prior years did not have experience working in diverse neighborhoods. Cultural diversity training would help officers better understand those they served, making their jobs easier.

I believed ethics training provided the opportunity to save officers' careers. The officers being arrested for criminal violations might have been saved if they had received some training in ethics. I had already decided to include ethics as mandatory training for all officers prior to the DOJ investigation. I did so because I read that the United States Marine Corps was including ethics training in their recruit training. I remembered being in Parris Island two and a half decades earlier and learning combat tactics, which always resulted in death and destruction. I believed it was a good idea that ethics should be mandatory when preparing for war. And if it is good in those situations, it should be beneficial to officers to help keep them from making errors in judgment that could destroy their careers.

My wife, Commander Cathy McNeilly, introduced me to verbal Judo training. I had practiced some martial arts including Judo and recognized that what could be accomplished physically could also be accomplished verbally. Since more than half of all complaints filed at the Office of Municipal Investigations involved rudeness, training officers in how to more effectively communicate with the public they served would enhance our relations with the community while reducing the number of internal investigations for rudeness. This training would also reduce the number of complaints filed against officers that could otherwise hinder their performance and record.

It was obvious that the intent of each of the three required training courses was to help the officer's career, ensure effective policing, and reduce complaints.

REQUIRED REPORTS

The only additional reports required of officers were to address (1) traffic stops, (2) search and seizure, and (3) use of force.

Traffic stop reports. As I explained earlier, any good officer already tracked information on any traffic stop including the time and date of the stop, the license plate number, a description of the driver, and the reason for the stop. In fact, policy already dictated that officers were to notify Communications of each stop and submit this information.

This is simply good police work. Failure to document, track, and evaluate traffic stops prevents a department from being able to defend itself against claims of racial bias.

Search/seizure reports. When my wife was the commander in Zone 1, a man walked into the station demanding his jewelry be returned to him. She had no idea what he was talking about. She checked the evidence locker where all seized property/evidence should have been located. There was no jewelry belonging to this man. She viewed all the police reports from the day before and found no mention of the jewelry.

She eventually learned that on the previous night, an officer had stopped this man, searched him, and seized the jewelry he was carrying in a handkerchief in his pocket. The officer told the man he would check burglary and theft reports and return the jewelry if he found nothing. He did not document the seized jewelry in any police report, and he failed to place the jewelry in the evidence locker.

Instead, he put the jewelry in his uniform locker. Cathy retrieved it and returned the man's jewelry. Anyone would be outraged to have one's jewelry seized and then find it difficult to have it returned. Search and seizure reports are simply good police procedure. Failure to document, track, and evaluate searches and seizures meant that a department was unable to defend itself against claims of unlawful searches and seizures and theft of property.

Use-of-force reports. It was incredulous that any police agency would not properly document something as serious as a use of force. I am certain anyone subject to a use of force would expect a thorough accounting of the level of force used and why that level of force was used. Failure to document, track, and evaluate uses of force demonstrates neglect on the part of a department. By not having that information available, our department was unable to defend itself against claims of excessive uses of force.

Although initially there were complaints from officers and the union about having to complete use-of-force reports, the exact opposite happened after months and years passed. Officers found they had better documentation of their use of force and were better prepared to testify in court as to the resistance offered by the person who was arrested and the actions the officer had to take to overcome that resistance. They were better prepared to explain themselves. The reports also helped the officer's defense when they were accused of excessive force.

Although the union argued about the need for tracking use of force, the initial reports showed that officers in the bureau didn't use force as many times as they were authorized by law and that the level of force they did use was lower than they would have been authorized to use. The union used the findings from those reports during contract arbitration hearings to argue they exemplified the exceptional job Pittsburgh officers were doing. It was ironic to see the union take advantage of the results of something they fought so hard to prevent. There was always the possibility that had the bureau captured use-of-force data during a previous administration, that data may have provided evidence that officers had used force appropriately. Not tracking use of force was a mistake for many reasons.

The Police Executive Research Forum titled "Guiding Principles on Use of Force," from the *Critical Issues in Policing* series, published in March 2016, listed the thirty guiding principles as "best practices" in use of force for law enforcement agencies.

The guiding principles included: principle #10, that agencies should document all uses of force; principle #11, that agencies should publish reports on uses of force; principle #18, that agencies should train all officers in communication skills to de-escalate confrontations; and principle #25, that agencies should provide access to and training for less lethal options.

The Pittsburgh Police did not adhere to any of these principles prior to 1996; however, my initiatives in 1996 and the consent decree requirements of 1997 provided for these "best practices" twenty years prior to the PERF publication. In law enforcement, it is best to set the highest standards early rather than face lawsuits, consent decrees, or public dissatisfaction and demonstrations to force a law enforcement agency to make the changes they should have made.

EARLY WARNING SYSTEM–PARS

The consent decree required an early warning system (EWS) to include data in the following areas:

- citizens' complaints
- officer-involved shootings
- commendations
- discipline
- training
- reassignments
- transfers
- mandatory counseling
- appeals or grievances
- criminal investigations
- civil or administrative claims
- all arrests
- searches/seizures
- use of force
- traffic stops
- discretionary charges (including public intoxication, disorderly conduct, resisting arrest, and obstructing law) since these charges were thought to be filed following "contempt of cop" situations.

In addition, we incorporated information to include: (1) vehicle collisions, (2) missed court appearances, (3) promotions, (4) sick leave, (5) absences without authorization, and (6) suspensions.

In a *New York Times* article titled "It did not stick" (4/9/2017), writer Sheryl Gay Stolberg included the following quote regarding early warning systems:

> Bob McNeilly was like a test pilot in the Mercury flight program, said Chuck Wexler, the president of the Police Executive Research Forum, a group of law enforcement professionals. No one knew what an 'early warning system' was, how to build it or what to measure.

We weren't only going to do what was required, but we were going to include more information that supervisors and managers would need to track, assess, and take appropriate action to ensure exceptional officer performance and to make corrections in any area not achieving the high standards expected of our bureau.

The early warning system was expected to not only identify developing problems early to prevent misconduct that could damage or destroy careers and to avoid liability to the city and the bureau, but it was to aid supervisors to obtain the help their subordinates needed.

The union president was opposed to the EWS, claiming it was like Big Brother. I had anticipated that claim and purposely did not include any information that could be considered personally invasive. The system only tracked the activity of officers when they worked.

INTERNAL AFFAIRS INVESTIGATIONS

Some changes to Internal Affairs investigations were required. They all were reasonable. They included the following:

- All sustained OMI complaints could not be changed by anyone in the police bureau. (The DOJ found that some members of the bureau had changed findings from sustained to not sustained, unfounded, or exonerated without any justification.)

- All sustained complaints mandated some corrective action to include discipline, counseling, training, or transfer. (The DOJ found that some officers who had been found guilty of misconduct received no corrective action. That is unconscionable.)

- Anonymous complaints now required an official investigation. (This drew the ire of the union. Union President Mickey Hughes said the city's investigation of anonymous complaints was a violation of an officer's rights. That was absurd.)

After explaining the need for investigations into anonymous complaints, I asked our supervisors what they would do regarding an anonymous complaint I received while working as a lieutenant on a night shift. A woman, who did not want to identify herself, called the station to report an officer driving a police car while intoxicated. She said he was swerving from lane to lane down the highway.

Not one supervisor said s/he would ignore the complaint. Everyone said they would have investigated the complaint to determine whether or not the officer was sober. The supervisors recognized that not investigating would be equivalent to negligence. Investigations into anonymous complaints are proper, done in other departments, and considered a best practice. Just because a department investigates an anonymous complaint does not mean that there will be any negative action taken against the officer. Only sustained complaints affect the officer.

One of Union President Mickey Hughes's major complaints was that all internal investigations were recorded. Mickey claimed that recording officer statements violated their civil rights. When he appeared in the courtroom of Judge Robert Cindrich, who oversaw the consent decree, he stated he would never require an officer to give a tape-recorded statement. He said, "Police are people. They have bad hair days. Sometimes they call people names. I've done that myself."

His testimony seemed to indicate that an officer's rudeness was acceptable if that officer was having a "bad hair day." He did not provide a good role model to his membership by saying this and by also admitting that he himself had been guilty of rudeness in the past. He also provided poor advice to the officers when he insisted that he would not require officers to provide statements during internal investigations if they were to be recorded.

On the day following the announcement that all officers would be required to abide by the bureau requirement and consent decree requirement to cooperate with recorded Internal Investigations interviews, three officers followed Mickey's advice and refused to have their interviews recorded. When I learned about this, I instructed their supervisors to give them a direct order to return to the Office of Municipal Investigations and cooperate with the investigation, and be recorded, or face disciplinary action that would result in suspension or termination. Two of the three officers claimed there had been a misunderstanding and that they wanted to provide statements. Those officers returned to OMI and agreed to have their statements recorded.

The third officer still refused and he was subjected to discipline. At his hearing, I gave him a one-day suspension rather than terminate his employment. I told him he would be ordered a second time to cooperate and if he did not comply, he would face termination. I needed to ensure compliance but did not want the officer to lose his job in the process as a result of being poorly advised by his union president. That officer's suspension was upheld. No other officer ever refused to comply. If Mickey had not provided a poor example to his membership, that officer may not have needed to be the test case.

OTHER CONSENT DECREE REQUIREMENTS

Annual performance evaluations would have to be completed for all members of the police bureau. Those evaluations would be used in promotions. Although this caused some consternation with the union, I explained that even people working in a fast-food business received evaluations. To suggest that an officer had the authority to stop someone, search someone, arrest someone, and use force, including the use of deadly force, without a supervisor's evaluation, was irrational. Officers should be evaluated on how well they perform the duties that impact on people's freedom and lives.

Officers were required to notify their supervisors when they were arrested. The first time an officer failed to do so resulted in that officer losing his job. That was never a problem again.

The bureau was required to have a full-time legal advisor. The police had had a legal advisor until the position was written out of the budget years earlier. If the bureau had kept a legal advisor, an attorney would have been available to review use-of-force reports, search and seizure reports, and other reports, and to notify the chief of police of developing problems. Failure to have an attorney for such a large department most likely led to many more lawsuits that cost more than the expense of having an attorney.

The rotation schedule, or transfer of personnel, was a problematic issue for many officers and supervisors who had become comfortable in their assignments. I believed rotations were good for many reasons including the following:

1. Some supervisors became too entrenched in their positions. Lieutenant Stanton, for example, was the only person in the Traffic Division trained and assigned to certain duties such as special events and collision reconstruction. He was virtually able to write his own overtime checks. Once he was transferred, other personnel had the opportunity to move into assignments that had been closed to them

beforehand. And the bureau had the advantage of an increased number of personnel knowing how to perform specialized duties.

2. Some officers working in what were considered to be the "fast" districts, such as Zone 5, complained they were left on the "front lines" too long and needed a rotation to another district. Zone 5 had a large number of calls for violent incidents and some officers said they were getting "burned out" due to constantly running from one bad call to another. To transfer officers out meant there had to be officers to be transferred in. Other administrations had addressed that issue by transferring in new recruits. Having so many recruits in a duty location, without more experienced officers to learn from, was a disservice to the recruits, the other officers, and the public. When we did do transfers, we permitted officers to choose their top three preferences of duty location. Only two officers throughout the entire bureau had a request for transfer to Zone 5.

3. On the other hand, some districts were considered "slower districts." Those districts did not experience the amount of violence, arrests, or shootings as "fast" districts. One officer, testifying in Federal Court when he sued the city, said Zone 4 was known as "Zone Snore" because of the totally different work environment. It was obvious that certain districts were considered more desirable than others. It seemed unfair that the same officers would remain in one of the desirable districts for decades.

4. There had always been rumors throughout the bureau that some supervisors either encouraged or looked the other way when officers failed to perform according to regulations. Continuously working for weak or unprincipled supervisors would taint nearly every officer on the shift. There were many examples of dark-blue supervisors who had influence over their officers and could hinder their careers if they thought they did not have to abide by regulations. Every officer benefits from not being regularly assigned to work for a dark-blue supervisor.

5. It provided learning experiences, especially for those who would be promoted.

The consent decree required all instructors and field training officers (FTOs) to receive proper training. Of course, this meant the bureau would have an FTO program. The prior chief's abandonment of field training had a significant impact on the rising number of complaints, lawsuits, vehicle collisions, officer injuries, and so many other costly consequences.

CONSENT DECREE WORKLOAD

The bulk of the workload following the consent decree was given to management. My wife was transferred to the Administration Branch to oversee all decree requirements. Although she was content with leading Zone 1 and requested to remain there, I knew I needed the use of her talents to benefit the entire bureau. This would include rewriting the entire policy manual, creating dozens of forms, and building an early warning system that would require regular monitoring and reporting.

Supervisors and managers were required to monitor all information contained in the early warning system, assess the information, and take all appropriate action to address any questionable performance. The early warning system would assist supervisors by identifying unusual officer activity.

ENSURING COMPLIANCE WITH THE CONSENT DECREE

The first consent decree requirement was that all officers and supervisors had to sign a statement that they received a copy of the consent decree and understood the requirements. I knew this was going to be the first step and I needed to ensure we would not be derailed in our initial effort. I was going to meet with every supervisor to explain the consent decree and have them sign that they understood it.

I scheduled seven training sessions so that I could meet with every supervisor. Every supervisor worked on Thursdays, so I scheduled two AM sessions, three PM sessions, and two night-turn sessions on a Thursday. Every supervisor had to attend one of the seven-hour training sessions.

All supervisors were required to bring their copy of the consent decree and their regulations manual. At the beginning of each session, I announced that the training session would last approximately four to five hours and that the supervisors who completely understood the contents of the consent decree would sign a statement that they understood and would be free to go home for the rest of the day.

However, I informed them if they did not understand some portion of the consent decree following my instruction, they should remain behind for the rest of the training session for individualized instruction. Of the more than 160 supervisors, no one needed individualized instruction. It appeared the instruction I provided was so clear that everyone signed the document.

I believed the training sessions were beneficial since they put me in the same room with every one of the bureau's supervisors. It gave me an opportunity to address them and have them ask questions or provide comments. I continued the training sessions in subsequent years and provided training in various subjects I thought were needed at the time. Other command staff assisted in providing some of the training those years. The only years I did not conduct these training sessions were 2001 and 2003 when I was called to active duty with the Coast Guard.

The mistake I made was to have each of the lieutenants and sergeants who signed they understood the consent decree to provide the same instruction to their subordinates and obtain their signatures. I should have realized that some of the dark-blue supervisors would not provide the same level of instruction. Although every officer signed, I would never know what they were told about the consent decree prior to their signing that they understood it. I should have had one or a few supervisors schedule training sessions at the Training Academy to provide that training.

PROGRESS

A selection process was developed to determine who the monitor would be for the consent decree. The DOJ provided some names and several auditing companies were considered. Dr. James Ginger, of Public Management Resources of San Antonio, was ultimately selected. For months, Dr. Ginger seemed to be everywhere. To avoid any resistance to Dr. Ginger's audits, I issued an order instructing all personnel that Dr. Ginger had the authority to enter any police facility, any room in any police facility, or any drawer or file in any cabinet to conduct his audits.

Dr. Ginger was experienced at police work and with audits. I knew he was reasonable and would access only what he needed. I also knew there were some disgruntled officers and supervisors who might attempt to hinder his work. My order was intended to be direct so I would not have to repeat myself and/or initiate disciplinary action. The benefit of being considered a disciplinarian while leading during a time of controversy was that people tended to believe you when you provided blunt direction.

Dr. Ginger attended one of the initial training sessions I had with supervisors to obtain their signatures signifying they had received and understood the consent decree. When Sergeant Sean McInerney objected to the early warning system tracking an officer's sick time, I firmly explained that I wasn't in attendance to debate what was in the consent decree but I was there only to explain to the supervisors what we were going to do. Although McInerney served the union and would eventually be the president, my position was that the union had already passed on their opportunity to have input. I assured all the supervisors that we would attain compliance with the consent decree and we would exit the consent decree only after the required two consecutive years of compliance.

The first quarterly progress report from the auditor, Public Management Resources of San Antonio, was in December 1997. It lauded the police bureau for the level of compliance, although noting that the Office of Municipal Investigations was not making progress. The auditor wrote, "After more than 100 similar projects, the auditor has yet to see a more committed, focused, open or candid city compliance team."

Each quarterly report indicated progress and that progress continued for years. To use ACLU Executive Director Witold Walczak's metaphor, sometimes progress requires the carrot and sometimes progress requires the stick. One quarterly report assessing the bureau's annual training stated that the bureau had neared the required 95 percent to achieve compliance.

Since we failed to achieve compliance with consent decree mandated training the first year, a review of each lieutenant was conducted to determine whose officers had failed to attend training. The review revealed that two lieutenants had failed to have their officers attend consent decree training. I do not know if this failure was due to the lieutenants' negligence or if it was due to their disdain for the consent decree. To me, it did not matter. All that mattered is they failed to do their jobs.

First, I ordered all officers under their command to attend the training sessions they had missed. I then wrote a memo to each lieutenant advising them that it was because of their failure to ensure their officers were training that the bureau failed to achieve consent decree compliance. I advised them that their duty was to ensure their officers were trained in the future and if they did not comply, they would face disciplinary action.

I knew both lieutenants well, especially Tom Douglas. Tom and I went to the police academy together and ate lunch together there. Tom was humorous and congenial and I considered him a friend. We regularly encountered each other when my duties brought me into the Zone 2 area where he worked much of his career.

The following year, the officers under the other lieutenant, Bob Horn, complied. However, Lieutenant Tom Douglas's subordinates still failed to attend required training. I reminded Lieutenant Douglas that he would be faced with disciplinary action. The discipline I intended to impose was reduction in rank to police officer. I realized I could not depend upon him as a lieutenant or a sergeant to supervise officers. He retired rather than risk losing his rank.

While one of the disciplinary reports he was faced with was neglect of duty for his failure to ensure his officers were trained, he was also being disciplined for sexual harassment, specifically, making inappropriate comments and showing a sexually explicit video in the station. Tom Douglas, who often brought humor to his shift as a police officer, failed to realize that as a shift lieutenant his actions would have more serious consequences.

By 1998, our bureau was in compliance with the consent decree except for the early warning system. It seemed computer personnel knew a lot about computers but not a lot about law enforcement. At the same time, the officers and supervisors in the bureau knew a lot about police work but not enough about computers. I detailed Commander Cathy McNeilly to those duties. Within weeks, our early warning system was operational. It had taken two and a half years to get there. This was our most important project and it was the most involved. Without her skills, I don't know how much time, money, or technical support would have been needed to get us there.

To reach an operable early warning system, we computer-wired every police facility in the city, installed computers at officer workstations and supervisors' offices, and developed the most complex officer performance tracking system there was to date. Not only did the system track all officer performance, but it could determine if an officer had reached a certain threshold for performance that would require a supervisor's attention.

With the early warning system in use, the first quarterly report indicated that twenty-two officers were identified to their supervisors by either a yellow or red indicator. This had the unanticipated impact of media inquiries. It seemed the media wanted to know the names of the twenty-two troubled officers. It was apparent the media had misinterpreted the findings of the early warning system. They believed that any indicator for any officer in EWS meant the officer had done something wrong. That was totally incorrect.

The data only did comparisons. The data listed some officers above two standard deviations. This was not necessarily negative. An officer in the city might lead in number of searches even if that officer had only conducted three searches. Notification of the yellow or red indicator was sent to the officer's supervisor for review. A review could, and usually did, show the officer conducted a legal search and the paperwork for the search was completed accurately. This was a case of an officer performing well.

In fact, 90 percent of all the indicators showed officers who were performing well. All the command staff met quarterly to discuss the officers with the most activity in their performance measures. This was the biggest reason the bureau was able to do more and better police work even though we lost 25 percent of our officers through department downsizing. We were able to identify the officers responsible for the most searches and transfer them to Narcotics. We could also see the officers responsible for the most traffic stops and transfer them to Traffic Division. Tracking officer performance proved to have many positives for the police bureau and for the officers.

From that time on, I would never refer to an early warning system by that name. It was misleading. I believed it was more appropriate to refer to any general system as an early intervention system since it was designed to intervene. More importantly, we always referred to our system as the PARS (Performance Assessment and Review System). Our system enabled a supervisor to track, assess, and review the officers' performance.

Most of the time the reviews indicated excellent officer performance and gave the bureau the information in each area of performance upon which to reward officers. Many officers were designated as officer of the month or officer of the year for their performance, based upon PARS statistics. In addition, the system protected managers from the terrible accusations and misconduct of dark-blue officers.

For example, Bob Smith, who was disciplined and removed from a detective position, submitted a transfer request to Traffic Division. Smith had had one traffic stop in the prior year. Officers who were transferred to Traffic Division had from eighty to more than three hundred traffic stops in the prior year. After the transfers were made and did not include Smith, he filed a lawsuit claiming age discrimination. He was my age and younger than some officers in Traffic Division. The data clearly exposed his lack of initiative in making traffic stops as the reason he was not transferred. His lawsuit was dismissed. Although I am convinced that he only filed the transfer request and the subsequent lawsuit because he was a malcontent dark-blue officer, his antics would not tie up city time and resources once we had the data to prove his frivolous allegation.

Dr. David Harris, a police accountability expert, believed an early intervention system was necessary to provide police accountability. In his book *Good Cops*, he cited Pittsburgh's PARS as an example of internal accountability. He wrote: "The PARS system in Pittsburgh represents the state of the art for early warning systems." An outside evaluation of the Pittsburgh Police Bureau conducted by the Vera Institute of Justice in 2002 found the PARS system to be "a model for police departments across the nation."

OFFICER RESULTS YEARS LATER

Nearly every officer was unsure what to expect when the consent decree was announced. The union's comments were not helpful to their own members and heightened their anxiety about how a consent decree would affect their jobs.

As much moaning and groaning as there was following the consent decree, as time went on many officers conceded that the consent decree had no effect on how they did their jobs. Those who performed well were given awards, granted specialty assignments, and promoted.

After two years, the sky-blue officers remained very productive. I contend they were more productive because the EWS had identified them as exceptional performers and they were transferred to positions where they excelled.

After two years, many officers said that the consent decree had not affected them. And it would not affect them as long as they were doing their jobs. Committed, hard-working officers will always find a way to do their jobs regardless of any barriers that others may introduce in an effort to prevent them from doing so.

I am certain many officers in other groups were apprehensive about doing their jobs. The light blue to the middle-blue groups were affected by the union president's baseless comments. They either wondered how they could perform their duties without facing negative consequences or they slowed their performance until they realized officers weren't being penalized wholesale as the union president had claimed.

Every negative prediction made by those dark-blue officers and supervisors did not come true. There was no federal takeover of the Pittsburgh Police, crime did not run rampant, no officer was ever fired for having an anonymous complaint filed against the officer, and officers did not leave the department in droves. In fact, the number of those separated, due to retirement, resignation, death, or termination, was lower than usual. The number of separations is illustrated in this chart.

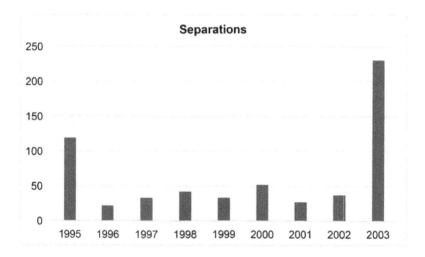

Separations

The separations in 1995 were due to the last group of officers taking advantage of the final offer to retire at ¾ retirement. From 1996 onward, retirement would be at ½ pay. The separations in 2003 were due to furloughs; however, those furloughed were returned to work when approximately 180 officers retired at the end of 2003 in order to maintain fully paid health care benefits, including during their retirement. Those retiring after 2003 would pay a portion of their retired health care benefits. The consent decree years (1997-2002) saw normal attrition rates.

Unfortunately, the disgruntled dark-blue officers do most of the talking about their agencies. And most of their talking is mere complaining without any facts to support their grumbles. As Shannon L. Alder said, "When dealing with critics always remember this: Critics judge things based on what is outside of their content of understanding."

RESULTS OF CONSENT DECREE

Dr. Ginger told me that Pittsburgh would set the record for coming into compliance with the consent decree and being released from the consent decree. More than twenty years later he was shown to be right.

Torsten Ove, in an article for the *Pittsburgh Post-Gazette* titled "Federal control of Pittsburgh police lifted—City force becomes model for nation" (4/6/2005), included Dr. Ginger's comment that the Pittsburgh Police Bureau was a model for American law enforcement.

Dr. Ginger was quoted as saying, "I routinely refer police managers and executives to the City of Pittsburgh to aid those executives in developing model practices for their individual police agencies." He also wrote, "The Pittsburgh Bureau of Police and the Pittsburgh Office of Municipal Investigations now have in place more than a dozen systems that are 'best practices' in American policing."

Vera Institute published a report in September 2002 regarding the Pittsburgh consent decree titled "Turning Necessity into Virtue: Pittsburgh's Experience with a Federal Consent Decree." Their findings included the following comments: "Our report... and the monitor's reports demonstrate that Pittsburgh made substantial progress in reducing police abuses by implementing innovative programs." The report also stated, "We attributed much of the success to a pro-reform police chief and the guidance the monitor provided to city officials."

A Community Oriented Police Services report titled "Federal Intervention in Local Policing: Pittsburgh's Experience with a Consent Decree" was written by Robert C. Davis, Nicole J. Henderson, Janet Mandelstam, Christopher Ortiz, and Joel Miller and released on October 11, 2005. According to the report, "The chief was the most important figure in implementing the decree. He was committed to a reform agenda, and the decree incorporated many of the initiatives that he wished to adopt. In fact, the decree was a boon to his efforts because it allowed him to avoid the inevitable political battles with the police union over the reforms, and it ensured that the city would provide the money to carry out the reforms."

EXIT FROM CONSENT DECREE

The terms of the consent decree required compliance for two consecutive years within five years of its issuance. We were in compliance for two and a half years when we were released from the decree. The Office of Municipal Investigations was not released at the same time because it was still reviewing the backlog of cases pending investigations.

I asked Mayor Murphy to permit me to send one commander, Commander William Grant, and several detectives to OMI to help them reach compliance. Once these officers were in place at OMI, compliance was achieved within five months. That was an outstanding accomplishment since OMI had struggled for five and a half years to achieve compliance.

When Federal Judge Robert Cindrich released the Police Bureau from the consent decree in 2002, he told me, "I think you deserve to be commended."

When I retired from the bureau, Michael Fuoco, in an article for the *Pittsburgh Post-Gazette* on January 9, 2006, wrote, "The Pittsburgh Police Bureau is 149 years old, but there may have been more significant changes in its makeup, operation and supervision during the past decade than at any time in its history."

The article also said, "Mr. Vic Walczak, … who filed the federal lawsuit … said the police bureau's culture has been greatly improved 'by the consent decree and by having a police chief committed to implementing those requirements. We give McNeilly a lot of credit. He wasn't perfect but nobody's perfect. He brought the department into compliance with the consent decree faster than anyone thought possible. One of the things we have learned in doing a lot of institutional reform cases, in trying to change how an entire agency operates, is that no matter how good the court order is, if the director is not committed to making changes, it's not going to happen.'"

The article added, "Although Mr. McNeilly was seen by many in the bureau as a rigid disciplinarian, his methods were regarded by supporters as necessary to enforce the consent decree and to weed out problem officers. 'It takes that kind of chief to keep the street-level officers abiding by the rules,' Mr. Walczak said."

COST OF CONSENT DECREES

Union members who resented the consent decree for whatever reason complained about its cost. They included the cost of computerizing the bureau as a cost of the consent decree. That was disingenuous. It implies that if there hadn't been a consent decree, the police bureau would never have computerized. Mayor Tom Murphy already planned to provide the bureau with computers since he knew the police would be able to work smarter.

Prior to the consent decree the city had a limited number of computers with none in the districts. The computers that did exist weren't connected, and there were no computers in police vehicles. We operated just as the bureau had decades before by leaving phone messages with a desk sergeant, written memos, and in-person meetings. The command staff did not even have cellphones to contact each other.

By the time the bureau was in compliance with the consent decree, every station had computers that were connected city-wide, each officer had an e-mail address, communications were primarily electronic, orders were issued daily, there were computers in police vehicles, and multiple members of the bureau had cellphones.

Even though the city was financially strained, Mayor Murphy was determined to enhance the bureau's ability to use computerized systems more efficiently. Most of the costs that detractors attributed to the consent decree were those associated with computerization that had been planned prior to the DOJ investigation.

The only real expenses connected to the consent decree were the costs associated with the auditor and the development of the early warning system. The expense for the auditor was much lower than expected since Dr. James Ginger's costs were only a fraction of the costs proposed by other auditing firms. His contract was for $392,000 for the five years of the agreement. Dr Ginger not only audited our compliance, but he provided expert advice that would have cost the bureau enormously to obtain from other sources. Dr. Ginger was extremely fair in his audits. He always provided us with an opportunity to correct a problem.

And the cost of the early warning system was minimal when one thinks of the efficiency it provided to the bureau in many ways.

First, PARS enhanced efficiency by identifying the high-performing officers and placing them in the right positions, which resulted in the bureau producing better work with fewer personnel. Even though the number of police bureau employees fell from 1,500 in 1995 to 1,000 in 2003 and the number of officers fell from nearly 1,200 to 900, the crime rate in Pittsburgh continued to fall. The cost of operating with only two thirds of the bureau personnel and three fourths of the sworn members would have been enough to justify a consent decree and PARS.

Second, PARS identified officers who needed assistance and their supervisors acted after receiving an alert and when they conducted their required quarterly review of PARS data. One can only wonder how many careers have been saved. That alone would have been worth the cost of a consent decree.

Third, PARS identified troubled or poor-performing officers and took corrective action that replaced lawsuits exceeding one-million dollars in 1995 with settlements of only $30,000 for several years following the consent decree. If the cost of lawsuits had remained over $1,000,000 annually, it would have cost the city $10,000,000 to $15,000,000 over the decade I led the bureau. The drop in number of lawsuits in Pittsburgh was noticeable. The same results were found in city after city following other consent decrees.

While I served as the chief in Pittsburgh, the Law Department provided me with the expenses related to the lawsuits and claims brought against the bureau. I used this chart during the annual training I provided to all bureau commanders, lieutenants, and sergeants. The charts explain the trend of lawsuits and settlements/awards from those lawsuits.

Lawsuits and claims as a result of police incidents

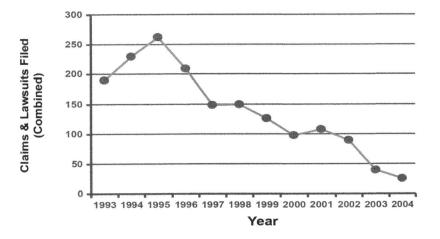

It was obvious the number of lawsuits was high and increasing from 1993 to 1995. Once accountability measures were introduced in 1996, the number of lawsuits began decreasing. By 2004, they were reduced by 90 percent.

Incurred losses involving the police bureau

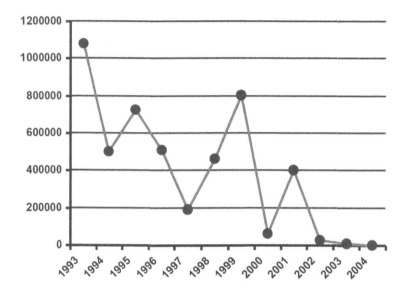

Again, it was obvious the amounts paid for lawsuits were high from 1993 to 1995. Once accountability measures were introduced in 1996, the amount of money lost due to those lawsuits began decreasing. By 2004, they were reduced by more than 90 percent.

John Worrall, a professor of criminology at the University of Texas at Dallas, published his study of consent decrees in an article titled "Data show consent decrees worth their costs." He explained that consent decrees reduced the risk of litigation. He also wrote the following.

> The City of New Orleans paid out $13 million in settlements to resolve a number of post-Katrina lawsuits over deadly police shootings. New Orleans eventually entered into a consent decree.
>
> The City of Cleveland paid $6,000,000 to settle a lawsuit following the shooting death of 12-year-old Tamir Rice. It was reportedly the largest police-involved shooting settlement. Cleveland eventually entered into a consent decree.

The City of Chicago paid $5,000,000 to the family of Laquan McDonald. Chicago eventually entered into a consent decree.

The City of Baltimore paid almost $6 million to alleged victims of police abuses in a four-year period and paid $6.4 million to settle civil claims from the family of Freddie Gray. Baltimore eventually entered into a consent decree.

Unfortunately, in Pittsburgh, news reports stated that between 2010 and 2015, the city spent $4,900,000 to settle more than twenty-eight civil-rights-related lawsuits against police. The city was nearing the $1,000,000 per year in lawsuits that it had spent prior to my assuming command of the police bureau and the changes brought about from either my initiatives and/or the consent decree. The negative trend experienced from 1996 through 2005 did not continue.

FAILURE TO EMPLOY BEST PRACTICES

I have constantly advised chiefs that to maintain control of one's own department, the department's leadership must be committed to constant change while researching best practices and taking whatever measures necessary to implement and maintain those practices. All anyone needs to do is review the many consent decrees there have been since 1997 in order to determine if one's own department fails to comply with any of those best practices. Not all consent decrees are between the Department of Justice and a municipality. The City of Wallkill, New York, and Niagara Falls, New York, both entered into a consent decree with the New York State Attorney General's Office.

Not all provisions of every consent decree will be applicable to every department but there will always be some areas in which a department can do better. Any department, believing they do not need to make any improvements (as did the union leadership in Pittsburgh in 1996), faces the same destiny as every department who has experienced a consent decree.

So, what can happen when a department cannot fix themselves? Someone else will come along and fix it for them. And the department probably will not like the experience. Being ordered to make changes will shine a spotlight on the deficiencies of the department and management. Police managers keeping up with best practices will make changes themselves rather than wait to have someone else force them.

Chiefs and elected officials need to determine the expenses necessary to ensure their police agency employs best practices. Failure to provide the funding can result in even more expense if forced to do so. From the beginning of the Negotiated Settlement Agreement in Oakland, California, in 2003 until August of 2019, the city had paid $16,700,000 for auditing and they were still not in compliance. Civil rights attorneys Jim Chanin and John Burris initiated the lawsuit in Oakland, California, that led to the consent decree. As Mr. Chanin pointed out, although that may seem like a lot of money, the expense needed to be compared with the expense of the payouts from allegations of police abuse. He said, "I 'd rather spend it on a monitor than on a family with someone who is dead or wounded."

There are even more consequences for agencies not ensuring best practices. In 2020 efforts were underway in many municipalities throughout the country to defund the police due to citizen dissatisfaction with police performance. In an effort to maintain an acceptable level of police service while ensuring changes in police practices, the U. S. Conference of Mayors released a report on August 13, 2020, with recommendations regarding use-of-force policies, bias training, handling of citizens' complaints, and collecting data on police stops, searches, and arrest. Fascinating! These are all consent decree requirements.

In many municipalities, the elected officials are contemplating city ordinances to codify the police department's policies. In August 2020, an assembly member in Anchorage, Alaska, proposed a city ordinance for the police use-of-force policy. This ordinance would set standards for the department and require public hearings for citizen input prior to any changes. The authority for a department's use of force would not rest with the department itself.

On June 15, 2020, an article in the *Rochester Democrat & Chronicle* titled "New York signs sweeping police reforms into law after George Floyd death" stated, "Gov. Andrew Cuomo signed into a law Friday a package of police reforms in New York that gives the public access to police disciplinary records and bans police chokeholds."

On June 7, 2020, the *Associated Press* printed an article about Minneapolis titled "Minneapolis council majority backs disbanding police force."

In June 2020, the *Chicago Sun-Times* reported that officers were retiring at twice the normal rate.

In August 2020, Seattle Police Chief Carmen Best announced her resignation when the City Council cut police funding including her salary. After George Floyd's death, she said, "Policing will never be the same as it was before."

During the same month, the *Los Angeles Times* reported that the National Association for the Advancement of Colored People (NAACP) and Campaign Zero were initiating campaigns in larger cities against police union contracts and state laws that provided union protections for officers. On June 15, 2020, an article appeared in the *San Jose Mercury News* with the headline "Major California police unions call for reforms, removal of racist officers." This was clear evidence the police unions saw a need for change.

A March 13, 2021, Police Executive Research Forum publication mentioned a March 3, 2021, report from the National Conference of State Legislatures, "According to the National Conference of State Legislatures, 36 states have introduced more than 700 bills addressing police reform since the killing of George Floyd, and nearly 100 have been enacted."

FUTURE OF CONSENT DECREES

There are more than eighteen thousand police agencies throughout the United States. It is the responsibility of each municipality or county or state to ensure their police agency operates properly. That requires a commitment to provide a department with the funding, leadership, and authority to ensure their citizens are served with fairness and respect. Not providing adequate funding and not ensuring competent leadership with the ability to do what needs to be done will result in costly failures. If the local officials are unable to correct their deficiencies, someone else will move to make the changes they should have made themselves.

There are many departments throughout the country currently struggling to improve. Many are burdened with problems beyond their control or ability to correct.

In an article for the *South Florida Sun Sentinel* (6/3/2020), Anthony Man wrote that Chiefs Sean Brammer, Michael Gregory, and Javaro Sims "indicated a willingness to cede some authority to outsiders, something police often resist. And they're looking for some federal and state involvement—something that's often disliked by local government officials—in their efforts to deal with problematic officers." It is obvious many chiefs recognize they need help to ensure accountability in their departments.

While police leadership and agencies are looking for help, some in positions of authority to provide that help have chosen not to do so. Prior to Attorney General Jeff Sessions leaving office, he signed a memorandum restricting the Department of Justice from becoming involved with consent decrees.

Two municipalities and their departments felt abandoned. Officials in Baltimore and Chicago objected when the DOJ threatened to leave. Baltimore Police Commissioner Kevin Davis said he considered it "a punch in the gut." Following the death of George Floyd less than two years later, there was acknowledgment from another Republican that it might be time for a return to the use of consent decrees.

On June 23, 2020, Bryn Stole, in an article for *News Break*, wrote, "'The sweeping federally mandated overhaul of the New Orleans Police Department could serve as a model for implementing reforms at other local police agencies,' U.S. Sen. Bill Cassidy said...." Senator Cassidy is a Republican senator from Baton Rouge, Louisiana.

The importance of consent decrees is explained by Dr. Samuel Walker (University of Nebraska at Omaha), a police accountability expert, and author of *Twenty Years of DOJ 'Pattern or Practice' Investigations of Local Police: Achievements, Limitations, and Questions.* According to Dr. Walker, "pattern or practice" investigations have provided the nation with "best practices" in police accountability in the following areas:

(1)   a state-of-the-art use-of-force policy;

(2)   the requirements that officers file complete and accurate reports about each use of force, and that their supervisors critically review those reports;

(3)   an early intervention system designed to track officer performance for the purpose of identifying officers who are engaged in repeated instances of problematic performance;

(4)   a citizen complaint process that is open and accessible to potential complainants.

Dr. Walker wrote, "Prior to the first DOJ consent decree (Pittsburgh, 1997) there was, to the best of this author's knowledge, no equivalent set of accountability-related best practices."

Obviously, the Pittsburgh Police Bureau was on the forefront of use-of-force best practices.

LESSONS LEARNED

1) If a department does not fix their own problems, someone else will. And those in the department probably will not like it.

2) Tracking employee performance should include, at least, each officer's:

    - use of force
    - searches
    - seizures
    - arrests
    - traffic stops
    - history/complaints
    - lawsuits filed
    - weapon discharges
    - missed court
    - sick leave
    - counseling
    - disciplinary action
    - vehicle collisions
    - transfers
    - awards
    - secondary employment
    - criminal investigations

      NOTE: The system should identify the diligent 20 percent of officers doing most of the work of providing professional service to the community and the 20 percent of officers who required some type of intervention to help them save their careers.

CHAPTER TEN

From Awards to No Confidence

"There is only one way to avoid criticism: do nothing, say nothing, and be nothing."

—ARISTOTLE

In 1996, shortly after my promotion from commander to chief, the union presented me with an award for "Compassionate Leadership" in recognition of my interaction with Zone 2 officers during my twenty months as commander of the zone. I appreciated the award for the support I provided to my officers. I had hoped that support would continue during my time as the chief, but I eventually realized that a reform chief leading a department that urgently needed change would not sit well with those who enjoyed the status quo. When I was sworn in as the chief, I commented that I hoped to maintain the support of the union and the rank and file.

Although I had a reputation as a disciplinarian, Union President Mickey Hughes noted that I had a reputation for being firm but fair. There was no question I had initiated disciplinary action for many officers when necessary.

It is difficult to maintain support in an organization when changes are required but its members believe there is no need to change. Change is important in an organization as society changes, community expectations change, laws change, and court decisions affect police procedures. I remembered the advice of my first partner who told me I'd have to adapt to change in the department or I'd go the way of the Dodo bird that couldn't adapt.

I am uncertain whether I was chosen to lead the department because I was viewed as a change agent, but once I was promoted to the chief's position, I found it necessary to become one. I realized change was difficult, but it was necessary for our department. There would be many impediments to change.

COLLECTIVE BARGAINING AGREEMENT'S IMPACT ON DEPARTMENT CHANGES

It is difficult to make changes in a department when the collective bargaining agreement is too broad. A collective bargaining agreement (CBA) is rigid since it dictates how police operations will be conducted. When I took over as the chief of police, the CBA was fifty-six pages long and covered topics such as how officers bid on the jobs they will work, how they can be transferred, timelines for disciplining officers, and the process the chief must follow to change policies.

For example, I could not require my officers to submit to drug/alcohol testing following a vehicle collision when the occupants of the other car were being transported to Traffic Division for Breathalyzer tests. Neither could I require an officer involved in a shooting to be tested for drugs/alcohol even though the community was demanding answers as to why those tests were not being completed.

It could take years for a contract arbitration to make those changes since the union was not inclined to make any changes unless there were increases in benefits such as pay raises. That would be difficult to arrange since the city was already struggling financially.

Collective bargaining agreements have continually increased in length and have reduced the ability of police management to initiate change. For example, some prior administrations were forced to cede management rights in lieu of pay raises during tight budget years. Sometimes during collective bargaining, arbitrators believe they need to cede some management rights to the union during every contract arbitration.

IMPENDING CHANGES

Mickey Hughes was elected to a two-year term as president of the local lodge of the Police union in March 1996. On April 2, 1996, Mayor Murphy announced I would be assuming the chief of police position for the City of Pittsburgh. I had known Mickey only as a Homicide detective for many years until his recent retirement.

I called Mickey to try to set up an initial meeting and to establish regular meetings. The first meeting was cordial. I asked him to prepare a list of changes he would like to see within the department. I told him that while he did that, I would prepare a list of changes for the department I would like to see and that I would like to discuss with him how we would go about making changes.

I knew the department was in trouble as evidenced by the 60+ lawsuits filed against the city the prior week due to police actions. The American Civil Liberties Union (ACLU) and the National Association for the Advancement of Colored People (NAACP) joined those lawsuits. There was considerable community outrage over many issues that eventually led to a call for a Civilian Police Review Board (CPRB) and a Department of Justice (DOJ) Civil Rights Division investigation into the police bureau.

The following week I met with Mickey again to discuss our lists. My list was easy. I had already prepared a list of changes I planned for the department when I was interviewed for the chief's position. When I inquired about Mickey's list, he said he did not have one. He said he did not have any changes he wanted to see during 1996 but noted that 1997 was a contract arbitration year and he would talk about changes during 1997 for the contract that would take effect on January 1, 1998.

I told him that his proposal would not work for me since I needed to make changes sooner than two years in the future. Waiting two years to make changes would not be acceptable to the citizens clamoring for change, the elected officials who were already enacting legislation affecting the police bureau, or the plaintiff and city attorneys involved in the lawsuits already filed against the city.

THE IMPACT OF ONGOING CHANGE

During 1996 there were many officers disciplined. The number of officers terminated far exceeded what the union and officers in the department had been used to seeing in the past. The level of disciplinary cases continued into 1997 and 1998 as discussed in chapter 8.

In addition, the City of Pittsburgh and the United States Department of Justice (USDOJ) entered into a consent decree in 1997. The consent decree created considerable displeasure with the union since it required many reforms within the department which the union opposed. This was discussed in Chapter 9.

Change was happening within the Pittsburgh Bureau of Police. Change can seem threatening to officers who believe that the same routines and tactics they have always employed have kept them safe. I realized that officers do not adjust well to change.

Dr. Kevin M. Gilmartin and John (Jack) Harris explain, in their training and in their book, *Emotional Survival for Law Enforcement,* how officers frequently develop a sense of victimization over time. They explain how over-identification and over-investment in their job cause them to link their sense of self to their police role—a role they do not control. While this builds camaraderie, it can also cause officers to eventually hate and resent the job they once loved.

In an International Association of Chiefs of Police (IACP) article published in *The Police Chief Magazine* in January 1998 titled "Law Enforcement Ethics: The Continuum of Compromise," Gilmartin and Harris described how officers survive the dangers of their jobs by being "hypervigilant." They wrote: "Hypervigilance coupled with over-investment leads officers to believe the only person you can really trust is another cop … a 'real cop,' that is, not some 'pencil-neck in the administration.' While officers first become alienated from the public, they can soon distance themselves from the criminal justice system and finally from their own department administration. 'I can handle the morons on the street, I just can't handle the morons in the administration,' is often heard among officers."

After attending the authors' training session during an IACP conference, I understood further what our officers were experiencing with ongoing change. I believed that their training was so important in police work that I required all members of the command staff to attend their training and mandated their four-hour training video for every new recruit class and every class newly promoted in the Pittsburgh Bureau of Police. I believed this training was so important that I personally conducted the training and led the discussions following each segment of the video. I even insisted that members of my family who were becoming police officers or marrying police officers view the video.

Mickey's unwillingness to work with me led to changes being made without him. Although by contract he had ten days to review any new policy and provide input, the union failed to make any recommendations. Much of the time union officials failed to open their e-mail to review the pending policies. It appeared easier for them to criticize a policy after it was issued than to participate in the hard work of developing policy.

From what I could see, Mickey refused to participate because he was angry that (1) he had given up the opportunity to be involved in the consent decree and the changes it mandated, (2) union membership was blaming him for not better defending the officers being suspended or terminated, and (3) the changes were creating rifts within the union itself.

UNION TACTICS TO PREVENT CHANGE AND PRESSURE POLICE CHIEFS

There are many measures a union can employ to retaliate against a police chief when displeased with the chief's leadership. The "no-confidence" vote is one tactic used by police unions to disparage a police chief. The tactic is designed to force the chief to cave into their demands or to force the chief from office if the chief will not submit to their demands.

Some of the other tactics employed include:

A. Making accusations of illegal and/or unethical conduct by the chief
On May 11, 2001, Union President Edward Gregson held a news conference regarding a letter he sent to the U.S. Attorney claiming I knowingly falsified the 1998 Annual *Subject Resistance and Use of Force* report.

The *Pittsburgh Post-Gazette* found evidence that Gregson's accusation was not truthful. According to the May 12, 2001, issue, "…court documents filed in connection with a lawsuit that Showalter filed against the city contradict Gregson's claims. In a deposition filed in connection with the court case, Faith Jones testified that she was the person who made the decision to eliminate the training recommendations from the report before it was sent to McNeilly. Jones said there was no need to include the recommendations because they were already covered in another report." One would think Gregson would provide a retraction and an apology but neither occurred. Of course, they did not since the purpose was to accuse and not to really prove any misconduct.

B.   Request for criminal investigations concerning the chief's actions

        a.   Armstrong Tunnel shooting even after two separate investigations into the shooting were already completed.

C.   Exaggerating claims of harsh disciplinary measures to give a perception of a chief's unfairness

D.   Grievances

        a.   Even though the city won grievances for transfers, the union continued to file more grievances to bog down police administration and to claim that the chief was acting unreasonably. The outcome of the grievances was not as important to the union as driving up the number of grievances.

E.   Complaints to the Labor Relations Board

        a.   It is common, and considered to be a best practice, to have outside agencies investigate a citizen's death while interacting with the police. A police officer involved in a shooting in Pittsburgh led to the union filing an unfair labor practice claiming the city was giving away their "work" by having those incidents investigated by another agency.

F.   Lawsuits

        a.   A union notice was posted which was authored by Officer Rich Richards, a union trustee. He notified officers the union paid the legal bills for several officers to sue the chief and the city.

G.   Complaints to elected officials

        a.   Complaints regarding transfers. Many detectives contacted city, county, and state elected officials complaining about their transfers. This included officers who failed to perform their assigned duties and believed they were untouchable because of their political connections.

H. Threatening a lack of political support for elected officials who support the chief

    a. This was common during the 1998 mayoral and council elections and during the 2002 elections. Councilwoman Teresa Hooks was a supporter of the mayor's opponent and accused the mayor and me of wrongdoing and being ineffective leaders. She eventually resigned from council and pleaded no contest to seventeen charges of corruption and ethics violations. She was sentenced to one to two years in prison on charges of channeling $43,160 of city money (earmarked for consultants) into her personal and campaign bank accounts.

I. Public hearings

    a. Councilman Monty Davis called for a public hearing regarding the no-confidence vote in the chief. Councilman Davis was elected in 1997 and was close to Ed Gregson, who would later become the union president. Davis was successfully elected to the Pennsylvania House of Representatives in 2000 where he clashed with the House Democratic Caucus. He switched to the Republican party in 2005 but failed to win the Senate seat that year. He was voted out of office in 2006. In 2009 he lost the race for district justice in Pittsburgh. Davis was twice accused and staff members were indicted for forging signatures on nominating petitions.

J. Internet postings critical of the chief

    a. Although this was a newer phenomenon in the 1990s, this is now common.

K. Complaints to media

    a. Mickey Hughes told the media that police would stop doing their jobs in response to the consent decree being signed. He claimed young black men would be lying dead in the street due to officers' unwillingness to perform their duties.

L.   Personal attacks on the chief's character

    a.   The first vice-president, Sergeant Kevin Massey, participated in rumors that I was involved in a domestic violence incident. He would eventually testify in federal court in 2003 that he spread those rumors because he "thought it was funny." This is further discussed in Chapter 11.

    b.   Registering a chief's e-mail address with organizations that would negatively affect the chief's image. On July 21, 1999, I asked the owner of a website to investigate my e-mail address with a password of "wifebeater" being registered to his website. The website sent out jokes to one's contacts. I notified him that the registration was meant to disparage and harass me through electronic means.

POLICE MORALE AFFECTED BY CITIZEN DISSATISFACTION

Much of the public in Pittsburgh was dissatisfied with the police bureau in 1996. That dissatisfaction brought about a move to amend the City Home Rule Charter to create a Citizen Police Review Board (CPRB) to investigate and recommend action regarding citizens' complaints of police misconduct. It seemed to me that union leadership failed to understand the intensity of the groundswell and believed they did not have to expend much effort to stop it. The citizens of Pittsburgh voted through a referendum to create a CPRB on May 20, 1997.

On September 10, 1999, the *Pittsburgh Post-Gazette* reported on the CPRB's first case. The CPRB sustained a misconduct case against Officer Veronica Chase for excessive force and false arrest. The Office of Municipal Investigations had already sustained charges against the officer. The CPRB recommended a ninety-day suspension which did not conform to the city's disciplinary measures. The city's final step in discipline was a five-day suspension pending termination.

The CPRB was expecting a 90-day suspension when they knew that was not possible. Someone at the CPRB was apparently attempting to placate some segments of the public by imposing lengthy suspensions. The CPRB executive director would have been limited to the same city disciplinary measures if they suspended one of their employees. They would have to choose between an oral reprimand, a written reprimand, a one-day suspension, a three-day suspension, or a five-day suspension pending termination. This put me in an impossible situation since they were demanding extensive suspensions that they knew I could not employ.

Ann Porter, then head of the CPRB, drew up a spreadsheet that claimed that a ninety-day suspension really meant a one-day suspension; a six-month suspension really meant a three-day suspension; and a one-year suspension really meant a lengthier suspension. I advised them that they should actually say what they meant and stay with recommendations that could be considered.

It did not surprise me that Ann was unrealistic. After being sworn in as chief in 1996, I met with many groups, including the city's Human Relations Commission. She was a member then and she questioned me as to why it would take up to six officers to arrest one person. I explained there were many instances when an arrest could take that many officers, for example, if the person was high on drugs or alcohol, was very strong, had had martial arts training, or offered considerable resistance. She told me she worked in the mental health field and that she could singlehandedly subdue any person she needed to. I realized then that if Ann passionately believed that, she could never be convinced otherwise and would never comprehend the dangers officers experienced on the street.

The CPRB, over the years, received little cooperation from the rank-and-file officers or from the police union which resisted all her

efforts. Since the CPRB was created via legislation, as chief I was required to ensure that officers attended the hearing. The union, and
some officers, resented being ordered to attend the hearings and they
resented the recommendations for lengthy suspensions.

The few officers who did establish a rapport with Ms. Porter were
those who were opposed to the consent decree, the chief, and even the
union. She must have believed she could win the support of officers if
she joined them in their criticism of me. Although the union continually complained about the CPRB, police review boards were common
among major U. S. cities.

Instead of Mickey Hughes attempting to manage the interactions with the board, he included the CPRB as one of the problems
affecting Pittsburgh officers along with the ongoing Department of
Justice investigation, which would lead to a consent decree, negative
comments made by the public, poor news media reports regarding
the police, and increased disciplinary actions. His panicked approach
to leadership instilled fear and anger among many of the officers. I
certainly would not have wanted to serve in a foxhole with someone
who handled stress so poorly.

NO-CONFIDENCE VOTE

Mickey Hughes was the union president in February 1998 when some
union members voted "no confidence" in my leadership. The union
stated that the reasons for the no-confidence vote were two-fold. One
was my not fighting the United States Department of Justice consent
decree. I believed the consent decree was a measure to improve the
department as explained in the previous chapter. The second reason
given for the vote was the union's claim of excessive discipline.

Following the vote of no confidence a newspaper editorial board
quoted me as saying, "I know officers are upset about a lot of things
and I can understand that. Anybody who has kids has heard them
say, I hate you." The editorial stated, "...Pittsburghers should regard

the union vote with the same equanimity that Chief McNeilly has demonstrated."

To stress that the vote did not impact my ability to perform my duties and that it was a popularity poll, I said, "I guess I won't be the homecoming king at the policemen's ball." My comments raised the ire of the local, state, and national union. A *Pittsburgh Tribune-Review* article on February 24, 1998, regarding the no-confidence vote quoted me as saying, "It doesn't mean anything."

In the article, I acknowledged that officers were claiming I was imposing too much discipline against other officers. They also quoted me as saying, "I think we've taken more disciplinary action than we have seen in the past, but I think it is long overdue. I think we should hold our officers accountable for their actions."

DISCIPLINE AS A REASON FOR THE NO-CONFIDENCE VOTE

According to an article in the *Pittsburgh Tribune-Review* on February 25, 1998, Hughes said, "Excessive use of disciplinary action against officers is the reason some are turning against McNeilly." Hughes cited the example that disciplinary action against an officer for not wearing a tie was leading to her termination. Mickey did not tell the entire story even though he knew the details.

I was leaving the U. S. Coast Guard office in Downtown after completing a day of active duty for training (ADT) as a reservist when I came across two officers walking down the street without ties. Wearing ties was mandatory with a long-sleeved shirt. I approached the two officers who recognized me. When I inquired why they were not wearing ties, they went back to their police car to retrieve their ties. I noticed they were operating a Zone 5 car but they were downtown in Zone 2. They were obviously out of their district, which would be a policy violation unless authorized by their supervisor. The officers said they were on their way to meet with a union attorney.

I called the Zone 5 supervisor and asked where his officers were. He did not know but said they were assigned to patrol a target area in Zone 5. Officers assigned to target areas were specifically instructed not to leave that specific portion of their zone without the express permission of their supervisors. A commitment was made to residents in target areas that there would be police assigned within those few blocks since there had been an increase in gang activity, shootings, and other violence. Obviously, the officers had not received permission to be out of their zone or the target area of patrol.

The sergeant initiated disciplinary action. The city had a five-step disciplinary process. The first was an oral reprimand, followed by a written reprimand, a one-day suspension, a three-day suspension, and finally a five-day suspension pending the officer's termination. When reviewing the disciplinary record of one of the officers, it was noted the officer had an extensive history of failure to obey orders and to patrol her assigned area. She had already proceeded through the stages of disciplinary measures and served two separate three-day suspensions for leaving her assigned post.

The second three-day suspension was obviously implemented so that the five-day pending termination did not have to be implemented for her continued defiance of supervisory direction and policy. She was spared her job when progressive discipline should have mandated her termination before I ever saw her Downtown. As it was, I did give her a five-day suspension without terminating employment but admonished her that one more infraction involving her leaving her assigned post would definitely lead to her termination. Fortunately for her, she finally realized how close she was to losing her job and never came in front of me for any other infraction.

I explained Mickey's allegation about the officer facing termination for not wearing a tie as akin to someone claiming the "Son of Sam" murderer was serving multiple life terms in prison because he committed a parking offense. The truth was, the murders committed by the Son of Sam murderer were eventually solved with the help of a parking ticket he received when he committed some of his murders. Mickey could make any claim he wanted, but once people heard the facts of the case, his accusations appeared disingenuous.

OTHER PERCEPTIONS OF THE NO-CONFIDENCE VOTE

On February 27, 1998, the *Tribune-Review* printed an editorial titled "Confidence confirmed." It said, "Pittsburgh Police Chief Robert W. McNeilly, Jr. has come up on the short end of a police union no-confidence vote. Gee, what took members...so doggone long? After all, the chief's been in office for almost two years now, there are strict new standards of accountability for officers and, get this, Bob McNeilly actually has had the nerve to hold disciplinary hearings." The editorial concluded, "We said Chief McNeilly was the right person for the job when the mayor named him in April 1996. He still is."

Whereas the union's only constituency is the group of officers they represent, the chief must be concerned with the department's officers, the community needs and expectations, crime rates, budgets, and internal corruption. It is difficult to maintain harmony with all groups in light of their conflicting needs.

MORALE PROBLEMS CREATED FROM TURMOIL WITHIN THE UNION

The union itself, with only one constituency, was rife with turmoil. During my nearly ten years as the chief of police, there were four different union presidents. The term for a president was two years. Mickey Hughes was elected president only weeks prior to me taking the helm of the department. He was followed by Edward Gregson, then by Marty Jackson, and then by Sean McInerney.

Mickey Hughes and I had many cordial meetings and I attended many union meetings since I remained a member of the union. I never stayed the entire meeting but made a presentation, answered questions, and left. After my first appearance at the meeting, Mickey applauded my presence there.

Mickey and I met regularly at first. However, as I had predicted when I was interviewed for the chief's position, I anticipated that officer morale would be the biggest problem within the department in the coming years. Eventually, some officers who had been counseled or disciplined resented my presence at the meetings. I stopped attending when Mickey asked me to.

Our lunch meetings stopped when some officers accused Mickey of being in bed with the administration. And Mickey stopped speaking with me after an officer who called himself the "Royal Knave" began attacking me on the Internet. Mickey told me that he had to be critical of me or the person writing on the Internet would start writing accusations about him next. I had to ask Mickey why he even cared what the officer wrote. Mickey could not take the pressure and instead of attending our regularly scheduled meetings, he began attacking me through press conferences.

Mickey's leadership came under attack within the union. He lasted two terms and was voted out in 2000 when some of his opponents accused him of wrongdoing.

On March 13, 2001, amid infighting within the local lodge of the union, the second vice-president, Bruno Bonaduce, resigned his leadership position and his union delegate position and delivered a blistering critique of other union board members. He accused the current union leadership of President Edward Gregson as "ineffective...and often unfocused and confused."

The second vice-president also accused the prior union president, Mickey Hughes, of being a "miserable failure" at obtaining a good contract and improving racial harmony. He continued that the "majority of the board is committed to mutiny." He also accused Mickey of not paying a union auditor when that auditor revealed past accounting violations on the part of the union lodge. Bonaduce stated that was "theft of services" and that the IRS was investigating. He added that there were men on the executive board of the local union who were neither decent nor honorable.

When Bruno Bonaduce was elected as second vice-president, a union official told me that Bonaduce had only three agendas. The first was that he hated the consent decree, the second was that he hated the early intervention system mandated by the consent decree, and the third was that he hated me. It became obvious his agenda was not the same as all the other elected officials in the union. He was continuously critical of the union, to the point that they referred to him in the union newsletter as "Officer Bimbo." They ridiculed him and referred to his not seeing much of the inside of a courtroom. Of course, that was a reference to his making few, if any, arrests.

Although Bonaduce challenged me to regular debates, I never accepted for two reasons. First, I knew he wanted a forum only to make accusations rather than to honestly discuss any issue. Second, he was not my equal. If I had any reason to respect his police work, I would gladly have debated him. His work record was dismal. Those who worked with me on the street would never say I did not work hard and would have acknowledged my making many felony arrests. I decided not to provide him instant credibility just because he could write well. I knew much of what he wrote was not true. He seemed to find it easy to accuse but not necessary to provide evidence.

Bonaduce eventually demonstrated his reluctance to assist with an arrest and was called out by another woman officer in Zone 4 where they both worked. He accused the officer of using excessive force as the reason he did not assist her. If that had been the case, he should have interceded. Instead, he became the object of scorn of many officers and retired.

I came to three conclusions from his resignation. First, I believed he was not strong enough to withstand the pressure that came with a leadership position and could never have handled a supervisory or management position in a large department. Second, some of those attacking the chief had a soft underbelly when they were criticized. Third, even when the leadership of an organization is committed to serving one constituency such as the union, there is always going to be disagreement, which can lead to accusations and attacks on another's character. As chief of police, I received media attention when disgruntled officers complained. I understood that those disgruntled officers were upset with more in life than my leadership.

The situation with the union leadership was so fragmented, so accusatory of each other, and so intent on outdoing each other that it was difficult to establish a working relationship. Mickey had been successful at making the administration the target of wrath to rally the officers behind him, just as political candidates identify a threat, either real or imagined, to rally support for their election. When Ed Gregson assumed the position of union president, he kept the same tone with the administration and directed a similar wrath toward other union members.

Steve Volk, in an article for the *Pittsburgh Magazine* on February 16, 2001, titled "The Thin Blue Whine," wrote about the inner workings of the union being similar to a "soap opera" and a "civil war." The article reported that union First Vice-President Joe London had threatened criminal charges against union president Edward Gregson and Second Vice-President Bruno Bonaduce. Bonaduce threatened to have London arrested for official oppression.

The article also reported that the union state lodge members attended the December 2000 union meeting and witnessed the chaos of "name-calling and unintelligible bellowing." Volk wrote that officers walked out of the meeting with one saying, "I can't have my name attached to anything I say about what's going on, because the union has gotten too ridiculous. If I say the wrong thing, someone might not protect me in the street."

A *Pittsburgh Post-Gazette* news article by Johnna A. Pro (2/23/2001) reported that the state union lodge ordered an investigation by a committee into the competing complaints. The president of the state lodge, according to the article, said that any action taken by the state lodge would depend on the outcome of the committee's investigation.

Of all the challenges I faced as the chief, I always wished for better relations with the union leadership. That was a difficult undertaking due primarily to fractured leadership within the union.

I was convinced Mickey Hughes at first wanted to work with the administration but was caught up in the antics of some dark-blue and midnight-blue officers who exhibited bully tactics.

His opponents made every effort to argue that Mickey was not tough enough with the administration since so many policies were being issued, more reporting was required for use-of-force incidents, and more disciplinary cases were leading to suspensions and terminations. His opponents won the union presidency and other positions during the union election in 2000.

CHIEF'S UNION MEMBERSHIP

On Friday, August 28, 1998, Channel 11 news reported that officers attending a union meeting voted no confidence in my leadership of the police bureau. My wife immediately resigned her membership in the union as did several other members of the command staff. Actually, I had been contemplating doing so for quite some time since my own contributions were being used against me. I was the highest paying member of the union since monthly dues were based upon hourly pay. This was the opportunity to exit the union.

On August 31, I resigned my membership in the police union. My membership was solely to maintain working relationships between police management and the police union. I was quoted in the newspaper the next day as saying, "Being the chief is not equivalent to being a union president. I also have to consider the needs of the community and what we are legally required to do."

ORGANIZING THE NO-CONFIDENCE VOTE

There were morale problems created from the department's poor hiring record. As previously discussed, the Pittsburgh Bureau of Police did a poor job of deselecting police candidates during the early to mid-1990s. Some were hired who should never have been hired.

In 1979 Johnny Weaver joined a Colorado police department. In November 1983, two ounces of cocaine disappeared from the evidence locker at the department. After an investigation, the chief of police came to believe that Weaver had stolen the drugs (*Pittsburgh Post-Gazette*, 3/19/2000). Weaver denied the allegation but refused a polygraph and refused to cooperate with investigators, according to the *Loveland Reporter-Herald*.

Weaver resigned from that department in November 1984. Five days later, the department issued a news release suggesting that Weaver's resignation cleared up the theft. The chief also dispatched detectives to Denver International Airport to search Weaver's luggage while the former officer waited to board a flight. Weaver sued the police department, and the city settled out of court (*Pittsburgh Post-Gazette*, 3/19/2000).

Weaver was hired as a Pittsburgh Police officer in March 1993 and worked at Zone 2 in the Hill District. He was one of those hired during a massive hiring effort. Had I been the chief in 1993, I would never have hired a police officer who had failed to cooperate with a police investigation into stolen cocaine.

Although Weaver denied being the author of a website launching attacks on his supervisors, he lived at the billing address and paid the bills when they arrived (*Pittsburgh Post-Gazette*, 3/19/2000). The website accused me of misappropriating funds and beating my wife. Although Weaver believed I harbored animosity to him, he appeared to be projecting his feelings onto me. I told a reporter, "Every Sunday in church, I pray for the people who write that stuff. Something evil has attached itself to their thoughts."

He constantly complained of retaliation due to his criticism of supervisors, including me as the chief. I believed he had illusions of grandeur that he needed to maintain to feel important. He was obsessed with me and my decisions as chief, but I had neither the time nor the inclination to concern myself with his rants.

At first, I believed it necessary to address the untruths circulating through the department that were being spread by multiple officers and union officials. I learned that the only person who did not have the right to speak was the chief. Any officer can complain about the chief and the chief's policies, but any effort I undertook to address the falsehoods led to claims of retaliation.

Even writing a memo to an officer subjected me to claims of retaliation. I eventually abandoned any effort to correct the lies since those responsible for them relished any response. Once our department had a public information officer in place, the department was able to distinguish fact from fiction through her office.

In February 1998, at one of the union meetings, some officers and retired officers took a vote of no confidence in me as the chief. Remarkably, there were news cameras interviewing Weaver after the union meeting.

Weaver's hate-filled, untruthful postings continued for about a year and a half. Following a shooting in a police station in Washington, D.C., where several people, including an FBI agent who had lived in Pittsburgh, were injured or killed, I began installing bullet-proof glass at police headquarters. Many unbalanced or angry people walked straight from the street into the police headquarter offices. Usually, the only people in the chief's office were secretaries and unarmed civilians since police officials had numerous meetings throughout the city. Weaver indicated on his website that the bullet-proof glass was installed specifically to prevent me from being shot.

Since Weaver inferred violence on his website to those managing the department, I put together a packet of information to send to the FBI's Behavioral Science Unit in Quantico to have their experts compile a psychological profile. I believed his supervisors needed to know if experts believed he was as dangerous as his postings threatened. The packet was ready to be sent on December 21, 1998.

SECOND AVENUE SHOOTING

A pursuit began in the early morning hours of December 21, 1998, that traveled through Zone 2 on Second Avenue heading towards Downtown Pittsburgh. Shortly before 4:00 AM, Officer Weaver said he got out of his vehicle and fired four shots at the fleeing vehicle. One of those bullets struck the driver, killing him. The car continued travelling before crashing. The driver was killed by a gunshot wound to the side of the head and the passenger was injured.

Homicide was called to the scene to investigate. I learned of the shooting as I arrived for work that morning. From the early reports I was receiving from members of the command staff, including Commander Robert Bradford who oversaw the Investigations Branch and the Homicide detectives involved in the investigation, the shooting did not appear to be justified.

I initially was told that investigators believed Weaver was out of his police car, leaning or lying across the hood of the car, and began firing at the car being pursued by other police units. I was also informed that Weaver initially told others on the scene that he fired on the car being pursued because it was speeding toward him and he could not get out of the way. Why an officer would place himself in front of a speeding car is unknown. That exemplifies extremely poor police tactics.

Although department policy did not at that time prohibit shooting at a moving car, Acting Sergeant Ken Ashford, who was in charge of and taught firearms training at the Pittsburgh Police Training Academy, had previously provided instruction to every firearms class, specifically to not shoot at a moving vehicle. He always explained that doing so would create a 2,000-pound projectile going down the street with no one in control.

The investigation revealed that none of the bullets pierced the windshield of the vehicle and the bullet that killed the driver of the car was determined to have entered the side window of the car. That appeared to contradict Weaver's version that he fired to prevent being hit by the car.

I was further advised that following the shooting Weaver indicated he needed medical attention and was granted permission to go to a local hospital. Once at the hospital, he left and went home. Supervisors had to go to his house to get him to return to the bureau to provide a statement. Weaver had changed out of his uniform. A police commander informed me he refused to turn over his uniform to investigators. Weaver's behavior was not what would be expected of an officer. Officers know they must stay on the scene during a homicide investigation and follow the orders provided by their supervisors. Command staff members informed me that Weaver was refusing to cooperate with the investigation.

My deputy chief and I contacted the Law Department to ensure that we handled everything properly. We followed their advice. Since it appeared the shooting may not have been justified, Weaver was informed of his constitutional rights and chose not to make a statement.

In order to comply with a City Council ordinance, I had previously made arrangements with the Allegheny County Police Department to supervise any investigation into any shooting involving a Pittsburgh officer. I was glad these arrangements were in place for two reasons. First, it is sound policy never to investigate one's own shooting incident since it may provide the appearance of bias in favor of the officer or department. Second, outside supervision into this investigation could ensure that the command staff would not be accused of influencing the investigation or its findings.

Due to problems encountered during this investigation, the county police notified us they would not supervise other investigations into other shootings unless they not only supervised the entire investigation but used their own investigators to conduct it. The union would eventually file an unfair labor practice at the Labor Relations Board, which was later withdrawn. I made arrangements with the district attorney's office to supervise any critical incident involving Pittsburgh officers since the council ordinance demanded another agency's supervision of critical incidents and the union was unwilling to agree to a complete outside investigation.

At a meeting the morning of the shooting incident to discuss our department's cooperation with the county police supervising the investigation, Commander Bradford informed me that he had spoken with Weaver before the shooting and that Weaver acknowledged being the author of the website accusing police managers of misconduct.

I forwarded all the information compiled for the Behavioral Science Unit to the Allegheny County police superintendent, who was ultimately responsible for supervising the shooting investigation. I believed that all information regarding an officer was important for a complete investigation. No information was to be withheld. The information contained in the website spoke for itself.

The website was described by Michael Miller writing for the *Pittsburgh Business Times* on February 22, 1999: "The site is strewn with skull-and-crossbones, references to Hitler and profanity aimed at Chief of Police Robert McNeilly. One page allows you to 'Punch Chief McNeilly,' illustrating the bloody effects of repeated fists to the Chief's image. The site is devoid of any humor. This is not satire or sarcasm, but rage and frustration spit like cobra venom." He concluded,

"It is ironic that a person supposedly committed to upholding the law would skip the suggestion box in favor of an anonymous, violent, libelous and unhinged method of expression."

DISCIPLINARY CASE RESULTING FROM THE SECOND AVENUE SHOOTING

Since Weaver had been openly critical of me as the chief and was responsible for the false attacks on his website and the no-confidence vote in me, I recused myself from any role in the disciplinary process. Deputy Chief Declan Mulligan handled that process, which concluded with Weaver's dismissal on February 9, 1999.

CRIMINAL CHARGES FOLLOWING THE SECOND AVENUE SHOOTING

A coroner's open inquest into the shooting resulted in Coroner Dr. Cyril H. Wecht recommending homicide charges against Weaver. Another officer and the passenger in the pursued car, who was the brother of the driver, testified the pursued car did not swerve out of its lane or appear to aim at Weaver, whose car was parked on Second Avenue. Other evidence, such as the driver of the car being shot through the side window, was not consistent with Weaver's version of events.

District Attorney Christopher Abrams accepted the recommendation. Weaver's charges included first-degree murder. A three-week trial in 2000 ended with Weaver being found not guilty.

LAWSUITS FOLLOWING THE SECOND AVENUE SHOOTING

The family of the deceased motorist filed a lawsuit against the city. Weaver filed a lawsuit against the city. They were both settled and Weaver received a pension. Two other officers filed lawsuits against the city over this matter.

One was Officer Showalter who claimed he was being prevented from testifying as an expert witness and was the target of retaliation. While assigned to the police academy, he was responsible for including all use-of-force incidents in an annual report. He completed the 1998 report indicating there were no Pittsburgh Police fatal shootings. Of course, that was incorrect since the shooting on Second Avenue occurred in December 1998.

Showalter continued as an officer and testified as an expert in some use-of-force cases for other municipalities. He represented a chief of police who had stepped in front of an officer at a police firing range and pulled the officer's loaded gun into his chest while questioning the officer. I was the use-of-force expert for the municipality. I testified it was improper for a firearms instructor to step in front of an officer with a loaded weapon and ready to shoot.

Showalter claimed it was common practice for the Pittsburgh police to stand downrange during live fire. I knew that to be untrue. He also said he taught it was considered proper by the National Guard where he claimed he was an instructor.

I sent a request to the City of Pittsburgh's Office of Municipal Investigations (OMI) since I believed he was being untruthful. If that had ever occurred on the firing line with the Pittsburgh Police, it needed to be brought to the attention of police officials to stop the practice. I knew one officer who had been killed at the range when checking weapons. I never received a reply from OMI.

I had been a qualified firearms instructor in the U. S. Coast Guard for twenty years and knew that one mishap would have ended a firearms instructor's career. Officer Showalter would never have served as a firearms instructor while I was chief had I learned of such negligence. I later learned he was providing instruction at the Allegheny County Police Academy and that one of the police cadets, under his supervision, accidentally discharged a shotgun. That one mishap could have cost people their lives. Ensuring that weapons are cleared is the first lesson instructors provide to students when handling weapons. His performance in this incident conflicted with his claim to be an expert.

Sergeant Arthur Lyman was the second officer to file a lawsuit related to the Weaver shooting. He was Weaver's immediate supervisor. His case was settled following Showalter's case. He claimed his support of Weaver's shooting was met with corrective action. It had been his responsibility to complete a use-of-force report if one of his subordinates was not capable of completing the report. No use-of-force report was ever completed following the shooting on Second Avenue.

Lyman went on to become the chief of police in a suburb of Pittsburgh in March 2009. One of the first news articles concerning his tenure there reported on his threat to take disciplinary action against an officer who spoke to the media.

While chief in Twin Oaks Borough, he came under fire in 2010 when he was accused of disrobing and allowing a prostitute to touch his genitals before making an arrest during an undercover operation. His actions led to an investigation by Twin Oaks Council and the Allegheny County District Attorney Christopher Abrams, but no charges were filed, and council took no disciplinary action (*Pittsburgh Tribune Review*, 6/20/2012).

Lyman's actions caused the Allegheny County district attorney to set clearer rules: Officers can take off their clothes in an effort to make an arrest; however, participation in a sex act could prohibit prosecution in the case (WTAE news, 11:49 PM EDT, Sep 21, 2016).

A WTAE news report said that eight out of nine prostitution arrests made by Lyman involved him disrobing, having a prostitute touch him, or him touching a prostitute in a sexual way. According to the news reports, he found the women online and arranged to meet them in a local hotel.

Dr. David Harris, an expert in police conduct at the University of Pittsburgh, explained that neither the law nor police procedure requires that anybody take their clothes off. He said it is highly unusual and unnecessary. He said such conduct opens officers up to cross-examination to determine what was really going on during the investigation.

I attended meetings of the Allegheny County Chiefs of Police and the Western Pennsylvania Chiefs of Police, where Lyman's actions were roundly met with astonishment and disapproval. None of the other chiefs said they would even remotely consider similar actions. It is surprising a chief of police would even become involved in an investigation of prostitution. There are officers or detectives who are specifically trained to conduct those investigations.

Lyman left the Twin Oaks PD in 2012 to take the chief of police position in New Franklin, PA, which was in a county abutting Allegheny County. He was terminated by the New Franklin Township Board of Commissioners in 2016. He announced that day he would sue the township. On September 6, 2018, the *Pittsburgh Tribune-Review* reported that Lyman received a $600,000 settlement from New Franklin Township.

Showalter and Lyman each saw policing from a different perspective than I did. I would never sanction personnel being downrange as officers were firing weapons and I would never sanction a chief of police engaging in sexual acts before making an arrest for prostitution. Our approaches to law enforcement were diametrically opposed. Unfortunately, subordinates can make any claim against a public official, but the public official is limited in any reply lest the official be accused of retaliation.

SHOOTING AT A MOVING VEHICLE POLICY

All policies of the Pittsburgh police were in the process of being reviewed, updated, and reissued, which is normal for a well-operated police agency. Many of the policies, including use-of-force policies, were updated and reviewed by the United States Department of Justice

(USDOJ) as required of the consent decree between the USDOJ and the City of Pittsburgh.

One policy scheduled to take effect on December 30, 1999, prohibited officers from shooting at a moving vehicle unless the occupants were using deadly force against the officers or another person by means other than the vehicle. I had attended the International Association of Chiefs of Police annual meeting just weeks before where this issue was discussed. The policy also coincided with the training being provided by the firearms section of our own Training Academy.

As soon as the order was issued, the union president threatened a court injunction to prevent the order from taking effect. He indicated that the union and officers believed the policy had something to do with Weaver's upcoming trial. I met with the union president and agreed to eliminate that portion of the policy until his trial was completed.

MODEL POLICY REGARDING USE OF FORCE AND SHOOTING AT MOVING VEHICLES

A nonprofit organization, the Police Executive Research Forum (PERF), was founded in 1976 as a police research and policy organization and a provider of management services, technical assistance, and executive-level education to support law enforcement agencies. PERF helps to improve the delivery of police services through the exercise of strong national leadership; public debate of police and criminal justice issues; and research and policy development (PERF website).

The Police Executive Research Forum issued "Thirty Guiding Principles on Use of Force" in March 2016 as part of the *Critical Issues in Policing* series. It presented guiding principles for policies, training and tactics, equipment, and information issues with respect to police use of force. The guiding principles were the result of eighteen months of research, field work, and discussions by hundreds of police professionals at all ranks. These guiding principles as they applied to use of force would reflect the best practices for police agencies.

The eighth guiding principle was that agencies should adopt a prohibition against shooting at or from a moving vehicle unless someone in the vehicle was using or threatening to use deadly force by means other than the vehicle itself. The prohibition on shooting at moving vehicles was previously in place in many agencies. It had been part of PERF's use-of-force recommendations to individual agencies for years and was included in the model use-of-force policy from the International Association of Chiefs of Police.

OUTCOME OF THE NO-CONFIDENCE VOTE

According to state union officials, chiefs of police generally don't last beyond two years after a no-confidence vote. That reminded me of a story I heard during PERF training at the Senior Management Institute for Police (SMIP) in Boston. It was about a chief leaving office and greeting the new chief replacing him. The outgoing chief told the new chief there were three letters in the desk drawer and to open them in sequence when the new chief encountered significant problems.

Of course, most people understand it takes time to make change in a department. At the end of one year, this particular chief encountered considerable discontent among some of the officers, elected officials, and members of the public. He opened the first letter. It told him to blame everything on the past chief. The chief did just that and it bought him another year.

At the end of the second year, the chief encountered even more problems. He opened the second letter. It instructed him to create a new initiative, such as community policing, and announce it would solve all the department's problems. The chief did that and it bought the chief another year.

At the end of the third year, the chief was confronted with even more problems. He opened the third letter. The instructions were, "Write three letters."

I was fortunate to serve nearly ten years as Pittsburgh's police chief and then as the chief of a suburban department for another eight years. I eventually left policing to work as a consultant and as one of the monitors for the consent decree between the USDOJ and the City of New Orleans. Chiefs can and do survive no-confidence votes. And some persevere longer than the average three-year length of service.

Chiefs of police have many critics within the department, as well as among elected officials, the public, and some reporters. A chief could spend a considerable amount of time worrying about critics and finding himself/herself unable to perform as a chief.

I opted to concentrate on the opinions of those who really mattered other than some disgruntled officers, many of whom I had disciplined. Some of the opinions I valued came from (1) the hard-working officers of the department, especially those I worked alongside in the streets, (2) successful supervisors and managers either working or retired, (3) my own command staff who voted "confidence" in my leadership following the union vote, (4) the attorneys supporting the department, (5) the consent decree monitor who oversaw department improvements, (6) U. S. District Judge Robert Cindrich, who, when releasing the department from the consent decree, said I should be commended, (7) the Vera Institute Report referring to me as "talented," (8) the International Association of Chiefs of Police where I provided presentations, (9) the Police Executive Research Forum for their ongoing support and for presenting me with a leadership award in 2003, (10) the Allegheny County Chiefs of Police who elected me as their president, (11) the Western Pennsylvania Chiefs of Police who recognized me with a leadership award, and (12) Mayor Tom Murphy whom I greatly admired and respected. I definitely did not want to disappoint him, given his trust and faith in me as his chief.

What made the difference between my lasting a few years or a decade was working for an honorable mayor. Mayor Tom Murphy led the entire city through some troubling times. I only had to lead one bureau through those troubling times. Mayor Murphy took the very tough steps, including layoffs and furloughs, to put the city on track for a brighter future.

RESPONDING TO A VOTE OF NO CONFIDENCE

I was surprised when I received a phone call one evening from a reporter asking me for a statement regarding the no-confidence vote some officers had taken that evening. Half of those regularly attending the union meetings were retired officers. I needed time to gather my thoughts before responding to that call.

Fortunately, I was a member of the Police Executive Research Forum and knew the executive director, Chuck Wexler, well enough to call him. I believed him to be, and still believe him to be, the most knowledgeable person as to police departments across the country, the leaders of those departments, and the issues those leaders face.

Not only was I to receive great advice from Chuck but he put me in touch with other police chiefs who had faced no-confidence votes. Their input was a tremendous help through what was one of the most difficult times a police official can encounter.

Drawing from all their advice, I created a short guide to help other police chiefs who later faced votes of no confidence. Police and fire unions use guides to get rid of chiefs. I have reviewed those guides and found them to be detailed. The International Association of Fire Chiefs provided information regarding union attacks on fire chiefs in a document entitled "Background Information: 'Fire Chief Under Attack.'"

In addition to the support provided by so many other chiefs, the Western Pennsylvania Chiefs of Police presented me with a leadership award for what I had accomplished in the department and how

I handled the union fallout. Their support was greatly appreciated. Years later I made recommendations during the chief's meetings to support other association chiefs who were under attack from officers and elected officials. I came to see that many of those chiefs were criticized by local elected officials who were determined to replace the chief with another officer within the department. There is no escaping bad politics.

LESSONS LEARNED

The no-confidence vote is a tactic utilized by police unions in recent times to undermine the efforts of a police chief. The no-confidence vote is merely one step in a series of efforts that may be employed by the police union to pressure a chief into capitulating to the demands of the union. The sequence of events will most likely unfold as:

1) A vote of no confidence in the chief of police. It is used to create media attention to the demands of the union and to the police chief's inability to "compromise" with the union

2) A series of press conferences to discuss difficulties working with the chief

3) A call for a public hearing, most likely in a local political setting such as a City Council meeting

4) A series of grievances filed on every imaginable issue in an effort to show how unreasonable the chief is or how difficult s/he is to work with

5) A call for the chief to resign

6) Attempts to sabotage the reputation of the chief when the chief applies for other employment

A vote of no confidence is usually merely a symbolic gesture. In most cases, it will have no binding effect on the chief's ability to perform his or her duties. As soon as the vote is taken, the chief can expect considerable media coverage, because that is precisely what it was intended to create. In many cases, the media may have been "tipped" to the no-confidence vote and will be present outside of the union meeting to report on this "late-breaking development." This is the union's effort to send a message to the chief by sending a message to everyone.

CHAPTER ELEVEN

Urban Legend

"Even a tiny bit of deceit is dishonorable when it's used for selfish or cowardly reasons."

—JEANNE BIRDSALL

O fficer Tony Esposito was not the first Pittsburgh Police officer to go to jail while I was the chief of police, but he was the first one to be convicted in federal court of perjury and to spend time in a federal prison, just like his father had before him.

To understand how this police officer would follow his father's path to prison, it is necessary to briefly explain who his father was. From 1985 through 1993, Esposito, Sr. made kickbacks from his construction business to a county maintenance director, Jim Solomon, in Allegheny County, Pennsylvania. The county director failed to include the kickbacks on tax returns, but Esposito listed the kickbacks as business expenses on *his* returns. When called before a grand jury in 1994 to discuss those matters, Esposito made false statements. Those false statements eventually led to his perjury conviction and incarceration.

I first got to know of his son, Officer Tony Esposito, Jr., when I assumed command of Zone 2 in July 1994. I had not been the commander of Zone 2 for long before two women police officers independently approached me in my office and asked that they never be assigned to work with him. In 1993 Esposito arrested a woman who had been involved in an argument with her boyfriend. At the hearing, a magistrate dismissed the charges. Esposito then filed the same charges against her under her previous married name. The city settled that case.

In 1996, the city paid $22,500 to a woman who sued him and the city. She said Esposito used unnecessary force when arresting her after a traffic stop in 1995.

At one point during my command of Zone 2, Sergeant Robert Button told me that a rumor was circulating that I had been suspended for one day due to a domestic violence incident in Las Vegas. According to the bizarre rumor, I had been arrested in Las Vegas. My wife and I had accompanied my mother and father to Las Vegas so we could meet my sister and her new husband. When I asked Sergeant Button who was the source of the rumor, he declined to tell me.

The blue wall of silence protecting officers extended from the streets to the station house, ensuring that ranking officers were not informed. I could have pushed the matter but realized the sergeants in the station might decline to offer further information they thought I should know. It would take years to learn who the officer was who either started or continued the rumor, but Esposito's future actions would eventually expose him.

Esposito had been involved in many actions that were not only bizarre but violated bureau policy and direct orders from a supervisor. His first corrective action stemmed from a police report he wrote about an assault and his subsequent interaction with his direct supervisor, Sergeant Doug Shiner, while they worked in Zone 4. Esposito noted on the incident report that he intended to obtain a warrant for the suspect. Sergeant Shiner ordered him not to obtain the warrant but rather to advise the victim to file charges with the local magistrate as was bureau practice at that time.

Esposito indicated that he would do this, but when the sergeant left the station, Esposito used white-out on the report to cover the text where the sergeant directed the victim to the local magistrate. Esposito then wrote on the report he would obtain a warrant as he had written before the sergeant redirected him. The sergeant initiated disciplinary action against Esposito. This may have been the reason Esposito was transferred from Zone 4 to Zone 2 where I was to assume command.

Esposito had run-ins with nearly every supervisor he worked for and accused each of them of some type of misconduct. He accused Assistant Chief Jake Matthews of retaliation for Esposito's arrest of Matthews's wife, who was also a police officer. Esposito claimed he arrested Matthews's wife for retail theft.

Esposito never interacted with nor arrested Jake Matthews's wife, Carolyn Matthews, who worked at Zone 2. Jake Matthews sought advice from an attorney about suing Esposito for slander, but the attorney told Matthews he would not take the case because Esposito had nothing to recover.

The first instance when I had to initiate discipline against Esposito was following his use of bureau letterhead to write a request for the state attorney general to investigate a case against an FBI agent in Pittsburgh. The attorney general, in his reply to Esposito, informed him he planned to notify the chief of the Pittsburgh Police of Esposito's improper use of bureau letterhead. Esposito then wrote a second letter on bureau letterhead to the attorney general, claiming he was authorized to use bureau letterhead by the chief of police because the chief had authorized him to conduct an investigation.

As the chief of police, I received the letters Esposito sent to the attorney general and the replies. I requested an internal investigation since I had never authorized Esposito to conduct any investigation or to use bureau letterhead. A policy was in effect that strictly prohibited anyone under the rank of commander from using bureau letterhead. And Esposito had in fact acknowledged, in writing, that he had read that policy and understood it.

I would preside over the first of three disciplinary hearings to which Esposito was entitled since the discipline called for possible suspension and/or termination. The first hearing was conducted by the chief of police, the second hearing would be conducted by the Public Safety director, and the third and final hearing would be conducted by a neutral arbitrator.

At his initial hearing, Esposito stated that I had ordered him to conduct an investigation into the FBI agent who had investigated his father's criminal actions. When I told Esposito and his attorney that I never authorized any investigation, Esposito explained that when I had been the commander in Zone 2, he was sent to the convention center downtown to work in a job fair booth. As fate would have it, Esposito worked the job fair booth with the same FBI agent who had investigated Esposito's father and whose testimony sent the elder Esposito to prison for perjury.

Esposito claimed that he interpreted the job fair assignment to mean he was supposed to investigate the FBI agent for wrongdoing. Because his explanation was so bizarre, and because the written correspondence allegedly defending his actions was in direct violation of bureau policy, I recommended his termination.

The second step of Esposito's appeal was to the Public Safety director who upheld the termination. The third and final appeal was to an arbitrator, who bought Esposito's claim that he had a drinking problem and ruled that the officer could keep his job if he first attended a 28-day alcohol treatment program.

Esposito would claim years later that he never had a drinking problem but that the union president, Mickey Hughes, told him to say that during the final hearing in order to save his job. The union regularly represented officers for violations and had saved the jobs of many officers by claiming they had drug or alcohol issues. The arbitrators would order substance-abuse treatment for first-time claims of substance addiction in lieu of suspension or termination.

Esposito dodged a bullet and saved his career. He filed a lawsuit in 1999 claiming retaliation for being a whistleblower, apparently in the hopes of being insulated from any future discipline or obtaining a large settlement. In that lawsuit, he claimed retaliation from nearly every supervisor he had, including Sergeant Shiner, Assistant Chief Jake Matthews, and me as the chief of police. Esposito claimed he had witnessed a domestic between me and my wife, Commander Catherine McNeilly, at my house.

As soon as Esposito testified in 2000 under oath during a federal deposition that he had been at my house for a domestic, I requested an investigation by the Office of Municipal Investigations. I asserted that if Esposito's statements were true, I should not be the chief of police, but that if Esposito's statements were false, he should not be a police officer. A joint investigation was conducted by OMI and the officers assigned to the Integrity Unit.

THE INVESTIGATION

The investigation revealed considerably more corruption on the part of many other officers. The officers and supervisors involved in the corruption undoubtedly had various motives including the desire for retaliation against a supervisor; fear and anger due to uncertainties about how a consent decree would affect them; and the desire to be part of the midnight-blue officers, a bully subset within the bureau— or else, to avoid being targeted by that group.

The investigation of Esposito's claims was as thorough as it was alarming. Esposito was being investigated not only for his accusation against me as the chief of police but also for distributing KKK literature while he was in uniform and on duty.

His claims regarding the domestic violence incident were very specific and included the name of the dispatcher who was working when the dispatch was made, the name of the sergeant in charge who was supposed to have responded to my house, Sergeant Kevin Massey, and the date of the domestic, which happened to be within a week of Esposito's marriage.

The investigation revealed that there was only one day when the incident could have occurred since there was only one day during the month when Esposito, the dispatcher, and Sergeant Massey were all working.

Sergeant Eric Evans was another sergeant who worked the same shift as Sergeant Massey. Evans and I were friends and talked on occasion. Evans wanted to let me know that he had heard the rumor but took no part in spreading it. Evans told me that according to the rumor, he was present at our home, but that was impossible since he had never been there. He said the rumor had Sergeant Massey as the acting lieutenant that day. I was grateful that Evans was honorable in not spreading the rumors and demonstrated decency by telling me about the rumor.

Commander Cathy McNeilly provided information during the investigation that we were on vacation in Florida the week Esposito claimed to have been at our home on a domestic call. The work records showed that Cathy and I were indeed on vacation, we had time-share records for the apartment in Florida, we had car rental papers in Florida, we had phone records of calls from Florida to Pittsburgh (family calls), and we had airline records of a flight to Florida and the return flight. All these records conflicted with Esposito's claims that he was at our house on a domestic.

During the investigation, Esposito had three different attorneys representing him at various times. Apparently, the first two became aware of the discrepancies in Esposito's claims and dropped the suit he had against the city. The investigation broadened to involve other officers in a conspiracy that fed what an assistant United States attorney would refer to as the urban legend of a domestic at the chief's house.

Esposito's first attorney, Bob Frankfurter, held a press conference while he stood on the steps of the City-County Building (the seat of city and county government) and claimed they had documents to prove there had been a police emergency call for domestic violence at our home, as Esposito claimed. The investigation eventually revealed what that supposed document was and why the first attorney dropped his suit against the city. The document was counterfeit.

★★★★

Officer Sharon Dalton was to eventually retire from the Pittsburgh Police with a disability. Dalton played a major role in the conspiracy to frame me as the chief of police and my wife as a police commander. Many officers who had been injured on the job were placed on compensation or brought back to work light duty in an assignment where they would not have to interact with the public. The city tried to return some officers to some level of duty by returning them to light-duty positions.

For some time, Sharon Dalton was assigned to work a light-duty position in the telephone reporting unit (TRU). Officers there were assigned by dispatch to take police reports over the phone. The TRU office was next to the 911 dispatch room.

On one occasion, later testimony in federal court case would present evidence that Dalton and another officer approached a dispatcher, Jim Flanders, about calls entered into the computer-aided dispatch (CAD) system. She asked him to enter a call onto his screen as though there was a call for a domestic at the home of the chief and the commander. He entered the information as the two officers requested. They then asked him to print out his screen. He did so but when he did, the words "Test Screen" appeared printed at the top of the printout.

Dalton asked Jim to print out the sheet without the words "Test Screen" at the top of the page. He explained that the only way he could do that would be to enter the information about a domestic into the computer as though it actually happened. Jim told her that he could not do that since it would be unethical. He said she told him it would be all right since they believed the call did happen but claimed the chief had been successful in having the information deleted.

When Jim refused to enter the information they requested, Dalton merely tore off the top of the page with the heading "Test Screen" and presented that fake sheet as a document to Esposito's first lawyer, Bob Frankfurter. That was the document the attorney held up as "evidence" on the steps of the City/County Building during his press conference concerning Esposito's suit against the city.

Cathy and I learned of what seemed to be a miraculous event following Jim Flanders's testimony. Between the time of Dalton asking him to enter false information into the CAD system and the FBI investigation, Jim had become extremely ill and was hospitalized. He told us he was not sure if he would survive.

Without Jim's testimony, no one would probably have ever heard of Dalton's unethical request to enter false information into the CAD system. And learning how the forged dispatch "Test Screen" document was created may not ever have been uncovered. But miraculously, Jim did survive his illness and did get to testify. I am grateful for the honorable and courageous dispatchers as I am for the police officers who demonstrate honor and courage.

During the investigation, a separate investigation revealed Esposito's motivation for his perjury. He had been friends with another officer, Dennis Coleman, who had scored high on the sergeant's list. Coleman heard from other officers that he should distance himself from Esposito because his association with an officer of Esposito's reputation jeopardized his own chances of getting promoted.

Coleman kept his distance from Esposito from that point on. Esposito became enraged and reported to the Integrity Unit that his prior friend was involved in misconduct. The report accused Officer Coleman of hiring prostitutes, taking them to his house for sex, and then returning the prostitutes to the Downtown.

When Coleman was questioned as part of that investigation, he knew exactly who had filed the complaint (Esposito) and why (revenge for staying away from him). Coleman explained all that happened. Since he had been friends with Esposito, he was able to explain motive. Coleman asked Esposito if the claims of his being at the chief's home on a domestic were true. Esposito replied they didn't have to be true, but he only needed to show there was a domestic at the chief's house and the city would pay him a lot of money.

Esposito appeared to be ignorant of the fact that some police chiefs across the country were already losing their jobs due to domestic violence. If the claims of domestic violence had been true, Esposito would not have been paid anything. It would have been much easier to replace the chief of police.

When I encountered Coleman in town while the Integrity officers were conducting the investigation, he told me I was putting him in a tough situation. I told him the only situation he was in was one of telling the truth. Although Coleman was forced to tell the truth to defend himself against the lies Esposito told about him, Coleman did not want to have to testify against Esposito even when he knew Esposito was lying about a domestic at the chief's house.

Here was Sergeant Coleman, who later became Lieutenant Coleman, fearful of testifying honestly against a troubled, dishonest, bullying officer. It is no wonder that so many officers go astray in their jobs because they have supervisors who are fearful of being disliked by other officers. I never received backup from dark-blue officers when I was a lieutenant and commander in the field, but I always had backup from the good officers when I needed it. And they far outnumbered those who would not provide backup.

It was obvious that Esposito was frequently in trouble with supervisors. He may have considered himself to be untouchable by any supervisor, merely by making a claim of retaliation for whistleblowing. Whistleblowers do exist and they serve an important purpose among government workers. When whistleblowers are successful in their suits, other supervisors are reluctant to take any disciplinary action against them since those supervisors could be accused of retaliation. They fear for their careers. False whistleblowers become insulated from disciplinary action as a result. Esposito's blunder was in not realizing there had to be real evidence to accompany an accusation.

THE ARREST

When the OMI investigation concluded, the finding was that Tony Esposito had fabricated the claim that he responded to a domestic at the McNeilly home. Another OMI investigation also concluded that Esposito did distribute KKK literature while he was on duty and in uniform at a local mall. That finding would have led to his termination also.

Integrity Unit officers obtained a warrant for his arrest. Charges included his perjury under oath during the federal deposition. Officers arrested him at his home. When they were escorting him to the police car, he requested to leave at home the swastika he was wearing on a chain around his neck. He must have felt that wearing a swastika to jail would be problematic.

RESULTS OF THE STATE CHARGES

Esposito hired Mario Rossi as his defense attorney to represent him at the preliminary hearing in front of a City Court magistrate. The city officers had amassed an overwhelming amount of evidence from their investigation. Rossi argued that state charges should not have been filed against Esposito because the perjury had occurred while Esposito testified in a federal deposition. The magistrate ruled to dismiss the charges. The assistant district attorney, the investigating officers, and my wife and I were incredulous but there was little we could do.

THE FEDERAL INVESTIGATION

Following the City Court magistrate's dismissal of the charges, I approached the U. S. assistant attorney general for the Western District of Pennsylvania. I explained the course of events following the investigation into Esposito's claims of domestic violence at my home. I asked the attorney general's office to review the matter since the City Court magistrate had ruled that only the U. S. attorney's office could address federal charges.

I explained that the perjury was part of Esposito's testimony under oath in 2000. That lawsuit was eventually dismissed in 2001, but the failure of Esposito's claim to be addressed was a threat to my ability to lead a bureau. I was worried about the likelihood of an investigation and prosecution since this was post 9/11 and the FBI was involved in many types of investigations including terrorism.

I was so grateful that the Western District of Pennsylvania United States attorney and the FBI agreed to investigate Esposito's claims. FBI agent Albert Ward thoroughly investigated the matter. He eventually filed charges against Esposito for perjury. Esposito was arrested and the trial was held in July 2003. Assistant United States Attorney Marilyn Brooks presented the evidence to the federal jury.

THE RESULTS OF THE FEDERAL TRIAL

Sharon Dalton had been fighting the city as it attempted to provide her with a disability pension since it seemed she was never planning to return to policing the city streets. She appeared content to continue working twelve hours per week while being paid for forty hours. If she was forced to retire, her retirement pay would be less than she was receiving.

As soon as the trial against Esposito concluded, I requested an immediate investigation into Dalton's actions that were brought to light during Jim Flanders's testimony as well as the forged document she created claiming a domestic call at our home. A *Pittsburgh Post-Gazette* article by Torsten Ove (7/11/2003) reported that the U.S. attorney's office planned to investigate other officers involved in the Esposito claims. The article mentioned Sharon Dalton as one of those officers.

The Public Safety Director informed me that as soon as Dalton's role in the conspiracy was uncovered by courtroom testimony, Dalton went to the pension office to move her contested disability pension to the top of the list so she could retire immediately. If she had not done this, she would have been the subject of another OMI investigation into her role in the conspiracy that may have led to her termination and possible criminal charges.

Computer experts who designed Pittsburgh's CAD system testified that only a few people were capable of deleting any CAD information and none of those experts were in Pittsburgh. Only a few people in the company that built the system had the expertise to remove anything from CAD and they resided in Chicago.

A representative from USAir testified that two people carrying the identification of Cathy and me boarded planes to and from Florida the week prior to and following the supposed date Esposito said he was at our house.

The trial was over in July 2003. Esposito was sentenced in October to a federal prison for one year. Halfway through his jail term, he asked for a modification of his sentence. Esposito brought a character witness with him in an attempt to modify his sentence. The character witness was an Irish priest who worked at Duquesne University.

The priest testified that Esposito had studied hard to become a third-degree member of the Knights of Columbus. In fact, the priest testified that due to Esposito's upstanding status, he had received the rare honor of becoming a fourth-degree knight. When the deputy U.S. attorney attempted to question the priest about the basis for Esposito's criminal conviction, Esposito's attorney objected and the judge ruled the priest did not have to respond.

FOLLOW-UP

I had been called to active duty with the United States Coast Guard Reserves in March 2003 when Operation Iraqi Freedom began. I remained on active duty until the end of July 2003. I was grateful to the USCG that my schedule was adjusted so that I could be in court with my wife during the Esposito perjury trial.

Due to officer furloughs in August 2003, many officers were reduced in rank and transferred. One of the detectives who was returned from a detective position to an officer position was Blake Samuels. Within months, he would request to see me regarding the transfer. We met in my office. I expected he would be enraged and demand a return to his detective position. What happened was a complete surprise.

Samuels said he was full of rage while in church during the 2003 Christmas season. He said he began reflecting on why he was angry and realized he was not angry with me as the chief but that he was angry with himself. He acknowledged it was not me who did anything to him but rather that it was he who had done it to himself. I did not understand until he confessed that he had started the rumor of domestic violence between me and my wife.

I was shocked and did not ask when it started, where it started, or why he started the rumor. What impressed me was that he specifically asked to meet with me to apologize. I had not known who he was, where he worked, or whether he had been one of the detectives returned to an officer position. I will never know if he thought I knew all along that he was responsible for the rumor and was remorseful or that he had experienced an epiphany while attending church services.

I accepted his apology and told the deputy chief, who attended the meeting, that I had a lot of respect for Samuels for coming forward as he did. It made me begin to think about the others who either lied or were part of the rumor mongering to seek revenge for the police management decisions we had to make.

One of those who most disappointed me was Sergeant Kevin Massey. I knew Massey when he worked a plainclothes position in #8 Station while I worked a plainclothes position in #7 Station. He worked in the same station as my wife for many years. I thought he was a stand-up guy. However, he testified during the Esposito perjury trial that he participated in the smear campaign.

Massey said the rumor about domestic violence between my wife and me had been ongoing for years. As a supervisor I would have expected he would either report it if he believed it was true or he would have instructed officers to cease the rumor mongering if he believed it was false. He did neither.

In fact, Massey testified that many officers questioned him whether the rumor was true because part of the rumor was that he was the supervisor on the scene and that he supposedly took me for a ride in a police car and later returned me to my home. All of that would have been in violation of bureau policy. Massey claimed that he initially told the officers that the rumor wasn't true but then began telling officers that it was. He testified in court that he did so because he thought it would be funny. Massey was not principled enough to apologize for his malicious acts, even after more than two decades passed. I am left to wonder if he would think it funny if someone did the same to one of his loved ones.

As of this writing, Esposito is continuing efforts to challenge his 2003 jury conviction for perjury. On March 24, 2008, he was listed as one of many who were denied a presidential pardon by President George W. Bush. On May 1, 2017, the United States Court of Appeals, Third Circuit (No. 16-4026) dismissed Esposito's appeal to overturn the jury verdict.

LESSONS LEARNED

1) Midnight-blue officers and supervisors, either due to lack of training or lack of character, are capable of unjustly harming the supervisors with whom they disagree. Most criminals would not think of doing anything that loathsome.

2) Midnight-blue police officers can input false information into police computer systems and present falsified printouts as legitimate documents. The midnight-blue officers derive pleasure from their illegal activities.

CHAPTER TWELVE

Furloughs

"Rudeness is the weak man's imitation of strength.

—EDMUND BURKE

"It is not the strongest or the most intelligent who will survive but those who can best manage change."

—CHARLES DARWIN

While I served with the Coast Guard in 2001 and 2003, Deputy Chief Declan Mulligan led the bureau. We kept in regular contact and he informed me in July 2003 there would be discussions regarding layoffs of city employees before the end of the year due to the financial crises the city was facing. Deputy Chief Mulligan advised me that he had mentioned the layoffs to Union President Ed Gregson. Chief Mulligan said Gregson laughed in response that the city would never do that.

During my meeting with the mayor in August 2003, he gave me the bad news that the city had only enough funds to pay salaries for everyone until October 2003. He informed me the Police Bureau would need to furlough 102 police officers and that I could furlough them at any time during the month of August. More than seven hundred city employees were either furloughed or laid off by the end of August.

Fortunately, all personnel I furloughed would be brought back to their positions when retirements or resignations occurred. Unfortunately for some other city workers, layoffs would be permanent.

I went back to police headquarters and met with members of the command staff to immediately begin planning. It was going to be a monumental task. Furloughs, according to civil service rules, would be in inverse seniority. Since the bureau's officers and supervisors chose their jobs according to seniority each year, most of the younger officers were working the night shift. We could not possibly permit the night shift to lose more than half the officers assigned to that shift.

We had 1,170 officers when I took over as the chief in 1996. Due to continual budget constraints, the number of officers continued to decrease annually. By 2003, we had already reduced the number of officers to approximately 1,000. We were able to redeploy officers annually as fewer officers were available for the annual job picks. Even with fewer officers, officers still responded to calls for service and the crime rate continued to fall.

The furloughs would occur in a matter of weeks and we did not have the time to post jobs for bids or to conduct the time-consuming bidding process. It became obvious there needed to be a complete restructuring of the bureau, and quickly. Once we did that, we could furlough all the officers at the end of the month instead of gradually doing so as the days of August ticked away. I believed the few extra weeks would allow officers who would be furloughed a chance to make plans and to, at least, have a few more weeks of pay than many other city employees would receive.

FINANCIAL CRISES A LONG TIME COMING

I remembered back to the mid-1980s when the city reduced the number of police stations from nine to six. The district boundaries were changed for most districts and the old districts were renamed zones. The initial plan was to reduce the number of zones to five, but the closure of the South Side station would not be possible due to the large number of businesses located in that zone. The businesses were well organized and politically influential.

The changes made a decade and a half earlier helped the city's financial position but, obviously, not enough. The declining number of police officers, and other city employees, was due to a continual loss of taxpaying residents. The city's population increased from 321,616 in 1900 to 675,000 by 1950. However, from 1950 on it declined so that by 2000 its population was nearly the same as it was in 1900. The population loss and the loss of the steel industry greatly reduced revenues. Pittsburgh went from being the eighth largest city in the U. S. in 1910 to being the fifty-ninth largest city in the country in 2010, with a population of 305,704.

Unfortunately, the politics of reducing a workforce in response to population loss was not acceptable to many residents and elected officials. Any time there was a discussion about closing a police station, a fire station, or any recreational facility, there was upheaval. I remembered the uproar when some stations were closed in the mid-1980s and knew we would experience this opposition again. Throughout my years with the bureau, I was always hearing about the days when there were 1,700 officers. There were 1,350 Pittsburgh Police officers when I joined the bureau in 1977.

Every year, regardless of the size of the bureau, there was a constant clamoring that there were not enough officers. Although the city's population was only half the size it was fifty years earlier, many residents and elected officials wanted to live as though we could still afford every police station and fire station. The truth was the city had been in decline for decades. This was not solely a problem in Pittsburgh in 2003. A National League of Cities survey in 2003 of 322 municipalities showed that one-fourth of municipalities were downsizing public safety at that time.

DIFFERENCE IN UNION LEADERSHIP

Some city operations were not affected by the downsizing. They included City Council, the controller's office, emergency operations, and the Fire Bureau. Of these, the Fire Bureau represented a large part of the city budget—14 percent.

The fire union president, Joe King, had once said he learned the art of negotiation from Union President Patrick McNamara. McNamara became the union president shortly after I became a Pittsburgh Police officer and served more than fifteen years in that position. I knew him well since I had worked a radio car with him during my first few months as a rookie officer. He was a strong leader who obtained great contracts at collective bargaining. And he did so while displaying utmost civility.

McNamara once told me that he criticized policies but never criticized people. I learned that first-hand as a lieutenant when he criticized my deployment of officers publicly and met with me shortly afterward. As critical as he could be, he was so smooth that he could criticize your decision but still meet with you afterward with a handshake and a smile. If he had not become ill, he would have been reelected to that position as long as he desired to remain active.

Joe King learned well from Pat. He was very outspoken and many times critical of city decisions but was always willing to meet to negotiate. As precarious as city finances were for decades, Joe King managed to negotiate union contracts with mayors. He negotiated in 1999 and 2001 the number of fire units the city needed. State law dictated how many firefighters were assigned to each. Because the numbers were already established by contract and state law, the city could not furlough any firefighters in 2003 since to do so would have cost the city more in overtime expenses.

While Joe King was negotiating on behalf of the firefighters, the police union leadership was publicly criticizing the mayor, the police chief, and members of the police command staff, as well as the number of police disciplinary cases, the consent decree, the early intervention system, council members who failed to vote as they were urged to vote, the Police Civilian Review Board, and the media.

Their behavior was diametrically opposed to how Pat McNamara conducted union business, which had been successful for so long. Since Joe King had learned the art of diplomacy, the fire chief did not have to plan any furloughs. I was left to determine how we could police with an overnight loss of 10 percent of our bureau and how we would handle all of those affected by the reductions.

DOWNSIZING

We had to consider many factors when downsizing. It was going to be important to maintain our ability to respond to emergency calls, to effectively address crime prevention, and to conduct investigations for crimes that did occur. Getting rid of the least productive parts of the bureau was the first step.

Staffing of one duty location automatically reduced the number officers on the street by a full-time equivalent of five officers, due to 24/7 coverage of the desk position at that duty location. If we were going to lose officers on the street, I needed to shift officers from desks into police cars. Each station required one commander, four lieutenants, nine sergeants, one crime analyst, one community relations officer, five full-time equivalent officers to staff the front desk, and two clerks/secretaries. Twenty-three staff positions needed to be filled before even one officer would be able to answer a call in the district. Closing a station meant that more than twenty officers would be available for policing on the street. One station closing placed four more officers in each of the remaining five zones for 911 response.

The 102 furloughs of police officers averaged seventeen fewer officers to respond to emergency calls in each of the six patrol zones. That would have accounted for approximately 20 percent of the officers available for 911 response. With reorganization, including the closure of two duty locations, we would be able to reduce that impact to two or three fewer officers per zone. It was important that response times to emergency calls would not increase.

The question became which station should close. There was only one patrol district on the North Side whose zone covered all the city north of the Allegheny and Ohio Rivers. Geographically, due to the rivers and the bridges, Zone 1 would remain operating as it was. Zone 2 was in the center of the city and covered from the Downtown area into the eastern neighborhoods. Zone 2 had already been merged with portions of two other stations in the mid-1980s. It would remain operating as it was.

There were two districts in the eastern part of the city. Both were large districts and both had incorporated neighborhoods from other districts when those stations were closed during the mid-1980s. There were also two districts in the southern part of the city, which covered all neighborhoods south of the Monongahela and Ohio Rivers. Neither of those districts was affected by any of the closures or mergers in the 1980s even though one of them had initially been planned for closure then.

What made the most sense was closing Zone 3 or Zone 4 to combine the southern neighborhoods into one zone as had been initially planned a decade and a half earlier. So the question was, "Do we close Zone 3 in the southern part of the city or Zone 4 in the southwestern part of the city?" Many factors were considered, including traffic, parking, access to the entire district from the station, and priority call levels. In the end, Zone 4 seemed to be the station to close.

The ideal location for a police station in the southern part of the city was a vacated army facility. It had been used as a reserve training center and the army was looking to get rid of the property. This was an ideal location for a police station for many reasons. It would be larger than either of our stations in the South Hills and it had plenty of parking for police vehicles in the front and for personal vehicles in the rear of the building. Its location on the boundary between Zone 3 and Zone 4 would make it the center of the entire southern part of Pittsburgh.

Another plus was that the property was at a traffic-controlled intersection, which meant it would be easy to access and exit. The main thoroughfare made it possible for police units to travel quickly to most parts of the new, larger district. Although this was clearly the ideal spot for a new police station, it would need renovations to make it operational. I presented this plan to the mayor and deputy mayor. I had hoped the renovations would be completed within one year. In the meantime, I needed to determine which of the two stations in the South Hills would serve as a police station until then.

Another unit we reviewed as part of the overall restructuring was disbanding the mounted unit. Four officers and a sergeant were assigned to the unit. The cost for one officer exceeded $100,000 per year at that time, taking into account benefits, training, equipment, and other annual needs. In addition, housing for horses at the county police barn was expensive as were other horse-related costs such as shoeing, veterinary care, and the trucks, fuel, and trailers necessary to transport horses to and from the city daily.

Mounted officers had considerable downtime since one officer spent the entire workday at the barn tending to the horses and their portion of the barn. With five officers who had various days off, no more than two officers were available to ride on most days. Most of the officers' time was lost to travel since they reported for duty within the city limits and then had to spend up to one and a half hours driving to the barn where the horses were housed. The horses then needed to be driven to the city and back to the barn at the end of the day. The estimated cost of having two officers walk their horses on the street for approximately two hours per day was about three-quarters of a million dollars.

When the City of Pittsburgh reduced the number of police stations from nine to six in the mid-1980s, the same concerns existed about response times and distances from the station. Over the following fifteen years Pittsburgh remained one of America's safest cities with steady reductions in crime.

RESTRUCTURING THE BUREAU

During my career from 1977 to 2003, the bureau reduced personnel from 1,350 to the 1,000 and then, following the furloughs, to 900. Each station had fourteen supervisors. The need for forty lieutenants and one hundred sergeants was not the same with 900 officers as it was for 1,350 officers.

I worked with several members of the command staff to determine how we could restructure the bureau. A check with the Personnel Department and the Civil Service Commission assured us that any officer furloughed would be placed onto a special eligibility list and rehired as soon as there was an opening. We received the same assurances for any personnel demoted during the restructuring that they would be placed onto a special eligibility list and regain their higher rank as soon as there was an opening.

To ensure we had the most officers on the street as possible and the necessary supervisory positions filled with the restructuring, we needed to revert three commanders back to the rank of lieutenant, nine lieutenants back to their prior civil service rank (either officer or sergeant), and twenty sergeants back to officers. In addition, twenty detectives from the Detective Division would be returned to the districts as officers. The detectives would be chosen by the assistant chief in charge of that division. This shuffling eventually reduced the available number of officers answering calls in the districts to only two or three fewer officers per zone.

We anticipated returning each furloughed officer as soon as possible as well as returning each supervisor to their prior rank as soon as openings became available. Due to changes in the collective bargaining agreement over the next two years, nearly 300 of the remaining 900 officers would retire between December 2004 and December 2005. All furloughed officers who desired to return to the Pittsburgh Police (90 percent of the furloughed officers) would be rehired within eight months. All supervisors temporarily demoted were returned to their ranks within two years.

Closing duty locations meant we had to change the numbering of the stations. Since Zone 4 was closing, Zone 6 was renamed Zone 4 effective the day of the changes. To coordinate with the renumbering, all the car numbers that began with "4" or "6" had to be renumbered. New patrol sectors had to be configured and officers assigned to those sectors. All call signs beginning with "4" or "6" had to be changed. The computer-assisted dispatch system (CAD) had to have the correct district for each incoming 911 call and the correct district car to dispatch with the correct car for backup. All these changes had to occur simultaneously at 7:00 AM on the morning of the changeover. The transfers for all personnel affected had to be effective at the same time that day. With the temporary demotions, the furloughs, and the reassignments, one-third (300) of all bureau personnel were affected. All of this occurred simultaneously without any problems.

THE FURLOUGH PROCESSES

On August 6, 2003, Mayor Murphy announced the furloughs or layoffs of 731 city employees. In addition, 113 vacant positions were left unfilled. The layoffs/furloughs represented 16.8 percent of the city workforce.

When the layoffs were announced, Union President Gregson was at a union conference out of state. Some union officials returned to Pittsburgh, but he stayed at the conference. The union membership was critical of him for not returning. He explained he stayed there to search for grant funding to save officers' jobs. No grant funding ever materialized. There was so much dissatisfaction with Gregson that Marty Jackson was elected president at the next union leadership election.

NO GOOD DEED GOES UNPUNISHED

I thought it would be compassionate to meet with all the supervisors who were being temporarily demoted and then with all the officers who were going to be furloughed. We held the meeting with the supervisors at the Training Academy a week prior to the effective date of all personnel changes. The academy classroom easily accommodated the 32 supervisors affected by the restructuring of the bureau. I explained that because the bureau was shrinking in size and we now had 900 officers instead of 1,300 officers, the number of supervisors needed to decrease.

I assured them the temporary demotions had nothing to do with anything they had done or had not done, but the demotions were being completed by inverse seniority according to rank. I assured them that each of them would be placed on a special eligibility list and re-promoted as a vacancy occurred.

It was one of the most difficult presentations I have had to make during my career. The only harder presentation would be the next one with the officers who would be furloughed. One lieutenant approached me at the end of the question-and-answer portion of the presentation and told me he knew that what was happening was not my fault and he thanked me for taking the time to bring everyone together to explain changes that were directly affecting them. I was encouraged that he received this change with dignity.

The meeting we planned for the officers could not be held in a city facility since approximately one hundred officers would be attending. We arranged to use an auditorium at one of the high schools. I invited a representative of the Personnel Department and a representative of the Law Department to answer any questions I might not be able to answer completely following my presentation.

I explained how the financial position of the city forced a large number of layoffs and furloughs. I assured the officers that although some city employees would not regain their city job since it was being eliminated, they all would be regaining their positions once a vacancy occurred. I told the officers I understood their concerns about how the furloughs would affect them.

We provided paperwork to help the officers obtain unemployment insurance due to the furloughs. The meeting went as well as could be expected and the officers were attentive and respectful.

I came from a family of railroad workers. Both of my grandfathers, my father, uncles, a brother-in-law, and I worked for the same railroad. We all knew that layoffs happened during slow times and call-backs happened when business picked up.

As we were leaving the meeting at the high school, we were met by a crowd of about two hundred, made up of officers, retired officers, and family members of officers. When I reached the front door, I was met with boos and catcalls. Although the media were not present for the meeting with the supervisors, they had obviously been informed of this meeting and they were covering the disgruntled officers congregated outside.

As I walked to my car, the crowd turned their backs to me and continued the booing and catcalls. I probably should not have been as amazed as I was by the behavior of the officers, being accustomed as I was to the antics of disgruntled officers, but their behavior on this day was truly bizarre. A reporter later asked me how I felt walking the gauntlet from the school to my car amid jeers, taunts, and ridicule. I thought back to the time I was sworn in as chief during Holy Week and told him that I drew my strength from my faith, remembering another who had to walk a gauntlet of jeers and ridicule when he did not deserve it.

I was told I should not have made that comment since it would open me to ridicule. I did receive comments from the public, including from one man who sent a note that said, "When someone of your stature makes comments like that, it causes Christianity to soar." I did not mean to make any grand pronouncements but only to explain, when questioned, how I was able to endure. Of all the gifts my mother gave me, her greatest was that of faith.

It did open me to more criticism within the bureau. But as I explained earlier, I was not concerned with the comments of malcontents. I was more concerned with the comments that were constructive, considerate, and respectful.

Kevin M. Gilmartin, Ph.D. and John (Jack) J. Harris, M.Ed. addressed the fallout from furloughs in *Emotional Survival for Law Enforcement*, and wrote about "the continuum of compromise" for *The Police Chief Magazine* (January 1998).

In the article, they explained the concept of entitlement versus accountability. They wrote about some officers feeling victimized and resentful toward supervisors—feelings that led to a sense of entitlement. That sense of entitlement made them feel that they deserved special treatment. The authors explained that the only way to counter a sense of entitlement is through accountability.

The newer officers in the auditorium did not express a sense of entitlement. For the officers outside of the school, their sense of entitlement was way off the chart. When I looked out at some of the officers present that day, I could see many whom I had disciplined or arrested. Unfortunately, due to my efforts to meet with those being furloughed, I gave the malcontents a forum to display their irresponsibility.

If their conduct was not bad enough outside the high school, the group called for a mass protest at the mayor's office. When they arrived at the City-County Building, they angrily pushed past the security officers trying to do their jobs at metal detectors and entered the building while armed. They took elevators to the fourth floor and congregated at the door to the mayor's office and in the hallway. Many of those present displayed cowardice, the likes of which I had never seen in my career. One officer, hiding behind another officer, shouted obscenities directed at the mayor and me. I kept looking in his direction so that he would know I had witnessed what he did, but he refused to show his face again.

It is not acceptable for officers to feel entitled to a free cup of coffee or a free lunch. It is truly shameful for officers to feel entitled to immunity from furloughs or to feel entitled to flout the law simply because they wear badges. Some trade union members later told me they thought the conduct of the officers at both the high school and the mayor's office was immature.

I instructed supervisors from Zone 1 to post an officer in front of the mayor's house after other city employees were interviewed by the media and their rage indicated they might become violent. I was not sure about some officers either. Mayor Murphy later asked me to remove them from his property since the officers were shouting vulgarities at the mayor's house from their car. Their pathetic behavior was the antithesis of the way police are supposed to act.

Those officers would have felt outrage if someone who disliked police had shouted vulgarities at their own homes. But due to the sense of entitlement some officers have, they believed they had the right to act disgracefully.

I apologized to the mayor for having the meeting with those being furloughed because of the opportunity it gave malcontents to act immaturely. He explained he could have forewarned me if he had known. I would always feel I had let down the person who had always been supportive of me during the professionalizing of our police bureau.

The dark-blue officers seemed to think they accomplished something that day. What they accomplished was to offer proof that a percentage of police officers can't be trusted to act professionally. It was such a disappointment to see some of the men and women whom we trust to maintain peace and order acting instead like immature whiners. They were protesting furloughs without regard for the many citizens they were tasked to protect who themselves might have been furloughed at some point in their lives.

STATE FINANCIAL OVERSIGHT

Following the layoffs, the City of Pittsburgh, having had its credit rating lowered to junk bond status, and operating deficits, petitioned the Department of Community and Economic Development (DCED) for, and was granted, distressed status in 2003. Pittsburgh was the twentieth municipality to enter Act 47 according to the Allegheny Institute.

Not to be outdone by a Democratic governor, the Republican-controlled state legislature required state financial oversight through the Intergovernmental Cooperation Authority (ICA). The city had two financial oversight boards.

Our law department informed me that the Act 47 mandate limited the number of detectives I could assign to Internal Investigations. Because of the mandate, I had to disband the Integrity Unit and transfer those detectives to other assignments. This restricted our police bureau from investigating possible corruption. Officers learned that Integrity testing would not take place any longer. OMI detectives were too involved investigating citizens' complaints to take on additional duties. Sergeant Sean McInerney, who was involved in union leadership at that time and who would be elected union president shortly after I left the bureau, always referred to the Integrity detectives as "cheese eaters," implying they were "rats" since they were investigating other officers.

I had to believe that those looking to cut costs for the bureau were pressured by certain union members to rid the bureau of Integrity testing. The union had tried to undermine their investigations in the past and finally convinced someone it was a good idea.

Liz Naratil, writing for the *Pittsburgh Post-Gazette* on July 17, 2014, wrote about a Pittsburgh Police homicide detective who was charged with theft after taking an envelope of cash from a 7-Eleven convenience store counter. A man in line in front of the homicide detective cashed his paycheck, put the money into an envelope, and forgot it on the counter. After he left, the detective approached the counter, noticed the envelope, and seeing no one around, put it into his pocket. He could have told the cashier about it and had the store recordings checked to identify the owner of the lost property. He could have made a report and notified his supervisor. He could have done several things to ensure the money was returned to the owner, who probably needed the money more than the detective did.

Instead, the detective walked out of the store and failed to tell anyone. Once the customer realized he had left his money at the store, he returned. The clerk checked the recording and could see that the homicide detective had taken the envelope. She had recognized the detective since the convenience store was only a block away from police headquarters and he stopped there often. She notified the detective's supervisor who retrieved the stolen money from the detective.

The detective was charged with theft since the Pennsylvania Crimes Code covers theft of property that has been lost or mislaid. Although the detective was not convicted of the crime, everyone knew what he had done. What this detective had done was in direct contrast to the time someone dropped a five-dollar bill on the floor at the Zone 4 Station and officers claimed no one would touch the bill for a week.

The city lived under state financial oversight by Act 47 from December 29, 2003, until it was released by the governor on February 12, 2018. It took fifteen years to put the city on a track to fiscal health. None of that would have been possible but for the courage of Mayor Tom Murphy, who knew the only option to keep the City of Pittsburgh from bankruptcy was to make the hard decision to furlough and lay off city employees. He did so, knowing it would cost him his job, which he often said was the "best job in the world."

OUTCOME OF LAYOFFS

Every furloughed officer was returned to duty within eight months. All temporarily demoted supervisors regained their rank within two years. Due to new collective bargaining agreements following the furloughs that would require retirees to pay a portion of their retired health care costs, approximately three hundred of the nine hundred remaining officers retired between December 2004 and December 2005. The police bureau entered a period of massive hiring very quickly. Only this time, I was determined our bureau would not make the mistakes made in the mid-1990s.

When one door closes, another one opens. Tom Murphy went on to serve as a senior resident fellow for urban development at the Urban Land Institute. He would travel weekly to many different countries, providing leadership in responsible land use. He had many successes in Pittsburgh, having redeveloped its communities over the course of twelve years.

In May of 2006 I met Mayor Murphy in New Orleans in the aftermath of Hurricane Katrina. while I was on active duty with the U. S. Coast Guard. Mayor Murphy was working with officials there planning land redevelopment. Cathy and I had just started a police management consulting company a few months prior. Mayor Murphy told me he had mentioned to the mayor of New Orleans that I was available to help their police department cope with the many police problems that arose following Hurricane Katrina.

I eventually wrote a letter to their police superintendent offering to assist. The NOPD superintendent never replied to my offer of assistance. Four years later, at the invitation of the New Orleans mayor, the DOJ began investigating an alleged pattern of civil rights violations and other misconduct by the New Orleans Police Department (NOPD website).

On March 16, 2011, the USDOJ issued their report titled "Investigation of the New Orleans Police Department." The report stated there was a "pattern or practice of conduct that deprives individuals of rights, privileges, or immunities secured or protected by the Constitution or laws of the United States." The city of New Orleans entered into a consent decree on July 24, 2012. The federal court approved the consent decree on January 11, 2013.

The NOPD website states, "On August 9, 2013, the law firm of Sheppard, Mullin, Richter & Hampton, LLP, was appointed, by order of the United States District Court for the Eastern District of Louisiana, to establish the Office of the Consent Decree Monitor." I began serving as one of the monitors in September 2013 and continued into 2021.

As much as the union argued there would not be enough officers to police Pittsburgh following the furloughs, they reopened the old Zone 4 in the southwestern part of Pittsburgh and called it Zone 6. This move was to alleviate the complaints from some residents in the western part of Pittsburgh and the elected officials from that area who wanted their own police station. Taking officers from the street to staff another district did not bring about any union complaints.

In 2018, the PBP assigned four officers to a new mounted patrol. In 2019 they moved the barn to a new location within the city limits. By doing this, they saved the four to six hours of daily travel time they previously spent going back and forth to the original barn. It is unknown what the expense is for the mounted patrol or the expenses related to housing and security for the horses at the barn. I had been advised that protecting the horses at the new barn would require a police presence—the full-time equivalent of five officers due to 24/7 coverage to protect the horses from fire, criminals who would harm the horses, or other dangers.

Although the union complained in 2003 that there wouldn't be enough officers on the street to provide for the safety of residents, it appears their fear tactics did not have a foundation since the police bureau has been able to provide optimal services with even fewer officers working the streets today.

LESSONS LEARNED

1) If an agency does not conduct their own Integrity testing, another agency should be responsible for doing so, whether it is a county, state, or federal agency. I am convinced that Integrity testing saves careers.

2) Departments need to ensure they operate with the five C's in mind: Cops, Community, Crime, Costs, and Corruption. When a department cannot control any of those areas, someone will come in to make the changes for them, and when they do, the department will most likely not like the changes that are made.

CHAPTER THIRTEEN

Moving On

"Whenever you see a successful business . . .
...someone once made a courageous decision"

—Peter F. Drucker

R ob Hall, a police chief from Oklahoma and columnist for the website www.police1.com, wrote an article titled "Three Harsh Realities of Being a Police Chief" (12/3/2015) in which he explained, "The average tenure of a chief of police these days is about two and a half to three years—40 years ago it was roughly twice that. Yes, it's possible that you could land your dream job and stay there for the next 15 years, but it's also possible you could win the lottery. The smaller the jurisdiction you go to—especially if you come in from the outside—the shorter your tenure is likely to be."

There is no question that maintaining a chief of police position is extremely difficult. That was obvious to me when I considered taking the position in Pittsburgh. My only request of Mayor Tom Murphy when he offered me the position was that he would seek a second term so that I could reach pension age before another mayor took office and chose another chief.

It is common for each new mayor to choose a new chief regardless of the qualifications the current chief may have. How long a chief of police stays in that position has absolutely nothing to do with his or her ability and performance. Politics is the deciding factor. That's the reason I never believed I would serve in a chief's position. I was blessed that the right mayor came along at the right time.

It was unusual to have a mayor like Tom Murphy who wanted to professionalize city departments rather than staff them with political supporters. That was especially true of the police bureau. He waited until Chief Amos retired two years later before making any changes. He used that time to gain an understanding of all aspects of police work so that he would be sure of what he wanted to change.

Right after Tom Murphy was elected mayor, retired Chief Dean Silverman invited me to his home to discuss his possible return to the bureau. He had been retired for less than four years and was gathering information from ranking police officials as to changes he would make to the bureau in the hopes of encouraging Mayor Murphy to bring him back as the chief. I gave him my list of all the bureau deficiencies I believe needed to be addressed. I was glad to do this since I appreciated his confidence in me by promoting me to the rank of commander and his desire for my input into bureau reforms.

Shortly afterward, State Representative Tony Russo, who lived across the street from my wife and me, invited me to his home. That was unusual since we had never been in each other's homes even though we lived there for years and knew each other only to say hello. It was obvious he had political and public support in the community. He told me he was one of the main supporters of Mayor Murphy and had delivered union votes to the mayor during his campaign.

In light of his political assistance to the mayor, Russo believed he would have input into Mayor Murphy's personnel decisions as a form of political payback. He had drawn up an organizational chart of those who he expected would serve in critical positions within the police bureau. His list included returning Chief Silverman to the chief's job and positioning Commander Bill Wyman as an assistant chief. I respected both men. Russo informed me he was going to have me assigned to Zone 4 which was the zone where we both lived. Russo also listed Bernard Mancini as his choice for the commander in Narcotics. I found that to be problematic. Russo already had his mind made up and was not asking for input.

I had previously observed Bernard Mancini at Russo's house on election day. He had helped Russo's campaign by driving people to the polls. Mancini was also the best man at the wedding of convicted drug dealer and murderer Freddy Proctor. Mancini testified in uniform as a character witness for Proctor at his murder trial, which caused an uproar in the police bureau and among the public. His appearance resulted in a change in policy regarding when officers could wear their uniforms and testifying in court. I believed some of Russo's choices were good, but Mancini in Narcotics would be tantamount to putting the fox in charge of the henhouse.

I later told Cathy about the assignments Russo intended to tell Mayor Tom Murphy to make. After hearing that Mancini might lead the Narcotics section of the bureau, I didn't want any part of the lineup. I told Bill Wyman that I needed to talk to Tom Murphy right away in order to prevent that from happening. I should have done this, but I didn't when Wyman told me Mayor Murphy was already aware of Mancini's reputation and of Russo's desire to see him in charge of Narcotics.

What I didn't know was that when Tom Murphy heard about the proposed lineup from Russo, he wondered if I was part of a shady group. Although Russo insisted that his personnel changes be made in the police bureau, Mayor Murphy refused. Russo became a vocal critic of Mayor Murphy and worked against him in future elections. It was no wonder Tom Murphy waited to make changes in the department. He needed time to learn who comprised the police leadership in the bureau and whether they were trustworthy and competent.

Years later, Russo would be convicted of extorting bribes while he served on the board of the Allegheny County Sanitary Authority.

The local newspaper reported: "U. S. Attorney Harry Litman revealed that Russo was associated with organized crime figures, including the late Gino "The Mooch" Caputo, a convicted criminal, and Pat "Sully" O'Sullivan, who is serving a federal prison term for operating an illegal gambling enterprise." (Torsten Ove, "…Former City Councilman extorted bribes, sold jobs," *Pittsburgh Post-Gazette*" (7/6/2000). Russo pleaded guilty to extortion, mail fraud, and tax evasion in April 2000 and was sentenced to forty-six months in federal prison.

I was impressed that Mayor Murphy abandoned political support in favor of doing what was honorable and in the best interest of the city. It was refreshing that Mayor Murphy hired the Police Executive Research Forum to conduct the search for the next police chief.

Mayor Murphy always protected me politically when I had to move dark-blue officers who had obtained their assignments during prior administrations and failed to produce any meaningful work product. They were show horses who needed to be replaced by work-horses. Mayor Murphy always insisted I make the moves in the police bureau even though he was aware he would lose political support for not interceding. When he supported me during the no-confidence vote by the police union, he told me, and announced during the Council meeting, that every one of the council members had approached him looking for "favors" within the bureau.

I felt privileged to work for such an honorable man and realized later that my nearly ten years serving as the chief was due to his support. In return, I would strive to ensure that the Pittsburgh Bureau of Police was transformed into a national model. The results were astonishing.

The information from the following charts was provided by the City of Pittsburgh in 2005 as I prepared my final course of instruction for all the bureau's supervisors. The information regarding lawsuits was provided by the Law Department. The charts show that the bureau was significantly different in 2004 from what it was a decade earlier. They illustrate accountability throughout the bureau that can only be attained though effective supervision and leadership. I was grateful for my command staff, the supervisors who led the department twenty-four hours a day and seven days a week, and the hard-working men and women from the sky-blue group on down to the many medium-blue officers who worked hard to provide for public safety through ethical and respectful service. The example set by Mayor Murphy filtered down to nearly all the officers on the street.

BUREAU PERFORMANCE

Police-vehicle-involved collisions decreased from 344 in 1995 to 132 in 2003. Numbers were not available for subsequent years, after I left the bureau. The number of collisions in 1995 was alarming since the bureau only had approximately three hundred vehicles at the time. It was obvious that the number of collisions was directly proportional to the influx of new officers who did not receive field training or adequate supervision, and for whom there was little accountability.

Reducing the number of collisions from 344 to 132 did not happen by accident.

It took time for the bureau to put measures in place, such as (1) a new reporting form to include supervisors' recommendations, (2) the categorization of collisions, (3) the establishment of a collision review board to determine officer responsibility, and (4) follow-up actions to include training, counseling, reassignment, and discipline.

Once accountability was established, the collision rate was dramatically reduced, as were the number of associated lawsuits and claims, financial settlements/awards, and officer injuries. The reduction in number of collisions meant that more police vehicles were available for patrol—and the vehicles were in better condition.

Vehicle collisions were taken into account in the early intervention system, the Performance Assessment and Review System (PARS), even though these statistics weren't required in the consent decree. I realized that once we worked our way through the lawsuits involving uses of force and searches/seizures, the next big liability would be vehicle collisions. I insisted we include collisions in PARS as an important component of tracking officer performance. The next three charts demonstrate the success we had in addressing vehicle collisions.

REDUCING VEHICLE COLLISIONS

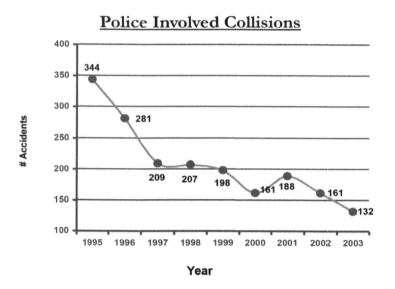

Police Involved Collisions

REDUCING FINANCIAL LOSS BY REDUCING VEHICLE COLLISIONS

The reduction in the number of lawsuits and claims related to vehicle operations was accompanied by a reduction in financial loss to the City of Pittsburgh. Hundreds of thousands of dollars were lost during the years 1993 to 1995, but the annual loss was reduced to much less than $50,000 in ensuing years. (There was only one exception when in one year an officer violated state law and bureau regulations by driving over a charged fire hose. The hose parted, injuring a man who suffered severe brain damage. The officer was terminated, returned to his job by an arbitrator, and subsequently terminated for violating a city and bureau residency requirement.)

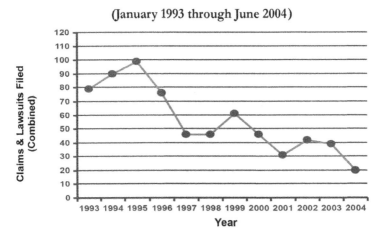

# of Lawsuits & Claims (combined) Filed
Based on Incidents Dealing with Police Vehicles

(January 1993 through June 2004)

REDUCING ALL LAWSUITS AND CLAIMS FOR POLICE-RELATED INCIDENTS

Just as the number of vehicle operation lawsuits and claims was reduced, so was the number of lawsuits and claims for all police-related
incidents. Although 1993 to 1994 saw the number of lawsuits and claims
increasing from nearly 200 per year to more than 250 per year, the number regularly decreased for the next decade to between 20 and 30.

# of Lawsuits & Claims (combined) Filed As A Result of Incidents
Involving Police Department   (January 1993 through June 2004)

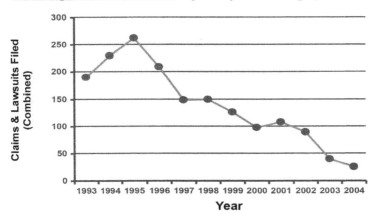

REDUCING FINANCIAL LOSS BY REDUCING LAWSUITS AND CLAIMS FOR POLICE-RELATED INCIDENTS

The reduction in the number of lawsuits and claims related to all police incidents was accompanied by a reduction in financial loss to the City of Pittsburgh. The loss, which amounted to more than $1,000,000 in 1993, was followed by hundreds of thousands of dollars during the years 1994 and 1995, but decreased steadily to much less than $50,000 per year by 2003 and 2004.

Incurred Loss Based on Incidents
Involving the Police Bureau

(January 1993 through June 2004)

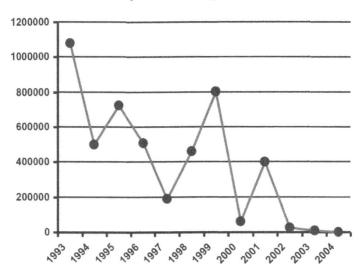

REDUCTIONS IN CRIME

Financial savings were important for a city that struggled with budgets annually. Budgetary problems developed into a crisis leading to hundreds of furloughs, layoffs, and other personnel actions in 2003. The Bureau of Police was reduced from 1,500 sworn and non-sworn personnel to only 1,000. The sworn strength was reduced from nearly 1,200 officers to less than 900 officers. The biggest success during this time was the continued reduction in crime. Crime rates in Pittsburgh continued to be low and trend lower. When comparing crimes per population, Pittsburgh was one of the safest cities in the United States. The following chart shows the crime rate trend in Pittsburgh from 1969 to 2004.

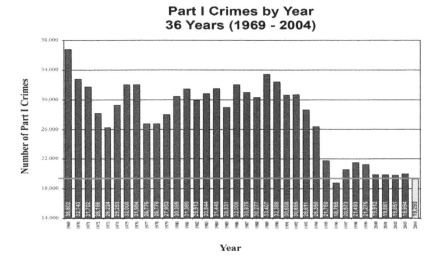

INCREASED CRIME SOLVING

The Uniform Crime Reporting Program collects statistics on the number of offenses known to law enforcement. Part 1 crimes include more serious offenses including homicide, rape, robbery, aggravated assault, burglary, vehicle theft, and theft.

Of the Part 1 crimes reported to the Federal Bureau of Investigation, Pittsburgh, with a population of slightly more than 300,000, solved, or cleared, each type of crime at higher rates than the solved crime rates of other cities of populations between 250,000 to 400,000 and/or the national clearance rates. Pittsburgh officers worked diligently to reduce the crime rate and worked hard at solving the crimes that did occur. This happened as the bureau shrank in size. The Performance Assessment and Review System (PARS) identified star performers who were moved into positions where they could be effective. Show horses were being replaced by workhorses.

2003 Clearance Rates by Category
National & Pittsburgh

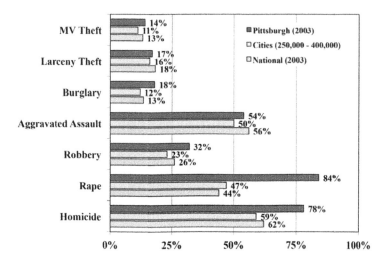

INCREASES IN GUN ARRESTS

PARS was able to identify officers who demonstrated initiative in conducting lawful searches that resulted in complete and accurate police reports. Many of those officers were transferred to units to investigate drug and gun crimes. The following chart illustrated the continuing successes those officers had in getting criminals with guns off the street. From 2000 through 2004 the seizures increased regularly and dramatically. Again, show horses were replaced with workhorses.

City of Pittsburgh
Gun (VUFA) Arrests by Month

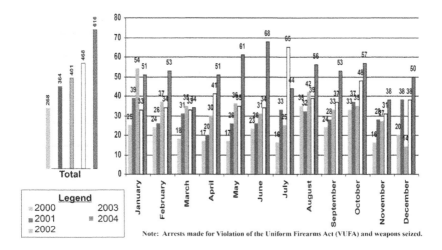

REDUCING OFFICER INJURIES

One important issue was the safety of our workforce and their families. By taking measures to prevent injuries, there is also a savings in medical costs, compensation payments, and overtime costs to replace an injured officer. The next two charts demonstrate a reduction in the number of officer injuries and the reduction in days lost for officer injuries.

Officer injuries were reduced from 335 in 2000 to 172 in 2004. The number of days lost per injury was reduced from 156 to 96 during that same time period. Increased safety among the workforce results from hard work on the part of many officers, detectives, supervisors, and managers and contributes to an increase in the number of crimes solved and a reduction in the number of guns in the hands of dangerous people on the street.

OFFICER INJURY RATES PER YEAR

Pittsburgh Bureau of Police

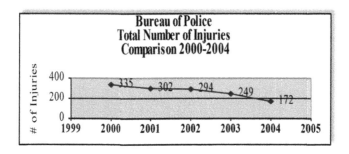

Cost of Injuries (for injuries that occurred in calendar year only) 2004 vs. 2003 =
27.8% decrease
$416,750.00 less in 2004 than 2003

AVERAGE NUMBER OF DAYS LOST DUE
TO OFFICER INJURIES

Pittsburgh Bureau of Police

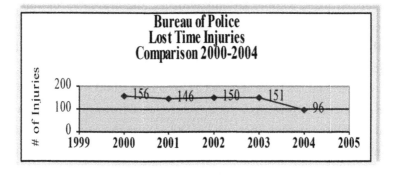

POLICE SUPERVISOR MORALE

Throughout my career, I have always heard that morale is either at "rock bottom" or it is "lower than it has ever been." While I served as a commander, officers were always expressing displeasure over the prior chief banning officers from wearing protective gloves while conducting searches and making arrests, the rationale being that they might look threatening to the public. The same rationale resulted in the lack of additional tools, such as collapsible batons, Tasers, and pepper spray.

I had expected officer morale to improve once officers received uniform items such as ballcaps and protective gloves, and other gear such as .40-caliber firearms, Tasers, pepper spray, and collapsible batons. However, there was still criticism from some officers that the batons, etc. had not been received soon enough or that they were not quite what they expected. Even when some officers were pleased with these items, other officers complained of low morale. Although I made sure all officers were paid 50 percent more for their off-duty details, the dark-blue officers complained they should have received more.

Despite the continued complaints on the part of dark-blue officers, the vast majority of officers seemed pleased with the changes being made and appreciated the time involved to make those changes. The problem was that it is not possible to assess officer morale without conducting a survey. I decided to do just that. Since I had been meeting with supervisors annually, I decided to survey all the supervisors during the 2004 training sessions. The first fifteen to twenty minutes of the training session were dedicated to completing the survey. Once the surveys were distributed, only the trainees were left in the conference room to complete them in private with no names attached. The surveys were tallied at the end of all training sessions. The supervisors rated their own morale level on a 1-10 scale with 1 being extremely low and 10 being extremely high.

The results of the survey were provided to all supervisors during the 2005 training session. Surprisingly, the surveys showed that morale among supervisors was much higher than anticipated. Forty-six percent of the supervisors rated their morale between very good to extremely high, 31 percent rated their morale between moderate to good, and 22 percent rated their morale between extremely low to somewhat low.

Pittsburgh Bureau of Police

Results of Survey on Police Leadership Morale (Sergeants & Lieutenants)

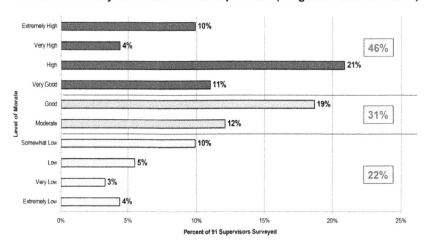

I decided to conduct the survey after reading an article regarding a study of employees in the United States. According to the report, 25 percent of employees loved their job, 56 percent said they could take it or leave it, and 19 percent said they hated their job.

I was impressed with the results of the PBP supervisors' survey when compared to the U.S. study. The comparison is listed in the chart below.

POLICE SUPERVISOR MORALE COMPARED TO U.S. EMPLOYEES MORALE

Pittsburgh Bureau of Police

PBP Supervisors v. Study of US Employees

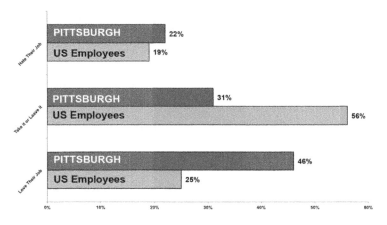

The PBP survey showed that the percentage of supervisors saying they loved their job was nearly twice that of U. S. employees. Those supervisors who felt they could take the job or leave it were fewer in number compared to the whole than the national statistics. The percentage of those who expressed hatred for their job was slightly higher than that shown by the national statistics.

Although the disgruntled segment in any department complains constantly and loudly, most people do not hear from the satisfied high performers who are committed to providing for the community's safety and security. The high morale among 46% of the bureau's supervisors meant that all the sky-blue and light-blue supervisors and some of the blue supervisors were included. Strong management, proper policy, enhanced training, greater recognition of excellent police work, replacing show horses with workhorses, computerizing an entire police agency, and supporting supervisors in the discipline they initiated—all these factors increased the morale of many supervisors, even amid chronic setbacks and complaints from the dark-blue officers.

The 22 percent of Pittsburgh supervisors who appeared to hate their jobs was near the 20 percent I would have expected from the dark-blue supervisors.

Many of those same supervisors who helped lead the Pittsburgh Bureau of Police through some of its most difficult times were still there inspiring the men and women they led with their can-do attitude and positive outlook. I was proud of the job they did and knew the PBP was in good hands with their leadership. The bureau would have even better days ahead as many of them moved into management positions.

The Pittsburgh Bureau of Police changed in many ways from 1996 to 2006. During that time the bureau raised the educational standards of training to require sixty college credits or equivalent. Training was required of any members who would serve in an acting position along with a checklist of duties to ensure they knew their responsibilities. Women comprised 37 percent of the command staff. When Commander Linda Barone attended a women's policing seminar, a presenter acknowledged that although women were breaking the glass barriers, they had not done so in three areas—Narcotics, Homicide, and Special Operations (Tactical). Commander Barone let the presenter know afterward that the Pittsburgh Police had women in each of those leadership roles.

I was proud that the accomplishments of the Pittsburgh Bureau of Police were formally recognized by many. Some of these accomplishments included: Certification through the National Institute of Ethics, a Webber Seavey Award for Financial Crimes Task Force, a Webber Seavey Award for Computerized Personnel Management System (PARS), and a Webber Seavey Award for Oral Drug Extraction Technique (ODET).

A national study titled *Improvement of Policing* was completed by the Vera Institute in March 2004. Many police agencies visited the Pittsburgh Bureau of Police to observe our operations, especially the computerized Performance Assessment and Review System (PARS) and the command staff meetings that addressed internal officer performance issues.

The final auditor report for the Pittsburgh consent decree and the Community Oriented Police Services publication regarding consent decrees discussed best practices employed in Pittsburgh. The PARS and the systems created to address officer performance were discussed in *Good Cops* by Dr. David Harris.

What we had accomplished led to our getting national attention. In addition, members of the command staff gave presentations throughout the country. It was a drastically different department from the one that existed in 1995.

Following the death of George Floyd on May 25, 2020, new laws were passed in Pennsylvania affecting police. Some of what the Pittsburgh Police accomplished from 1996-2006 would be mandated by all departments in the state in 2020. The requirements included cultural diversity training and annual training in de-escalation. Two other bills which passed the Senate included the requirement for police agencies to report and track use-of-force incidents, to train officers in use of force, and to ban chokeholds.

It is unfortunate that terrible incidents occur before so many police officials, local elected officials, and state lawmakers take action to force police agencies to employ best practices. The Pittsburgh Police were doing all these best practices more than twenty years ago.

GOOD TO GREAT

Jim Collins's book, *Good to Great,* was a #1 bestseller with over a million copies sold. The book discussed how some good organizations failed to move forward to become great organizations while other similar types of businesses soared past the good companies to become great companies. This book should be required reading for middle management and upper management police officials. The Police Executive Research Forum discussed the book at an annual training seminar. PERF Executive Director Chuck Wexler formed a group of chiefs to study how Jim Collins's approach could be used in police agencies.

Some of the principles endorsed by companies that became great are the same as those endorsed by great police agencies. One of those principles is leadership. Jim Collins discussed the concept of "a level five leader." Every great organization that he studied had a level five leader that could be identified by certain characteristics: (1) understanding that it's not about the leader but about the organization, and (2) having the "steel fist with iron resolve to do what is necessary to change an organization from good to great."

Supervisors often know how to handle crime issues but not personnel issues. Personnel issues may very well be the most difficult issue that any supervisor must face in running an effective and efficient shift or duty location. Fortunately, there are many good leaders in policing. However, there are also many show horse leaders who are more focused on their own advancement than on that of the agency they have been appointed to lead.

★★★★

In the private sector, a chief executive officer has responsibilities that mirror those of his or her counterpart in a police bureau/department: reducing costs; operating under budget; reducing the number of lawsuits; reducing the incidence of employee misconduct; improving the product (reducing crime rates); improving employee productivity (solving crimes higher than the national average, continually seizing more firearms, etc.); reducing employee injuries and the severity of their injuries; and achieving much higher supervisory morale than national levels.

The public sector doesn't necessarily adhere to standards of excellence or employ best practices. Instead, politics determines the leadership and the direction of the agency. City Council President David Bailey was the mayoral candidate who opposed Mayor Tom Murphy in prior elections in 1997 and 2001. During the 2001 election, Bailey sent a letter to all city police officers advising them that if he were elected, he would replace me as the chief of police.

I sent a letter to Councilman Bailey listing the accomplishments of the bureau and asserting that he had the wrong impression of police morale. I concluded the letter by saying, "The best part of working for Mayor Tom Murphy has been the absence of political influence in law enforcement. Officers are not being promoted or transferred to various positions due to friendships or relationships with elected officials or others of importance. Each has attained their position due to dedication and motivation. I'm as proud of each of them as they are to work for our Bureau."

In January 2001 the *Pittsburgh Post-Gazette* printed an editorial that read: "What Mr. Bailey appears to be doing is promising to deliver the chief's head to a union in return for political support. That is outrageous." The editorial continued: "What Mr. Bailey doesn't understand is that the new chief will figure out quickly that the best policy, if he or she wants to keep the job, will be to appease the union and its members. On that day, you can kiss effective discipline good-bye." The editorial concluded: "Mr. Bailey still has the chance to show that his glad hand won't be a bad hand for the city of Pittsburgh."

When Mayor Murphy did not run for a fourth term, David Bailey was elected mayor. I contemplated returning to a commander position to remain with the Pittsburgh Police because it had always been the department I wanted to work with and because my wife was still a commander there. However, knowing that the department was definitely going to backslide with the new political appointees, I was sickened at the thought of watching what we built be dismantled. The show horses were going to be prancing through the bureau again, bragging of their connections. I knew I could help other departments by moving on.

I retired on January 3, 2006, the day Bailey was sworn in. It was obvious to me Bailey was bringing in a new chief. It would, most likely, be someone who had helped him with his campaigning.

An article by Michael Fuoco in the *Pittsburgh Post-Gazette* on January 9, 2006, quoted Chuck Wexler, executive director of the Police Executive Research Forum, a Washington, D.C.-based think tank that has worked for the U. S. Justice Department and police departments: "The Pittsburgh police department today is light years better than it was because it has put in place systems, policies and practices which not only have made it a better department but have made it recognized across the country as a model." Wexler added, "Pittsburgh's policies and procedures are now hailed as models in law enforcement."

When referring to me, Chuck Wexler wrote, "He was the right guy at the right time in the right place to make a difference that will be felt for years to come…. The fact he encountered obstacles and challenges within the department should surprise no one who understands the hurdles in changing an organizational culture. For the next chief to decide to reverse those actions would raise eyebrows around the country and certainly within the Pittsburgh community."

A few days later another editorial appeared in the *Pittsburgh Post-Gazette* (1/11/2006). The editorial, titled "Good chief," stated that Bailey's spokesperson said they wanted to take the police in a new direction, but they didn't know what direction that was. The editorial included the following comment: "Because Mayor Bailey declined to retain a chief with a good record, he now owes the city something better. The position of police chief is far too important to go to a political crony. Show us qualifications and lay out the department's new direction, Mayor."

★★★★

Politics being what it is, many decisions are made for reasons other than those presented to the public. Some within the police bureau knew of the connections David Bailey had within the bureau. He demanded that some police personnel receive favorable assignments or promotions even if they were not competent.

David Bailey was the opposite of Mayor Tom Murphy. As much as I admired how Tom Murphy filled assignments according to capability, it was apparent that David Bailey relied on politics.

One has to understand Bailey's connections and the people he surrounded himself with to foresee the direction the police bureau would take under a Mayor Bailey. Fred Raymond was a perfect example of someone who received special treatment because of his relationship to the mayor.

Years later, another chief would reveal that he was ordered to make Raymond a detective. Raymond would be involved in more incidents leading to complaints and discipline. In 2011, it was determined that he had called off work *thirty-seven times* in four years to work side jobs. Reports from the Office of Municipal Investigations listed dozens of complaints of conduct unbecoming, verbal abuse, and excessive force. One of the complaints of excessive force was in 2011 following an incident at PNC Park, which received considerable media coverage. In March 2018, Raymond was involved in another incident while working an off-duty detail in uniform, which led to Mayor Allen Lewis demanding Raymond's termination. That incident also received considerable media coverage and provoked negative comments from citizens.

Considering Raymond's poor performance and behavior, one has to wonder how he not only maintained his position but was later promoted to detective. Raymond's sister, Eileen Walsh, was the secretary to David Bailey. I did not meet her until early in 2002 after David Bailey had lost the election to Mayor Tom Murphy. During Mayor Murphy's "state of the city" address, I sat behind a woman whose vulgarity could be heard by many in attendance. I learned that the rude remarks were made by Ms. Walsh. That was not the only connection Raymond had to Bailey. Ms. Walsh was reportedly living with Dylan Stevens who served as Bailey's campaign manager.

Dylan Stevens was a man whose threats overstepped his authority. Stevens once told an officer at Zone 3 to advise her commander, Brianna Waters, to allow a tire company to violate ordinances. Apparently, the tire company had friends in the mayor's office and the mayor didn't have a problem with tire company employees conducting business on the street even if neighbors complained. Stevens warned that failure to back off would lead to the commander "walking a beat." Since only officers walked beats, Stevens was essentially threatening the commander with demotion if she insisted that the business comply with ordinances. It was Stevens who ordered another chief to promote Raymond.

Stevens would later convince the mayor in office at that time, Allen Lewis, to appoint him as the Public Safety director. Stevens's appointment had the support of Union President Sean McInerney. Of course, it did. It meant that the union would have someone in charge who oversaw all disciplinary cases. Even before Stevens was appointed, he served as the acting Public Safety director and overturned the termination of Sergeant Mike Henderson, who had been fired by Chief Dean Romano. The union had to be ecstatic about overturning a termination case.

When the bureau heard that the mayor was going to push through the nomination of Stevens the next week, Commander Cathy McNeilly sent an e-mail to Mayor Lewis advising him of the danger of that appointment and the potential lack of discipline in the police bureau that could result. She cited as an example the thirty-seven times Raymond had called off sick to work secondary employment. She explained that disciplinary action was quashed and she suspected Stevens's influence. She gave Lewis several days to respond to her decision and informed him that if she didn't hear from him within that time, she'd contact City Council.

Mayor Lewis never responded so she notified City Council members. Lewis suspended Stevens and demoted Commander Cathy McNeilly to Lieutenant McNeilly. She was represented by attorneys Timothy O'Brien and Jere Krakoff as well as ACLU attorneys Vic Walczak and Sara Rose in her whistleblower lawsuit.

On January 10, 2007, Chief Judge Ambrose granted a preliminary injunction to Catherine McNeilly, reinstating her as a police commander. The city eventually settled, which included restoring her position as commander.

A DIFFERENT BREED

When I was sworn in as a police officer in 1977, I never imagined I would be promoted to any supervisory position and eventually be chief of police. A Triblive news article by Jill King Greenwood on Thursday, Jan. 12, 2006, quoted Dean Romano as saying, "When you become an officer, you aspire to be in the highest position in the police department."

Dean Romano started as a Pittsburgh Police officer in 1979. I remembered him working plainclothes on the North Side of Pittsburgh while I worked plainclothes on the South Side of Pittsburgh. Dean seemed to have a way of ingratiating himself with high-ranking police officials. He had worked as a plainclothes officer under Commander David Faust who was later promoted to assistant chief. Romano always seemed to turn up at numerous functions whenever the chief of police was in attendance.

When Chief Dean Silverman was promoted, Dean Romano was assisting with the organization of a dinner to recognize the new chief. When Chief Amos replaced Chief Silverman, Romano was assigned to a Narcotics position. He would often show up on a call when Commander Cathy McNeilly was the Afternoon Watch commander or when I was the Night Watch commander. We found it disheartening that as a sergeant he would have a city-issued cellphone while we did not. We not only outranked him, but our duties required us to make phone calls throughout the shift. We would have to find a public phone when a superior officer, a district station, or 911 requested we contact them. Issuing equipment and assigning positions were, at that time, done on a personal basis instead of rank, assignment, or duty requirements.

Chief Amos, prior to his retirement, had many sergeants and lieutenants promoted to commander. Romano, who had been a sergeant, was promoted to commander and assigned to Special Operations where he would oversee tactical calls. He still held that position when I took charge of the bureau. As I was moving to upgrade training throughout the bureau, I instructed him to prepare training for the command staff so they would understand their responsibilities and duties when they arrived at the scene of a critical incident and/or took command of it.

I attended the PERF training, Senior Management Institute for Police, in June 1996. As explained in a prior chapter, I returned early from that training when Officer Jack Lyons was injured. During the same week when Lyons nearly lost his life, Commander Romano managed an incident in which the subject was thought to be barricaded in his house. After waiting many hours without a response, Romano gave the order to use tear gas prior to entering the house. The officers in the rear had been sitting on the wrong house and so they shot tear gas into the wrong house. As if that wasn't bad enough, when the owner appeared following the incident, he was outraged. The officers' response was to arrest the owner of the house for disorderly conduct. The owner of the house had a right to be upset and to voice his displeasure. The incident was poorly handled.

On June 26, 1997, Commander Romano authorized the use of pepper spray grenades in an abandoned house for a training exercise. Two grenades were used during the Tactical entry exercise. The pepper spray drifted throughout the community, affecting twenty-eight people, including children and elderly who received medical aid. This incident created considerable controversy especially since it happened in a minority community. I formally counseled Commander Romano, the lieutenant, and the sergeant for using pepper spray in the community and ordered the supervisors to offer an apology to the community.

Romano never did create a training course for the department's supervisors as I had instructed him. Initially I could not understand what was taking him so long but eventually came to believe he just did not know enough about managing tactics to be able to train the command staff. By 2000, I was committed to transferring all commanders and assistant chiefs so that they would have the opportunity to develop new skills in new assignments.

Commander Romano was transferred to Zone 6 and Commander McNeilly was transferred to Special Operations. Soon after her transfer, she and I attended the International Association of Chiefs of Police course "Advanced Tactical Management for Supervisors and Managers" taught by officers from the National Tactical Officers Association.

We created a one-day course of instruction for all bureau supervisors and provided the instruction in the fall of 2000 during the annual supervisors' training. The training explained that every Tactical incident would have (1) an incident commander, (2) a Tactical commander, and (3) a negotiations supervisor. The negotiations supervisor was to report to the Tactical commander who in turn was to report to the incident commander. Each of the three commanders would have additional personnel reporting to him or her.

Commander Brianna Waters was transferred to Special Operations during the summer of 2001. She would oversee all tactics during critical incidents including one that was to happen on Republic Street.

REPUBLIC STREET

On February 20, 2002, when I had been on active duty for a few days at the U. S. Coast Guard District 8 headquarters in New Orleans, I was notified of an incident at a house on Republic Street in the Homewood section of Pittsburgh. Carl Bragdon was wanted on a warrant and suspected of having drugs and weapons.

Detectives were attempting to arrest Bragdon when he fled to the roof of the house while officers surrounded the property. He would stay on the roof for three hours. He was armed with a 9mm pistol. Romano was directed by the incident commander, Assistant Chief Jake Matthews, to act as the negotiation supervisor. Romano's responsibility was to supervise the primary and secondary negotiators at the scene. He was to report to Commander Waters, the Tactical commander.

The training I provided to Romano included instructions for the negotiation supervisor to maintain effective communications with the Tactical commander and the incident commander.

However, when Romano arrived at the house, he removed Sergeant Reginald Houston, who had been conducting the negotiations, and began conducting the negotiations himself. That was not the only error Romano was to make that day.

Romano gave orders to the Tactical team as to where they should be and how far away from the scene they should be. The officers abandoned their positions so quickly that they left some weapons behind. Romano was not authorized to give instructions to the Tactical team. Orders to the Tactical team were to be provided only by the Tactical commander or the incident commander.

Romano then failed to maintain regular communications and he failed to report to Commander Waters on the situation as it unfolded. Commander Waters knew that Romano was creating chaos and attempted to contact him by radio and phone. Romano did not answer her.

Commander Waters went to the incident commander, Assistant Chief Matthews, to have him provide direction to Romano as to the proper handling of the incident. Matthews failed to take any action. Romano had also failed to maintain communications with Matthews and did not comply with Matthews's initial direction. Instead of Romano acting as the negotiation supervisor, he assumed the duties of negotiator and began ordering the Tactical team to leave the area—in direct opposition to the direction from Commander Waters whom he should have been reporting to.

During Romano's negotiations with Carl Bragdon, he utilized a mirror in order to prove to Bragdon that he was negotiating with him alone in good faith and that the Tactical team was not in the room with him. In fact, the Tactical team was nearby. The use of the mirror jeopardized the safety of the entire Tactical team. A critical incident review board would later conduct an internal investigation into this incident that found Romano's use of the mirror actually gave Bragdon the advantage, rather than giving the advantage to officers on the Tactical team. The report stated Bragdon had more information about the Tactical team than the team had about Bragdon.

Romano also failed to have a surrender plan and failed to relay any information surrounding that surrender plan to the incident commander, the Tactical commander, and the Tactical team. Failure to have a plan and implement it placed all the officers in a dangerous situation. Romano also placed himself and other officers in a dangerous situation by conducting negotiations face to face. Face-to-face negotiations were prohibited by bureau regulations.

Romano made other poor decisions. For example, he permitted a television reporter to be inside the inner perimeter and to engage in face-to-face negotiations with Bragdon. It was expressly prohibited to allow anyone inside the inner perimeter. Romano's failure to comply with bureau regulations put him in direct conflict with Commander Waters, to whom he should have been delivering regular updates. But she was not given any updates, nor was she ever asked for permission to allow the reporter inside.

Romano eventually instructed Bragdon to put his weapon on the chimney of the house and to enter the house through a window. He promised Bragdon that he would not be met by a Tactical team that would take him to the ground to arrest him. Bragdon climbed through the window.

The danger was obvious. Romano's order for the Tactical team to immediately leave the room meant that sub guns were left behind. The Tactical team was outside of the room when they realized that Bragdon would have access to those sub guns as soon as he entered it. Realizing the danger to other officers nearby, the Tactical team immediately re-entered the room. Bragdon produced a second firearm he had concealed. Romano turned to exit the room and was shot by a bullet that lodged in the base of his brain.

The first Tactical officer on the entry team was shot three times in the chest. Although he suffered an injury, he was saved by his bullet-resistant vest. The next officer dropped to his knee to return fire. A bullet fired at him by Bragdon went past his head. That officer shot Bragdon five times. No one died that day, but there were serious injuries and the situation could have been much worse had Bragdon been able to grab one of the sub guns.

At my first regular meeting with Mayor Tom Murphy upon my return to Pittsburgh, I provided details of what happened on Republic Street. He told me that when he was at the house the day of the incident, he could tell that Commander Waters was upset with Assistant Chief Matthews. Her displeasure was due to Commander Romano's actions and Matthews's failure to order Romano to cease the way he was mishandling the incident.

As with any critical incident such as this one, a board was established to review the incident. Their job was to conduct a thorough review and make any recommendations regarding training, tactics, and discipline. The review board found that much of the incident was handled correctly but that some aspects of it were not.

According to the board's findings, "Commander Romano's failure to communicate with other members of the incident command and his failure to formulate a surrender plan enlarged a window of opportunity for Bragdon to carry out his plan." The board recommended that Romano be disciplined. As chief, I wrote a memo that would suspend Romano for ten days when he returned to work and prohibit him from being part of any other tactical incident until he received additional training.

Romano had conducted successful negotiations in the past and he seemed to enjoy the media attention he received from these incidents. It appeared he wanted to be the one in charge to defuse the Republic Street incident even though he was not in charge and he was not the person designated to be the negotiator. Had he permitted the negotiator to continue performing his duties and had he followed proper protocol, Romano would not have been injured and the incident might have had a better outcome.

The manual for the IACP training course, "Advanced Tactical Management for Supervisors and Managers," reported that the average barricaded-person incident lasts between four to six hours. Time was on the side of the officers in the Republic Street incident since the area had been secured, Bragdon was unable to escape from the inner perimeter, he was on a roof in the rain, and he would eventually become tired, thirsty, and hungry. Instead, Romano's failure to adhere to department policy and training led to chaos and injuries.

A copy of the disciplinary paperwork was sent to Romano. The suspension was never served because Romano never returned to work as a commander. He remained on compensation from the day he was shot until the day he accepted a disability retirement. Romano would move on to accept a Public Safety director job in a suburb. He could work that position while collecting a disability pension as a police officer since it wasn't a sworn law enforcement officer position. Receiving disability pay from one police position would not be possible while working another police position.

A police friend of Romano would submit his name and a biased and inaccurate version of the Republic Street event to the National Law Enforcement Memorial in Washington, D. C., where Romano was named "officer of the month" due to his actions on Republic Street. I eventually spoke with the executive director inquiring how Romano could receive this recognition when his own agency had not submitted his name and did not agree with the version described in his award. Furthermore, the bureau planned to discipline Romano for contributing to the tragic consequences of the event on Republic Street. The executive director explained that the version of the incident that he received came from another officer in another department who didn't accurately portray the details of what transpired. He said they would change their policy to ensure that the chief of the officer's department would be contacted before any officer received an officer-of-the-month award.

Carl Bragdon was found guilty of attempted homicide in April 2003.

THE NEXT CHIEF

Bailey did not conduct a national search for the next Pittsburgh Police chief as Mayor Murphy had. On January 13, 2006, Bailey named Dean Romano as the chief, declaring that he had chosen Romano because he was a "go-to person." Union President Marty Jackson said that the union was pleased with Romano's appointment. Jackson said, "The union is going to have more say in the direction of the bureau."

The Black Political Empowerment Project wrote to Mayor Bailey, urging him to name Assistant Chief Jake Matthews as the chief instead of Romano due to the errors made on Republic Street. A *Pittsburgh Post-Gazette* article by Rick Lord on January 14, 2006, titled "Romano named police chief," quoted Emma Adams, of the Black Political Empowerment Project and the Black and White Reunion, as saying, "I'm flabbergasted" at the appointment of Romano and that the process of choosing the next chief 'was not an open process….'"

The same *Post-Gazette* article reported that Romano had said he did not suffer health problems from the bullet. On January 20, another *Post-Gazette* article by Rick Lord titled "City will have to wait for its new police chief" reported that Romano would have to start as a civilian in his new position. That was because Romano was not current with police training to be certified as an officer.

According to a *Post-Gazette* article by Jonathan Silver "Incoming chief spent 6 of 25 years as a city police officer on worker's comp" (1/21/ 2006), Romano had spent six of his years with the Pittsburgh police on compensation including the time from the Republic Street shooting until he accepted the Public Safety director position in another municipality. Romano ceased receiving compensation pay when he accepted the new position. It was then that Romano received his service-related disability pay.

The article also explained that Romano's disability retirement required three doctors to declare he was disabled. With Bailey being elected mayor and appointing Romano as chief, Romano had to see three doctors to be medically cleared to return to work. The article quoted retired Sergeant Rich Lee, the pension fund's secretary and treasurer, as saying, "It's a miracle."

Dean Romano would only serve as police chief for approximately eight months, from January 2006 until September 28, 2006. Mayor Bailey would die on September 1, 2006.

Reporters Dennis B. Roddy and Rich Lord, writing for the Pittsburgh Post-Gazette on September 28, 2006 reported, "In an interview outside his Stanton Heights home this afternoon, Mr. Romano said the aftereffects of the shooting incident made it impossible for him to continue in the job he has held since just the first of the year." The same article reported, "Though both Mr. Lewis and chief attributed the retirement to the medical condition, longtime Romano friend and former Police Chief Richard D'Angelo said he believes the mayor likely wanted to appoint his own person to the position."

ANOTHER NEW CHIEF

City Council President Allen Lewis would replace Romano with his choice for chief, Jake Matthews. Matthews would serve as the chief slightly more than six years, from October 31, 2006, through February 20, 2013. Chief Jake Matthews pled guilty in federal court on October 18, 2013, to diverting $31,987 of public funds for his personal use. He was sentenced to a federal prison for eighteen months. He was released from prison in May 2015.

ANOTHER NEW CHIEF

Allen Lewis served as mayor from September 1, 2006, to January 6, 2014. Steven Hill was sworn in as mayor on January 6, 2014. In a *Pittsburgh Tribune-Review* article by Bob Bauder (5/15/2014) titled "Pittsburgh Public Safety chief will have free hand to attack cronyism," Mayor Hill described the culture of the police bureau as "mediocrity at best and corruption at worst." It was sad to see the mayor of Pittsburgh describing his police in this manner. But he wasn't the only person to see significant backsliding in the police in just eight years.

A *Pittsburgh Post-Gazette* article by Robert Zullo (7/6/2014), "Hill: Pittsburgh committed to fixing problems," discussed the state of the police bureau.

The article included statements by Withold Walczak, the legal director of the Pennsylvania American Civil Liberties Union. He said there had been "substantial backsliding in holding officers accountable for misconduct since the departure of former Chief Robert W. McNeilly, Jr. in 2006."

According to the article, "Mr. Walczak said the more immediate concern is that the department is not taking enough initial action against wayward officers." Mr. Walczak said. "There's plenty of cases where they don't impose discipline or it's just a slap on the wrist.... They need to be more vigorous and aggressive and diligent about making sure the police officers don't break the law."

The same article said, "Officer Richard Younger, president of the local lodge of the police union, doesn't see a problem with the city's disciplinary process."

It is apparent the union was successful in having more input into bureau operations, especially those related to discipline. That had been forewarned in the *Post-Gazette* editorial of January 11, 2006.

Hill hired Taylor MacPherson as the next chief on September 15, 2014. MacPherson served as chief for little more than two years until he resigned on November 8, 2016. When he was hired, Hill said of MacPherson that he "...most certainly will have to restore the trust with the community. He must rebuild the morale with the rank and file, and he must make the Pittsburgh Bureau of Police a national model."

It's noteworthy that Hill said the morale of the bureau was low even though the union had tremendous input over the prior eight years and Mr. Walczak had observed many cases "...where they don't impose discipline or it's just a slap on the wrist."

The union claimed morale was low during my ten years at the helm due to what they said was too much discipline. Years later, the mayor explained officer morale was low even when there was little discipline in the bureau.

Chief MacPherson was subject to considerable controversy on several matters. On December 31, 2014, MacPherson was photographed holding a sign that said, "I resolve to challenge racism @ work #endwhitesilence." This drew criticism from the union and from rank-and-file officers. On April 13, 2016, the union said officers were not well equipped at a Donald Trump rally at the convention center. MacPherson agreed.

On July 26, 2016, Chief MacPherson spoke in uniform at the Democratic National Convention. On September 2, the CPRB said MacPherson broke bureau rules by appearing in uniform at the convention. On September 14, the union voted no confidence in Chief MacPherson. On November 4, Mayor Hill announced he was going to talk to Chief MacPherson. Later that day, MacPherson said he'd be stepping down. Chief MacPherson's last day on the job was November 8, 2016.

I will always be grateful that Mayor Tom Murphy stood with me when I experienced the no-confidence vote in 1998. Mayor Hill apparently did not provide the same support to Chief MacPherson eighteen years later.

ANOTHER NEW CHIEF

Mayor Hill promoted Steve Simmons to chief on November 8, 2016. Simmons is still serving as of this writing.

As Steve rose through the ranks, I noted his ability. As a lieutenant, he attended command staff meetings to represent his commander. In

2005, I sent him and some other rising stars to the Police Executive Research Forum's annual training sessions—The Senior Management Institute for Police. Many who attended that training became assistant chiefs and commanders in Pittsburgh and senior ranking officers of other police agencies.

LESSONS LEARNED

1) Politics run everything. Good elected officials ensure that the best leaders are chosen for a police agency, workhorses receive important assignments and are promoted, and best practices are employed for efficient operations. Weak elected officials choose a chief and upper rank officers as repayment for political support, show horses receive important assignments and are promoted due to friendships or family connections to politicians, and best practices become less important than political loyalty.

2) Police chiefs are regularly replaced regardless of their abilities or achievements. Every chief taking office should have a game plan for the day s/he will move on.

3) Every chief should read the Police Executive Research Forum book titled *Chapter 2: How Police Chiefs and Sheriffs Are Finding Meaning and Purpose in the Next Stage of Their Careers.*

4) Every municipality interested in having a professional police agency should conduct an open-minded and thorough search for their next chief.

5) Every chief hired from the outside should expect to overcome obstacles that an internal chief would not experience.

6) Dark-blue officers from one department will work with dark-blue officers from another department to undermine a chief.

7) The tactics used to undermine a chief are the same in a large department as in a small department.

8) The officers who claim they are doing what is "ethical" are usually the officers who are not.

9) The number of grievance and unfair labor practices are not as much a reflection on the chief of police as they are on the union.

10) As bad as it is for a department to have a dark-blue officer, a dark-blue supervisor is worse.

11) The absolute worst scenario is when a dark-blue officer becomes an elected official.

CHAPTER FOURTEEN

Best
Practices

"Every society gets the kind of criminal it deserves. What is equally true is that every community gets the kind of law enforcement it insists on."

—ROBERT F. KENNEDY

There are around 18,000 police departments in the country with more than 800,000 officers in the United States. I contend that 1-2 percent of officers are in the midnight-blue group. That means they number between 8,000 and 16,000 officers in the United States. They should have never been hired as officers and should not be permitted to continue serving as officers.

There are reasons those officers remain in their jobs. Responsible police managers may know what needs to be done but they lack the political support to accomplish the difficult tasks of disciplining and terminating problematic officers. Second, with 75 percent of departments having fewer than twenty-five officers, budgets may be limited for conducting searches for the best chief and for providing that chief with the training needed to lead a department. Many times, a municipality will sacrifice training funds for a department at the first sign of a budget crisis. This is penny wise and pound foolish. Third, some police managers do not have the courage required for dealing with problematic officers and will not venture to jeopardize their careers by taking the measures that could result in significant back blast.

If elected officials can hire the best available candidate for chief, provide sufficient funding for training and supervision of that chief, and offer support when discipline is necessary, the municipality will have taken the first steps toward having an excellent department.

Unfortunately, most municipalities will opt to promote from within because it is less expensive and more politically beneficial. Conducting sufficient testing and background searches of officer candidates is imperative. Although it may be expensive and time consuming, it won't be as expensive as the lawsuits, the expenses related to disciplining and termination of officers, and the amount of citizen dissatisfaction when complaints are filed.

Municipalities must have sufficient training funds. In both agencies I led, I requested doubling and quadrupling training funds. I would rather have had fewer but better trained officers than more officers with less training.

I've always said that when an officer gets into trouble, 95 percent of the time it's the fault of the department that didn't provide good policy, sufficient training, adequate supervision, or appropriate corrective action (including counseling, retraining, reassignment, or discipline). A municipality can help their department avoid future problems if they provide for the immediate needs of their department and their officers.

Although my observations do not include every possible best practice, it is a good start to protect one's community, its police agency, and the officers working for the department.

RECRUITING

The two most important steps a municipality can take to ensure it has a good police department is (1) hiring the right chief and (2) hiring the right officers. As Jim Collins explains in *Good to Great*, "The old adage, 'People are your most important asset' turns out to be wrong. People are not your most important asset. The right people are." I would much rather have inexperienced people who have the right attitude and motivation than officers who are experienced and well-trained but will pollute the workplace with their negative attitude and lack of motivation.

There are many ways a municipality can ensure they have the best chief. A legitimate search should be conducted by an organization such as the International Association of Chiefs of Police, the Police Executive Research Forum, a state chiefs of police organization, or a company specializing in searching for police chief candidates.

A good chief should excel in these three areas: technical skills, people skills, and conceptual skills. Technical skills for police include emergency response driving, handcuffing, and use of firearms. People skills are being able to listen, communicate well, and work well with others. Conceptual skills enable a person to develop creative solutions to complex problems.

The municipality must hire a workhorse chief who can get things done rather than someone who is considered a good street officer or who has good people skills. An officer who excels in technical skills will be one of the best performing officers in the department. However, if that officer does not also have good conceptual skills, the officer will not be able to perform the chief's job as well as s/he performed as an officer.

The chief who has good people skills will be viewed as a "nice person." Even if that chief is not capable of doing what needs to be done, the community will probably keep this chief because s/he is well liked. Again, without conceptual skills and a strong ethical base, the chief probably won't survive the first crisis.

Once a chief is in place, the chief and the municipality must hire the best candidates for police officer positions. The time and effort expended during the hiring process will help ensure that only the best qualified candidates are hired. The interview process should seek to establish the reason(s) a person chose to become a police officer. The interviewer should ask questions to determine whether the candidate's motivation is in line with that of sky-blue and light-blue officers. The first step to avoid having bad officers in your department is to make sure you don't hire them in the first place.

Mass hiring should be avoided. If it is unavoidable, screening of candidates is imperative in conjunction with additional training, adequate and accountable supervision, immediate and appropriate discipline for violations of policy and training, and a means of tracking employee performance.

POLICY

A good chief should have access to publications from a variety of sources to develop best practices and incorporate them into policy. A Police Executive Research Forum membership provides access to the most recent studies, best practices (including thirty recommendations on use of force), ongoing executive training, and daily publications that provide access to the latest information and best practices. The International Association of Chiefs of Police (IACP) provides access to model policy, publications, training sources, and meetings. The Community Oriented Police Services (COPS) Office has a wide variety of free publications, including the final report of the "President's Task Force on 21st Century Policing" published in May 2015.

Other free resources containing best practices can be found in any of the United States Department of Justice consent decrees. A chief reviewing the requirements listed in the consent decrees can determine if his/her agency is lacking in any area. If so, the chief will know exactly what to fix and how to fix it since the consent decree will include all the requirements to bring that agency into line with national best practices regarding use of force, citizen complaint investigations, custodial interrogations, photographic lineups, domestic violence investigations, officer assistance, and other critical areas.

Dr. Sam Walker, professor emeritus of criminology and criminal justice at the University of Nebraska-Omaha, has said there is no excuse for any department in the United States to be sued by the Department of Justice in areas covered by consent decrees since the best practices have been available to everyone since 1997.

TRAINING

I came to realize that most officers and supervisors who failed to perform properly can attribute their failures to inadequate training.

Every officer should receive initial and ongoing training in the areas of ethics, cultural diversity, and communication skills. Officers benefit from being reminded that ethical conduct is important because they'll be confronted with temptations that cause too many officers to lose their jobs, get arrested, or commit suicide. As society changes, officers need regular diversity training to ensure they can interact well with every segment of the community. Regular communication skills training should lead to effective interaction with those they serve. More than half the complaints in Pittsburgh were about officer rudeness. The second vice-president of the union in Pittsburgh told me that the verbal judo class helped him not only on the job but in his personal life when interacting with family at home.

Field training should be provided to new officers and officers not performing to standards. Field training should only be conducted by the best officers in the department. Many careers were damaged or destroyed because of improper field training by officers of questionable character.

Specialized training should be provided to personnel expected to perform jobs beyond patrol. They include officers assigned to tactical positions, detective positions, and positions where specialized equipment is used. There should be lesson plans, officer manuals, checklists of duties to be learned, and testing for each specialized position. The department is better served if officers work in varied assignments during their careers. They will be more well-rounded as officers and more knowledgeable as supervisors if promoted.

All personnel, especially supervisors, need training to work with the media whose portrayal of the department can become a source of stress for officers. Training should enable personnel to handle interaction with the media with more ease once they realize the needs and the timelines of reporters. Too many times officers and supervisors are reluctant to speak to the media for fear of making a mistake or violating policy. It's important to train personnel in media policy and encourage them to cooperate with the media to get the police explanation of an incident on record. Supervisors shouldn't judge harshly if an officer does make a mistake. To do so could discourage other officers and supervisors from future media interactions.

One of the critical areas requiring training should be addressed through "Active Bystandership for Law Enforcement" (ABLE) training or "Ethical Policing is Courageous" (EPIC) training. These courses are designed specifically to teach officers to save their careers and those of other officers by intervening when they observe officers involved in unacceptable conduct. Although the New Orleans Police Department has provided EPIC training for years, the urgency of that training has been paramount since 2020.

Critical incident training is especially important. The Integrating Communications Assessment and Tactics (ICAT) training includes the latest effective methods of teaching officers how to handle use-of-force incidents.

SUPERVISORY TRAINING

Departments need strong policies and training regarding bias-free policing and sexual harassment. Supervisors need specialized training to know how to avoid even the appearance of inappropriate comments or actions. Thorough investigations are needed when complaints are filed, and the disciplinary process must be used for violations.

Every police supervisor and manager should read or view Gilmartin and Harris's *Emotional Survival* training program and read Jim Collins's book *From Good to Great*. Although departments train for the physical dangers of police work, *Emotional Survival* training is vital to the emotional health of officers and their families. *From Good to Great* is an excellent training source for those leading any part of a police department. The best classroom training I ever attended was the Police Executive Research Forum course "Senior Management Institute for Police." The course is taught by experts and stresses leadership in changing and challenging situations.

Formal training in all aspects of supervision is essential to performing a supervisor's role well, including submitting officers for awards, conducting investigations into citizens' complaints, and initiating disciplinary and non-disciplinary corrective action. Annual training should be provided to all supervisors to provide them with the tools they need to manage disruptive officers.

Supervisors should not be assigned to supervise any subordinates until the supervisor has received supervision training and field training for new supervisors. As personnel rise through the ranks, their responsibilities change. Each new rank should include training specific to that rank. As the promotions above first-line supervision occur, the person should receive management training. Having a well-trained and experienced mentor greatly increases a supervisor's effectiveness and chance for success.

SUPERVISION

The best policies and training do little to serve the public without effective supervision. Supervisors need more than training to be effective. They must also have the moral courage to confront officers who have demonstrated a lack of productive work and to hold them accountable for their attitude, motivational level, and actions.

Supervisors should be evaluated according to how well they prepare and assess the performance of their subordinates, how they enforce adherence to policy, how they provide direction and train officers on a daily basis, how they use the early intervention system, and how well they address deficiencies through counseling, training, and discipline.

Staff meetings are critical to any agency. They not only provide an opportunity for the chief to give direction but they also provide a forum for discussion, so that ranking officers can keep the chief informed of problems within the department, including what officers are feeling and whether the needs of the community are being served. Every department should have regular staff meetings.

Performance evaluations and positive discipline are the primary tools that supervisors should use to keep their subordinates informed as to their performance. All departments should conduct performance evaluations for all officers and supervisors.

DISCIPLINE

Some states, such as California, have a Peace Officers Bill of Rights and confidentiality laws that limit the department's ability to disclose internal disciplinary measures to the community. This may leave the community with the idea that discipline is non-existent or not effective. Unfortunately, without a change in the law or collective bargaining agreement, many people will continue to question the fairness of any police discipline.

In Pittsburgh, an arbitrator ruled that officers' disciplinary records are subject to specific reckoning periods. Records of oral reprimands are permanently removed after one year. Written reprimands are removed after two years and suspensions after five years. Some officers have been dishonest enough to claim they were never subjected to any discipline once those records were removed from their files. Reckoning periods hide continued poor performance.

Many unions and many officers will oppose any effort to make changes. Even though an officer can accuse the chief of wrongdoing, a chief is powerless to provide a balanced picture of the complaints being made since the chief is prohibited from discussing personnel matters and officers' disciplinary records. The public hears only one perspective. If transparency is considered a good thing when an officer makes accusations about a chief's performance, then transparency must also apply to the accuser's performance so that the community and elected officials can form educated opinions.

UNIONS

Police unions may be referred to as fraternal associations, benevolent associations, or protective agencies, but they are essentially unions. Many arbitration decisions are based on previous arbitration decisions rendered in non-police union cases. In some municipalities officers are represented by the Teamsters Union.

Police unions can serve an important function and have contributed to better benefits for officers in some departments. Caution is needed when making decisions to ensure that management rights are not given away during collective bargaining or in establishing a precedent. Some municipalities may trade away some management rights, such as setting work schedules, to save money during austere years. Management rights that are traded away will have a cost later. Departments that trade away work schedules may not be able to later adjust work schedules to conform to the policing needs of the community without paying enormous overtime costs.

Some union members equate seniority with better policing. There is a benefit to seniority if it brings experience and poise. However, having experience does not necessarily make a senior officer more motivated or knowledgeable. Seniority is important to assure officers of fairness, but it can't be the sole factor in deciding training opportunities, assignments, or promotions.

One department assigned minority officers to work with a federal agency investigating street gangs in minority communities. The police union filed a grievance and the arbitrator sided with the union. All the young minority officers had to be withdrawn from the task force. Sending older, white officers instead to infiltrate young, minority street gangs was a preposterous decision that effectively hindered the success of the investigation.

A union president in Pittsburgh insisted that access to all training be determined by seniority. He believed that an older officer assigned to patrol who was retiring in a year or two should be given the first choice of available homicide training instead of a younger homicide detective who was only recently assigned to the Homicide unit.

A conflict of interest exists when supervisors and officers belong to the same union. One sergeant once told me he could not investigate a complaint against two of his officers since they were union brothers. It is difficult to wear two hats—as a supervisor and as a member of the same union as one's subordinates. A supervisor attempting to discipline an officer must be cautious when dealing with a union representative since that representative may be the same person who will be needed if the supervisor should be subject to a complaint, investigation, or discipline. Good supervisors may find a way to wear both hats, but it will create some conflicts for them.

A municipality should not assume that the number of grievances filed by a union reflects the chief's abilities. Grievances also provide evidence of the union's intentions.

Establishing and maintaining a good working relationship with the union(s) can create an environment that serves both the personnel the union represents and the public.

ARBITRATION

An article titled "Police in misconduct cases stay on force through arbitration" (Associated Press, 6/24/20) included this quote by Michael Gennaco, a police reform expert and former federal civil rights prosecutor who specialized in police misconduct cases: "'Arbitration inherently undermines police decisions. It's dismaying to see arbitrators regularly putting people back to work.'" Until another system is developed, many police agencies will be forced to abide by arbitration decisions that have extremely limited chance for appeal.

Generally, anyone who makes a workplace decision must justify that decision with a superior. Officers answer to supervisors. Chiefs answer to elected officials. Elected officials answer to voters. There is no clear-cut superior authority for arbitrators. The best method to ensure accountability for an arbitrator's decision is to make that decision public.

At the conclusion of each arbitration decision, the public should be informed of:

- The charges against the officer
- Disciplinary recommendations
- Adjudication of charges and measures employed, including discipline
- Each appeal and the ruling of the decision-maker
- The name of the arbitrator, the arbitrator's decision, the history of the arbitrator's decisions in favor of the officer (or union) and in favor of the municipality

EARLY INTERVENTION SYSTEMS (EIS)

Some of the officers who appear to have the most potential in police agencies damage or destroy their careers through poor decisions that were not detected and acted upon by superiors. If those officers had obtained help through an early intervention system, many would have saved their careers or, in some cases, their lives.

An early intervention system does not need to be elaborate. It can consist of spreadsheets for every officer, having a separate page for each of the following:

- accident
- arrests
- awards
- citizen complaints
- traffic stops
- use of force
- searches
- off-duty employment hours
- civil claims
- lawsuits
- promotions
- officer counseling
- disciplinary action
- missed court
- injuries
- criminal investigations
- transfers
- weapon discharges
- sick leave
- suspensions

The EIS can identify officers in need of training, counseling, transfer, and discipline. Perhaps even more importantly, it can identify the high performers, the 20 percent doing most of the work. The information culled from the EIS can help to determine the best use of available training funds and the best candidates for assignments, transfers, or promotions. The information can aid in the defense of management decisions and in the defense of the department if and when lawsuits claim the department knew or should have known about officer deficiencies.

Early intervention is common in policing today, so much so that the IACP has developed a model policy for the use of EIS by police agencies. In the foreseeable future, agencies without the ability to track, review, and base management decisions on essential numbers related to officer performance may be regarded as lacking the "best practices" or even "acceptable standards" in managing their employees.

INTERNAL INVESTIGATIONS

The International Association of Chiefs of Police has conducted studies regarding the best practices for investigating citizens' complaints. One study, "Protecting Civil Rights: A Leadership Guide for State, Local, and Tribal Law Enforcement," was published in September 2005. I participated in that study and I presented two portions of the IACP annual workshop presentation covering the investigations of citizens' complaints and the use of early intervention systems.

The investigation of citizens' complaints has ten main parts:

1) Establish a citizen complaint process. This applies to small departments just as much as it does to large departments. I encountered many small departments who did not have a process in place.

2) Establish clear policies for investigating complaints. Again, many small departments do not have policies.

3) Have a central authority clearly responsible for the investigation and resolution of complaints. The person conducting the investigation should be different from the person who will determine follow-up actions, which may include discipline. Since the chief will, most

likely, decide the appropriate follow-up action, someone else in the department must oversee the investigations.

4) Complaints should be classified. A decision will need to be made as to whether a complaint should require an administrative investigation or a criminal and administrative investigation. A criminal and administrative investigation will entail two separate investigations. The complaint should also identify allegations of major or minor misconduct. Administrative action, such as a suspension, may be needed for serious allegations of violations.

5) The department should accept all allegations of misconduct. Mandating that a complainant come to the police facility and make a sworn statement can be viewed as an attempt to prevent the citizen from filing a complaint.

6) Establish fair, thorough, and transparent investigations. These investigations should be as fair, thorough, and transparent as any homicide or sex crime investigation.

7) Select and train investigators specifically to conduct investigations into citizens' complaints. Only trustworthy and morally courageous officers should be selected to conduct these investigations.

8) Protect officers against false complaints. Body-worn cameras have proven to be instrumental in identifying untruthful allegations against officers. The department will need to consult with the municipal attorney and the district attorney to determine follow-up action against any person filing a false complaint.

9) Track and analyze complaints to assess overall performance. The results of the analysis should identify officers in need of intervention, policies needing to be updated or clarified, and departments needing training.

10) Make summary reports of data available to the public, elected officials, and the media.

I would also suggest that the chief not arbitrarily change the findings of any internal affairs investigation any more than s/he would overrule the findings of a homicide or sexual assault case.

EXTERNAL INVESTIGATIONS

To ensure transparency, another police agency should investigate any incident leading to critical injuries or deaths.

External sources may be necessary to investigate internal police corruption in a large agency. For a small police department, only an external agency can be effective in preventing officer corruption.

Corruption extends beyond unscrupulous police officers to a department having ineffective regulations, lack of proper training, ineffective supervision, and lack of appropriate disciplinary action. Unbelievably, there are many police agencies operating without written manuals or a method to address citizens' complaints or a system to track uses of force, searches and seizures, and other important matters.

These failures may be identified and addressed if an agency seeks accreditation through the Commission on Accreditation for Law Enforcement Agencies (CALEA) or their state system for accreditation. Those departments not seeking accreditation should have either a state or county organization or private company review their policies and procedures to ensure they comply with best practices.

Without a method of ensuring that a municipal department is operating with best practices, the department is only one bad incident away from being dissolved.

INTEGRITY–REPORTING/UNITS/TESTS

Officers need a place to report wrongdoing anonymously so they aren't labeled or ostracized by other officers. A great deal of improper pressure is sometimes placed on officers who attempt to do what is right by other officers and supervisors within the department. Those conscientious officers are actually betrayed by the officers pressuring them. Many police officers will not report misconduct when they experience it firsthand since they still must work with the same officers and for the same supervisors. They depend upon those officers for backup in dangerous situations and they can be sabotaged by the supervisors who are supposed to be looking out for them.

Every police department should have either an Integrity Unit or an external agency to report undue pressure from corrupt police officers. Once officers know it is safe for them to report corruption, they will use the system. If an agency does not conduct their own Integrity testing, another agency should be responsible for doing so whether it is a county, state, or federal agency.

Integrity testing helps all officers avoid temptations. Good officers will pass an Integrity test and not worry about the results. Some officers will be hesitant to succumb to temptation since they don't know if the temptation is a test. It will help them stay straight.

CIVILIAN REVIEW BOARDS

PERF Executive Director Chuck Wexler spoke with Sam Walker, professor emeritus of criminology and criminal justice at the University of Nebraska-Omaha, about his extensive research on police oversight and civilian review.

Chuck wrote, "Professor Walker noted that while many people today are calling for civilian review boards to have more authority, including the power to impose discipline, his research has found that civilian boards tend to be more lenient on officers than police executives are. He believes that to enhance accountability, final decisions about police discipline should rest with the police chief and that departments should be subject to a strong auditing body."

Civilian review boards that are created solely to appease a community demanding police accountability but lacking the tools to investigate and take action will probably have too many weaknesses to accomplish what the citizens expected.

Civilian review boards need to operate as though they are conducting a fair investigation with unbiased hearings. The review boards that begin by accusing officers of wrongdoing or whose executive directors immediately denounce officers without having conducted an investigation may appease the 20 percent of the community that dislikes policing and police officers, but they won't garner the respect from most citizens to be taken seriously.

Review boards that are not empowered to interview officers are only empowered to conduct half of the investigation. There is no way they can reach an accurate assessment of the complaint.

Police chiefs are restrained in available disciplinary measures by municipal guidelines, collective bargaining agreements, or a police officers' bill of rights. Review boards that make disciplinary recommendations that exceed the chief's ability to impose discipline may appease the same police critics, but they won't establish a record of having meaningful impact on police misconduct.

Review boards without the authority to impose discipline themselves can recommend any disciplinary measure to emphasize how "tough" they are toward the police. If the officer and union can appeal to an arbitrator, the review board should either be forced to present the case to the arbitrator or should make meaningful recommendations to those who will present the evidence to the arbitrator.

MEDIA

All officers, especially ranking officers, should take advantage of non-threatening situations to develop relationships with the media. In the event of a critical incident, there is not enough time to establish a connection that will include mutual trust. Lack of a good working relationship with the media gives police critics a one-sided view of events.

Departments need to demonstrate transparency, especially regarding critical incidents. It does not take much effort to inform the public that an investigation is being conducted and the results will be relayed as soon as possible.

An annual report should be published and distributed listing important department measures such as:

- police budgets
- use of force incidents
- lawsuits/claims
- citizens' complaints
- vehicle collisions
- officer injuries
- officer awards
- crime rates
- clearance rates for crimes committed
- traffic stops
- searches/seizures
- number of officer sick days used
- arrests
- weapons discharges
- traffic citations
- calls for service
- personnel strength
- overtime expenses
- promotions
- agency accomplishments
- citizen surveys (if completed)
- officer morale surveys (if completed)
- number of disciplinary cases (with findings)

★★★★

In addition to accountability, the main characteristics of a successful police department are a competent chief, well-disciplined and motivated officers and supervisors, an elected body that supports the chief, and the resources the department needs to operate with best practices. Any municipality providing for these needs will be rewarded with an ethical, efficient, and well-respected department. That department will be made up almost entirely of sky-blue and light-blue officers. That is what the public deserves for its trust and its taxes.

WA